Vernacular Modernism

Vernacular Modernism

Heimat, Globalization, and the

Built Environment

Edited by   Maiken Umbach

and   Bernd Hüppauf

STANFORD UNIVERSITY PRESS

Stanford, California   2005

Stanford University Press
Stanford, California
© 2005 by the Board of Trustees of the
Leland Stanford Junior University

Published with the assistance of the Graham Foundation
for Advanced Studies in the Fine Arts, the University of
Manchester, and the Faculty of Arts and Science, New York
University

Library of Congress Cataloging-in-Publication Data

Vernacular modernism : Heimat, globalization, and the built
environment / edited by Maiken Umbach and Bernd Hüppauf.
     p. cm.
   Includes bibliographical references and index.
   ISBN 0-8047-5154-4 (hardcover : alk. paper) —
   ISBN 0-8047-5343-1 (pbk. : alk. paper)
     1. Vernacular architecture. 2. Regionalism in architecture.
3. Architecture and globalization. 4 Architecture, Modern—
20th century. I. Umbach, Maiken. II. Hüppauf, Bernd-Rüdiger.
III. Title.
NA208.V52 2005
720'.9'045—dc22   2005009493

Printed in the United States of America
Original printing 2005
Last figure below indicates year of this printing:
14   13   12   11   10   09   08   07   06   05

Typeset at Stanford University Press in 10/13 Galliard

Contents

Contributors

STANFORD ANDERSON teaches the history of architecture and is head of the Department of Architecture at MIT. He was educated at the University of Minnesota and the University of California at Berkeley and received his Ph.D. in art history from Columbia University. He was director of MIT's Ph.D. program in History, Theory and Criticism of Architecture, Art and Urban Form from its founding in 1974 to 1991 and in 1995–96. Anderson's research is in architectural theory, European and American architecture and urbanism, epistemology, and historiography. He is the author of *Peter Behrens and a New Architecture for the Twentieth Century* (Cambridge, Mass., 2000), the editor of *Planning for Diversity and Choice: Possible Futures and Their Relations to the Man-Controlled Environment* (Cambridge, Mass., 1968), and *On Streets* (Cambridge, Mass., 1978), and the editor and translator of Hermann Muthesius's *Stilarchitektur und Baukunst* (Mülheim-Ruhr, 1902), under the title *Style-Architecture and Building-Art: Transformations of Architecture in the Nineteenth Century and Its Present Condition* (Santa Monica, Calif., 1994). Anderson has been a Fulbright fellow at the Technische Hochschule in Munich, a fellow of the John Simon Guggenheim Foundation and the American Council of Learned Societies, Commissioner of the Boston Landmarks Commission, and a member of the Board of the Boston Preservation Alliance and of the Designer Selection Panel of the Massachusetts Port Authority. He is currently on the boards of directors of the Boston Society of Architects, the Fulbright Association, and the Batuz Foundation.

MARDGES BACON teaches architectural history at Northeastern University. She was educated at the Universities of Delaware and Michigan and

received her Ph.D. in art history from Brown University in 1978. Thereafter, she taught Fine Arts and American Studies at Trinity College, before moving to Northeastern University in 1988, where she became Matthews Distinguished University Professor and professor of Architecture in July 2002. She has also been a fellow of the John Simon Guggenheim Foundation. Her major book publications include *Ernest Flagg: Beaux Arts Architect and Urban Reformer* (New York, 1986) and *Le Corbusier in America: Travels in the Land of the Timid* (Cambridge, Mass., 2001).

JOHN CZAPLICKA is based at the Center for European Studies, Harvard University. He has taught art history in Hamburg and at Harvard University, Humboldt University in Berlin, the University of New Hampshire, and Amherst College, and has published on the imagery of Berlin, Americanism in Germany, and commemorative practice in Germany and central Europe. In 1996, he curated an exhibition for the Österreichische Galerie in Vienna on Austrian exiled artists and published a catalogue. His current project, "Divided Cities / Divided Histories," compares the historical imageries of Berlin, Gdansk, Riga, and Vilnius. He is also in the process of editing collections of essays on the city of Lvov and on writing urban history. Czaplicka is co-chair of the Study Group on Culture and Politics in Central Europe and the German Study Group at the Center for European Studies at Harvard.

KENNETH FRAMPTON is Ware Professor of Architecture at Columbia University. He was educated at the Architectural Association in London and has worked as an architect in England, Israel, and the United States. One of his housing designs, for the Urban Development Corporation of New York State, was built after being exhibited in the Museum of Modern Art in 1972. From 1964 to 1972, Frampton taught at the School of Architecture at Princeton University. He spent three years at the Royal College of Art in London and has since taught at Columbia University. Frampton has been a visiting professor at numerous universities worldwide and has been awarded fellowships by, among others, the Graham Foundation, the Harvard University Graduate School of Design Loeb Fellowship, the Institute for Architecture and Urban Studies in New York, the Guggenheim Fellowship, the Wissenschaftskolleg Berlin, and the American Academy of Arts and Sciences, as well as having won numerous awards. He is a founding co-editor of *Oppositions*. Major books include *Modern Architecture: A Critical History* (1980), *Modern Architecture and the Critical Present* (1993), *American Masterworks* (1995), and *Studies in Tectonic Culture* (1995), as well as

edited volumes and collaborative studies on contemporary European, Japanese, and South and North American architecture, as well as on individual architects such as Richard Meier, Frank Lloyd Wright, Philip Johnson, Aldo Rossi, Le Corbusier, and Calatrava.

BERND HÜPPAUF lives in New York and Berlin. He teaches at New York University's German Department and is director of NYU's Deutsches Haus. He received his Ph.D. from the University of Tübingen and taught at the Universities of Tübingen, Regensburg, and NSW, Sydney, before coming to the United States, and has been a visiting professor at several universities. He is the author and editor of numerous books and essays, among them *War, Violence and the Modern Condition* (Berlin, 1997), *Globalization and the Future of German* (Berlin, New York, 2004), *Skepsis und literarische Imagination* (2003), *Methodendiskussion: Arbeitsbuch zur Literaturwissenschaft*, 7th ed. (Frankfurt a/M, 1991), with Jürgen Hauff et al., and *Signale aus der Bleecker Street 2: Neue Texte aus New York* (Göttingen, 2003).

FRANCESCO PASSANTI lives and works in Cambridge, Massachusetts. He studied mechanical engineering at the Politectico di Torino and art history at Columbia University, where he also received his Ph.D. He went on to teach the history of architecture at the Massachusetts Institute of Technology, in the program on History, Theory and Criticism of Architecture. He is currently completing an extensive monograph on Le Corbusier, focusing on the process by which Le Corbusier constructed his modernist architectural concept during the years 1910–25.

MICHAEL SALER teaches in the History Department of the University of California at Davis. He received his Ph.D. in history and humanities from Stanford University in 1992 and spent a year as a visiting fellow at Stanford's Humanities Center in 2001–2. He is the author of *The Avant-Garde in Interwar England: Medieval Modernism and the London Underground* (New York, 1999) and has published on many aspects of the artistic and literary history of modernism. Saler is currently preparing a book on modernity and enchantment.

MAIKEN UMBACH teaches modern European history at the University of Manchester (U.K.), and holds visiting appointments at University College London and the Universitat Pompeu Fabra, Barcelona. She studied at the University of Cambridge, where she received her Ph.D. in 1996. Her research is located at the intersection of political and cultural history. Her first book, *Federalism and Enlightenment in Germany, 1740–1806* (London, 2000),

explores the role of architectural and landscape metaphors in defining the distinct regional identities of the smaller German states. Umbach has published widely on issues of regionalism and visual culture from the eighteenth to the twentieth centuries; she is editor of *German Federalism: Past, Present, Future* (New York, 2002), and she is completing a monograph on regionalism and modernism in Germany, 1880–1924. She has held visiting appointments at Harvard University's Center for European Studies and the Australian National University.

Vernacular Modernism

Vernacular Modernism

BERND HÜPPAUF

MAIKEN UMBACH

Theories of Modernity and Space

The built environment has played a pivotal role in shaping the modern world and in defining perceptions of modernity. Key elements of the modern condition, such as rationality, secularization, or disenchantment, were in no small measure modeled on the ideal-typical "functionalism" and "internationalism" projected by modern architecture.[1] Consequently, the crisis of modernity is closely intertwined with the evolution of an architecture that is postmodern in the wider sense of the term. Not just questions of style, but fundamental notions of building and dwelling are being transformed. Older theories of modernity narrated a teleological story in which time replaced space, and universalization eliminated place and the local particularism characteristic of the premodern condition. During recent years, this narrative has been questioned. A new uncertainty about the role of space in modernity has emerged. We no longer take for granted that modernization gave rise to the domination of time over space. Authoritative paradigms of the modern are giving way to a rediscovery of concrete experience. This trend is reinforced by a revival of the locality and a sense of place in everyday experience and politics. Thus, theories of modernity and attitudes to space are in flux.

The essays of this volume contribute to a new evaluation of the difference of place, which we call the vernacular.[2] We dispute that this vernacular was an inevitable victim of spatial modernization. Instead, we suggest that, in spite of its virtual absence from theories of the modern, the vernacular lived on as a strong subcurrent of modern praxis. The essays are concerned with its alleged continued presence. By examining some of modernity's

characteristic sites and buildings—real and imagined—they shed light on the role of the vernacular in the modern. Clearly, there is a danger of disproportion. Set against the fundamental problems addressed in the current debate about modernity, space and, in particular, the small-scale places denoted as vernacular, could appear insignificant. Understood in this way, a modern vernacular would trivialize the substantive problems of modernity. The essays of the volume conceptualize the vernacular differently. It is not difficult to concede that space and a sense of place never disappeared during the process of modernization. We pose questions in relation to space in a different manner: what can the vernacular, as category and concrete experience, reveal about the nature of modernity? It is not the discovery of the vernacular per se, we contend, that makes it interesting. It is, rather, the negotiation between, and the interdependence of, the regional and the global, concrete locality and border-devouring abstraction, that can generate a new and more complex narrative of the modern.

Conceiving of the vernacular as a space within the modern is inescapably enmeshed in ambivalence and ambiguity. The common denominator of the essays in this volume is that they locate and analyze the vernacular empirically, within specific spatial configurations of modernity. The vernacular and internationalism or globalization are not treated as mutually exclusive. On the contrary, their interdependence is a central theme of this book, which we explore from various disciplinary angles. The vernacular is of interest to us where and when it elucidates how local and regional identities are constructed within—rather than against—the context of the modern.

This perspective challenges some assumptions made by the anti-globalization movement. The political instrumentalization of the vernacular in the hands of the critics of globalization has a tendency to solidify that which we want to define as fluid and constructed. Searching for places of identity that may have survived the destructive power of rationalization is an epistemological trap. It entails a nostalgic idealization of a past that never actually existed. There is no hidden liberating potential lingering in the discovery of hitherto suppressed vernacular spatiality. Moreover, it would be naïve to assume that modernity is reversible. Fundamental differences between modern, internationalized and premodern, place-bound civilizations are indisputable, and to downplay them would imply not only theoretical oversimplification but also a dangerous political decisionism. In recovering a spatial perspective on modernity, we do not wish to blur the boundaries between modern and premodern experiences and conceptualizations of space.

The concern with the concreteness of the vernacular should not lead us to abandon theoretical approaches that help us understand the complexity

of modern civilization. We hope to avoid the danger of substituting one master narrative of modernity for another, but also do not propose to do away with theory altogether. We advocate an opening up of theory, with a view to reintegrating spatiality as a defining dimension of the modern. What makes the vernacular interesting cannot be captured in terms of intrinsic qualities such as its concreteness. We argue against the notion of the vernacular as a "stable identity," which is often posited in contradistinction to the free-floating denominations of the global age. Spatiality, and new ways of "thinking space," are the result of complex mental reconfigurations in modernity, and not of a shift of attention from one object to another. The modern vernaculars at the center of our investigation retain properties of their spatial origin, yet they are at the same time implicated in the abstract reality of the modern world.

Modernization theories conceived "the modern" first and foremost as a temporal category.[3] They interpreted modernity as being different from all preceding periods in that it marked a radical break with tradition, being, instead, the destination of history defined by progress. It was driven by continuous innovation and a fixation on the future. In Göran Therborn's words, modernity was an epoch fundamentally different from "and possibly better than the present and the past. The contrast between the past and the future directs modernity's semantics of time, or constitutes its binary code."[4] In this grand vision of historical progression, change on the micro-level, affecting the ways individuals relate to space and time, was interpreted as a consequence of transformations on the macro-level, resulting in a "functional" understanding of time and a corresponding modern subjectivity. In his classical account, E. P. Thompson argued that, with the rise of modern capitalism, life came to be organized around the clock and calendar, a theme that was subsequently taken up by many other authors.[5] Reinhart Koselleck proposed a similar, yet less economically determinist thesis by suggesting that during the decades following the seminal "modernizing" event of the French Revolution, the experience of time "accelerated."[6] Thus, this theory contends, time and speed became the constitutive features of modernity, and, correspondingly, a major theme in cultural modernism. Futurism's obsession with speed, movement and technology was only the most blatant example of this general trend.[7] Stephen Kern has suggested that the spirit of the period from 1880 to 1918—which encompasses the origins of modernism—could best be captured in terms of "the miles of telephone wires that criss-crossed the Western world [which stand for] the vast extended present of simultaneity."[8] What emerges from these theories is a sense that modern existence was signified by abstractness as a consequence

of making life flexible and fluid by subjugating it to a standardized international time. The condition of modernity required a life independent of place and experienced time, the seasons, movements of sun and moon, or the individual's inner physiological sense of time.

The International Style in architecture, these theories imply, was the outward manifestation of the changing parameters of Western civilization, in particular its continued reduction of the relevance of space. For modernization theories characterized the outlook of modernity as *cosmopolitan*, the style of modernity as *international*, and the archetypal site of modernity as the *city*—"where we can interact with strangers without becoming friends," Richard Sennett wrote, paraphrasing Georg Simmel.[9] The city here figures, not as a concrete place, but as a disembodied, ideal-typical sphere of rational discourse, whose participants remain anonymous and develop no emotional attachments to the physical and social environment. Modernity provides no home—domesticity is the antithesis of this concept of the modern.[10] Jürgen Habermas famously described this configuration as the "structural transformation of the public sphere."[11] In the public sphere of modernity, reasoning individuals engaged in a universal process of emancipation from absolutism, feudalism, obscurantism and, last but not least, the restrictions of place.

In political terms, too, modernization was associated with shifting geographical scales that imply progressive abstraction. Modernization theorists pointed to nineteenth-century European nation-building as the first stage of a universalizing process that led from premodern to the modern political affiliations.[12] Identification with the nation-state, which overrode older loyalties to the sphere of one's immediate social experience in the locality or region, turned, to use Eugen Weber's famous phrase, "peasants into Frenchmen."[13] At the same time, it meant that the collective that defined one's identity was no longer one that could be experienced in any concrete sense—it was not the lived environment of the locality, but the imagined community of the nation, which existed only in abstraction. A century later, this transformation evolved to the next stage, when even the nation-state was dismissed as too delimited, and replaced by pan-national institutions and global networks as the organizing paradigms of modernity. The economic, social and political changes thus classified in turn effected changes in lifestyle, requiring individuals to sever links with concrete places for the sake of mobility and flexibility. It is no coincidence, then, that in the discourse of modernity, time, acceleration and corresponding changes in attitudes and mentalities marginalized place as a category of social debate.

The Disintegration of Theory

In recent decades, the edifice of modernization theory has been systematically dismantled. Its inherent teleology and Eurocentricity in particular have become targets of a concerted critique.[14] The fundamentals of this debate, however, predate modernization theory, in that they evolve around the underlying concept of modernity itself. Enlightenment theorists defined history as a continuous and irreversible movement in time. However, from the late eighteenth century on, their critics questioned this concept of homogenous time, and attempted to reclaim place as a historical category. In this process, Romantics in particular invested the vernacular with polemical connotations, by positing particularity against universalist claims of temporality, abstraction and rationalization. This dichotomy persists. Postmodernists today are engaged in dismantling narratives that treat modernity as the *telos* of universal development. A rapidly expanding literature emphasizes heterogeneity and the plurality of modern experiences—cultural and political.[15] Modernity, we learn, is not a rational system, but, rather, "a matter of movement, of flux, of change, of unpredictability."[16] Bruno Latour, in analyzing the discrepancies between grand theories of modernity and its reality, concluded that *we have never been modern*.[17] Not all scholars find that the concept is entirely without content, yet most agree that older theories of modernity and modernization require conceptual revision.[18] New answers range from those that want to resolve the heterogeneity of modernity in terms of multiple stages, such as Marshall Berman,[19] and those who regard heterogeneity and ambivalence sui generis as the operative principle of modernity.[20]

Similar tropes can be found in the globalization debate. The idea of modernity posits the existence of a self that exists above and beyond "cultural differences." Francis Fukuyama's thesis of the "end of history" is predicated on the assumption that this self has reached its ultimate actualization under the conditions of liberal capitalism, so that no further change is desirable or indeed conceivable.[21] Skeptics have attacked this universalism as a tool of Western political and economic hegemony, an ideological veneer designed to prop up neo-imperialist politics.[22] Postcolonial theory rejects the identification of one particular value system with the whole, and tries to recover spatial as well as temporal difference.

If the built environment played a decisive role in constructing theories of modernity, it was also instrumental in their dismantling. Architectural discourse has significantly contributed to ongoing academic and political de-

bates about the modern. The International Style and what, after Charles Jencks, was dubbed "heroic modernism," have lost their hegemonic status and moral kudos.[23] In their place, a new architecture of cultural difference now promotes the disintegration of transcendental subjectivity. This process has deeply affected the discipline of architectural history.[24] Increasingly, its practitioners have moved beyond the view of modernism as a style, and focused their attention instead on its power of construction; modernity's "generative principles" have become the subject of controversy.[25] Architecture is no longer perceived as an *expression* of the modern, but rather as a collection of (necessarily heterogeneous) strategies, designed to cope with, make sense of, master, or create the "modern condition."[26] Indeed, the built environment in its entirety has come to be seen as a field for the construction (and destruction) of modernity very much in its own right.

Among those who have written on modernist architecture as an embodiment of the spatial politics of modernity, Michel Foucault's work has proved particularly influential. He understands modernization in terms of the rise of "liberal" or "neo-liberal" forms of government. Liberal regimes are characterized by a retreat of direct political rule for the benefit of subtle political manipulations—material and discursive—of the environment that we inhabit.[27] Foremost among these indirect forms of government is the organization of urban space, which affects the way we see, move, and think as citizens. In the age of "liberal governmentality," the management of space thus became a "technology of government."[28] The open and abstract character of space in the city is designed to educate us to govern ourselves, that is, to control and manage our own conduct, according to a set of principles that we have come to believe are rational, self-evident, and universal. Thus, "a free society is created, running according to its own laws and patterns, and the leviathan socio-technical intervention maintaining it [remains] hidden."[29] Much of the literature written in Foucault's wake concerns the infrastructure of the city, in which orderly civic conduct can be performed against a background of political interventions, from abattoirs to sanitation, from street lighting to public transport.[30] Yet aesthetics, too, play an important role in this conditioning. The technical infrastructure of the liberal city finds its analogue in an architectural idiom that promotes "functionalism." Functionalism figures here as a way of portraying modernity as transparent and rational, disguising its cultural specificity behind a façade of universalism.

The Foucauldian critique of the modernist city has political subtexts that, according to its critics, rehash the politics of nostalgia and threaten to undermine the emancipatory and democratic achievements of modernity. It is true that postmodernists often seek out a vantage point "outside" the promodernist consensus, from which a coherent critique of modernity can be articulated.[31] More specifically, the contention that premodern regimes tended to exercise power directly and openly, while modern "liberal" governance tends to be indirect and hidden,[32] could be taken to suggest that the modern state is somehow more dangerous than its premodern counterpart. Politically committed historians have therefore interpreted this postmodern critique as a threat to the modern ideas of universal human rights, political emancipation, and social justice. In particular, they have criticized a sense of nostalgia with which those who censure the cultural costs of modernization often hark back to an idealized premodern world.[33]

It is true that the critique of modernity has given rise to a spate of publications and exhibitions devoted to "rehabilitating" aspects of the non-modern that were long shunned as reactionary.[34] In these debates, the vernacular often figures as a rhetorical standpoint from which the impact of modernization can be rejected. This use of vernacular as a trope of resistance is not, however, the concern of this volume. Beyond the opposition of domination and resistance, we want to focus on a more fundamental issue by raising the problem of an indeterminacy of the modern: the simultaneity of internationalism and the local, of abstraction and its opposite, the concreteness of the vernacular. Keeping anti-modernism and postmodernism analytically distinct, we ask whether we can recover a sense of the vernacular as praxis beyond its instrumentalization for political anti-modernism.

Locating the Vernacular and Rethinking Modernity

The final decades of the twentieth century witnessed multiple revivals of the particular, the local, and the regional, evident, for example, in a resurgence of regional languages, such as Frisian, Catalan, and Basque. They have outlived the dual processes of nation-building and globalization and appear to have gained new energy.[35] Vernacular cultures are flourishing in the postindustrial world. A powerful resurgence of local and regional "identity politics" has been observable in the West in recent decades. At the same time, parallel changes in the former Soviet bloc have confounded modern-

ization theorists. This indicates, we contend, that the vernacular itself is one of the generative principles of the modern condition. We call this constellation "vernacular modernism."

In investigating "vernacular modernism," we not only face the difficulty that the two constitutive concepts—modernity and the vernacular—are notoriously fluid. They are also difficult to correlate due to a categorical difference. The vernacular denotes particularism and, by extension, a specific attitude of sensitivity to *place,* whereas modernity denotes both a historical period and a general mental disposition. Thus, any attempt to provide a consistent definition of vernacular modernism runs into semantic problems. Vernacular modernism is better understood in terms of praxis. In other words, its significance is best captured by examining its role in those cultural fields that participate in the construction and performance of space and place. The individual, the emotional, and the regional are, it transpires, constitutive parts of the political and cultural project of "modernity" in ways that we are only just beginning to recognize. As much as the theories of the postmodern lay claim to thinking diversity, rupture, the nonidentical, and the nonrational, this "other" of modernity has been part of its history from the beginning—albeit largely excluded from modernist theory, and generally less visible than the teleological optimism and triumphalist narratives of time, progress, and emancipation. To conceive of the vernacular within the framework of modernity therefore not only gives us a new handle on the dubious concept embodied in the German word *Heimat* (native place). It also opens up a repository of alternatives for dealing with the challenges of modernity in the age of globalization.

In recent decades, research in cultural geography has reexamined the experiences and practices that have customarily been associated with non-European civilizations and anti-modern attitudes. This literature emphasizes both the contingency of our own notions of place and the process by which other cultures draw upon "Western" pictorial conventions and material artifacts of the global market and use them to express agendas quite different from those for which they were originally intended.[36] Similar observations have been made in relation to the creative appropriation and transformation of consumer culture in the context of postcolonial vernaculars.[37] As the authors of a new study of American culture abroad conclude, globalization is not a one-way street: "greater homogeneity *and* greater heterogeneity are . . . simultaneously at work in the often chaotic negotiations between groups and cultures" in the age of globalization.[38]

The mutual dependence of the vernacular and the global is at the center of our investigation. Yet we have chosen a different focus from cultural anthropology and postcolonial theory. We do not investigate modernity's other, but the alternative—vernacular—potentialities within modernism itself. To do so, we revisit the definitional core of the project of the modern, both in geographical terms, by focusing on the "West"—that is, Europe and America—and in terms of genre. We suggest that the built environment was key to the way the spatial politics of modernism were constructed.

Foregrounding the vernacular as a defining moment of modernism conjures up problems of semantics. The term "modern" is universally recognized and has close analogues in all European languages. The same does not apply to the term "vernacular," which is neither universal nor unambiguous. In fact, in the English language, "vernacular" is used to refer to an extremely wide variety of practices and meanings, ranging from the native language or dialect of minority groups to the artifacts of everyday popular culture.[39] The term has no linguistic equivalent in most European languages—especially in those not predominantly derived from Latin—and none that would encompass an equally wide array of different meanings. To enable cross-national comparisons of the role of the vernacular in modernism, we need to reduce a dazzling array of meanings to certain core features. It is worth reminding ourselves that "vernacular" originally derives from the Latin *verna,* which referred to slaves born as children of slaves into the household of their owner, as opposed to those acquired on the market. More generally, the term meant things naturally belonging to or pertaining to the domestic sphere—as opposed to matters of state, the *res publica.* From this time onward, the term "vernacular" expressed a tension between the closed domestic sphere and the public sphere. Vernacular referred to the endemic, signifying characteristics of belonging to a specific region, of ethnic qualities, of a disease restricted to, or of a language spoken in, an area with discernible borders. To "vernacularize" used to be a verb for adapting to or making someone adapt to the specificity of a region, to make the person feel at home.

Read in this way, we can discover clear analogues to the vernacular in other European languages. German is a case in point. The closest analogue to the sense of place signified by vernacular is the word *Heimat*. Linguistically, *Heimat* is related to home. It associates a conceptual status akin to the vernacular but draws on emotional connotations. *Heimisch* or *einheimisch* refers to a space defined in terms of a mental and emotional place of be-

longing and, by implication, exclusion of others. In aesthetics, the vernacular, that is, a locally or regionally specific style, is called *Heimatstil* in German. In combination with knowledge or information, *heimlich* means secret, known only inside a closed circle and concealed to others. *Heimisch* in the sense of being at home, being familiar with, or dwelling at a place is the opposite of being alien, *fremd*. *Einheimisch* is translated as native or indigenous, but it has connotations that cannot be captured by these translations. *Einheimisch werden* is not the same as "to naturalize," as it contains the word *Heim*, which transforms it from a legal to a more emotional term — not unlike that which underpins the related notion of *Heimweh*, homesickness. The term *Heimweh* first appeared in Johannes Hofer's *Dissertatio medica de nostalgia, oder Heimweh* (Medical Dissertation on Nostalgia, or Heimweh), published in Basel in 1688, which deals with a condition affecting mind and body. After 1800, this notion was individualized and psychologized. For the romantics, *Heimweh* signified a subjective psychic disposition, the state of the lonely soul, of an ego that feels exposed and experiences a longing for a place called *Heimat*. At that time, the modern imagery of *Heimat* emerged in German literature, art, and architecture. Even more so than the English word "homesickness," *Heimweh* located the condition at the center of the psyche, designating an emotional reaction against the modern notion of abstract and homogenous space.

The legacy of the nineteenth-century discourse on *Heimat* is still to be felt today. Romantics and fin de siècle cultural pessimists looked to *Heimat* as a locus for resistance to the "alienating" effects of industrialization. Globalization as we understand it today was unknown to these critics, but they anticipated much of the physical and psychological destruction that it would entail, not least because they were wary of the link between modernity and the "global market."[40] While the idea of local resistance to trends of internationalism and cosmopolitanism was just as prominent in Germany as elsewhere in the West, the term *Heimat* gave it a dubious emotional twist with reactionary connotations. Hence, German historians and philosophers on the political Left, while engaging in anti-capitalist rhetoric, were loath to incorporate *Heimat* into their political vocabulary.[41] *Heimat* not only has overtones of political nostalgia — the same is true of the vernacular idioms invoked in England and America by Arts and Crafts reformers, who had little tolerance for progress, urbanism, and democratic pluralism. But in Germany, *Heimat* came to play a prominent role in the *völkisch* "Blut und Boden" ideology of National Socialism. The career of the Wilhelmine *Heimatschutz* proponent Paul Schultze-Naumburg, who became a major

figure in Nazi cultural politics after 1933, is often cited to illustrate the connection.[42] Even where scholars have refuted the notion that the history of *Heimat* in Germany can simply be written as the prehistory of fascism,[43] it remains true that any essentialist definition of *Heimat* fosters political exclusion, and it is often invoked to legitimate violence against the other. German institutions like the Bund Heimatschutz were ideologically wedded to idealization of an authentically "German," rural past that also informed Nazi racial thinking, even if Wilhelmine reformers could not have foreseen such consequences.[44]

Heimat, then, is not an idea to be toyed with light-heartedly. Yet it is equally problematic to skip too hastily over the fact that the ideological purposes served by the political mobilization of *Heimat* were not identical with lived experience. To tarnish all instances of regionalism and community-based sentiment with the brush of racism obscures the fact that such vernacular sentiments, while not "modern" in the orthodox sense, provided emotional means for dealing with the anomie caused by industrialization and urbanization. The longing for a home—a *Heimat*—in modernity cannot be denied legitimacy. It was more general than any one political movement, any one decade, or any one country. As long as modernity is exclusively equated with emancipation from ties to the specific and with embracing universal truths, an important constituent of the modern psyche is repressed. The essays in this volume are based on the contention that "vernacular modernism" was not an extension of reactionary politics and did not serve the hunger for stability and an end of time. It expressed, in the various historical, intellectual and political constellations examined, a mode of dialogical engagement with the natural and human environment and provided a sense of orientation in time and space. In this specific sense, the vernacular was an integral part of the history of the modern. It complemented abstract modern categories by producing concrete shapes and cultural meaning. Thus, the vernacular productively coexisted with the city: consciously or not, architects created a vernacular modernism that provided an important corrective to the trajectory of the International Style. In the city, modernity's locus classicus, the vernacular became commensurate with reason and self-determination. It placed sensitivity to experience, emotion, and tradition in a relationship with dimensions affirming the modern condition.

One reason for the exclusion of the vernacular from the modern in most theoretical debates is the allegation that the vernacular posits "timelessness." In this volume, we argue against the myth of *Heimat* as a time-defying con-

tinuum. Architectural vernaculars embody memory, and their grammar differs from that of academic history. But this does not make them amodern by definition. Rather, we contend, the vernacular reconstitutes memory under the specific conditions of modernity. From this perspective, the vernacular influenced even those architects and institutions whose work is often defined as "high modernism" or "International Style"; the examples investigated in this volume include Le Corbusier, and the Museum of Modern Art in New York. Our anthology demonstrates that the vernacular is present in such work, notwithstanding that its minimalist aesthetics eradicated visible traces of vernacular narratives: particular materials and particular proportions conjure up place-based memories. Viewed from this perspective, the notion of a faceless and abstract modernism was much less hegemonic in twentieth-century architecture than is often assumed. More typically, the vernacular was employed, consciously or inadvertently, as a corrective to modernity's universalism. This interpretation reverses the positions. Whereas essentialist definitions of the vernacular emphasize the absence of change, in our interpretation, temporality is located in the interplay between modernity's internationalism and the vernacular as a cultural memory.

The debate about the achievements and pitfalls of the vernacular, its relationship to time, and the relationship between global space and concrete place continues unabated. A recent example is *Empire* by Michael Hardt and Antonio Negri.[45] The alleged analogy between the space of modern globalization and the space of the Roman empire notwithstanding, the authors argue that globalization is the product of real-time communication and abstract networks, and therefore has no regard for the reality of place. Moreover, they suggest, in contrast to antiquity, late capitalism has no need of a center. This position has met with criticism. Globalization, critics argue, is predicated on power. Thus, even if there is no single point of convergence, centers of power like New York, Tokyo, and London create a special order around them—they structure the system of globalization geographically. Globalization, in this view, continuously establishes hierarchies and exclusions, and limits contingency. The privilege of determining criteria for these limitations and exclusions is defined as power. The execution of this power requires a place, a nodal point for flows of information and capital. Globalization is thus predicated on a fiction: the fiction of placelessness, of anonymous benevolence, and of changes from which no center benefits. Read in this light, it represents little more than another phase in the age-old coalition of knowledge and power, which Francis Bacon defined as a chief

signifier of the modern age: like the absolutist state, globalization, too, presupposes privileged places where knowledge is produced, ordered, and disseminated. Foucault suggested an extension of Bacon's proposition by arguing that there are no power relations without a corresponding field of knowledge and no knowledge that would not at the same time constitute power relations.[46] Should he be correct, globalization is as much dependent on space as the period of nation-state formation, which created a dual structure of center and periphery. In the age of virtual space, this dualism is seemingly dissolved. Yet even on this advanced level of abstraction, the system needs privileged places. Their counterpart may no longer be the periphery; it is, instead, a desire for the vernacular, a new imagination of place.

Such a view is borne out by historical chronology. The late nineteenth century, heyday of nation-state building and industrialization, saw a proliferation of vernacular revivals. In 1990, Celia Applegate published a book entitled *A Nation of Provincials*.[47] It sparked off a new trend in nationalism studies that has identified localist or *Heimat* sentiments as constitutive of the nation-building process. Far from standing in the way of national integration, as historians long assumed, it now appears that an imagery of the vernacular helped ordinary men and women imagine the abstract category of the nation.[48] The local sphere of experience came to be seen as integral to the invention of the nation. It is therefore neither surprising nor paradoxical that we find vernacular revivalism peaking precisely when popular nationalism was at its height: before and during World War I. Not only did idealized representations of the (rural) homeland play a crucial role in war propaganda, but in the shape of countless associations aimed at protecting and reviving local customs and traditions the notion of *Heimat* attracted an unprecedented mass following from the 1900s onward, and it is obviously experiencing a revival at present.

It is clear, then, that the desire for *Heimat* emerges within the parameters of modernism. Architectural historians have often portrayed the vernacular revival around 1900 as a "springboard" for the development of modernism proper. Even traditional scholars such as Nicholas Pevsner acknowledged that the English and American Arts and Crafts movements in particular helped wipe away the aesthetic "clutter" of historicist revival styles of the nineteenth century, and thus prepared the ground for modern functionalism.[49] While the truth of such trajectories is beyond question, this volume proposes that they contain only a partial truth. They reduce the role of the vernacular in modernism to a purely transitory one, which ceased to be rel-

evant as soon as high modernism developed. Moreover, this reading also divorces the vernacular from its sociopolitical contexts—notably the sense of place—and posits a purely aesthetic influence, where folkloristic simplicity helped pave the way for the even greater, ideal-typical simplicity of modern abstraction. Such a reading of the vernacular revival is not only unduly teleological; it also perpetuates a unitary narrative of modernity and modernism, which we consider no longer tenable. In this volume, we propose an alternative reading, based on two hypotheses. Firstly, we hope to show that the evident influence of the vernacular in the early modernism was not (only) a tool for "tidying up" historicism but itself an agent of modernization and, in many ways, already a product of globalization. Secondly, we hope to demonstrate that the vernacular, in order to be appropriately understood, needs to be interpreted in terms of ambivalence, because even in the period of high modernism, it continued to play a constitutive role in defining a sense of place. Against this background, we can appreciate the renewed attention that "postmodern" architects paid to vernacular idioms—commonly referred to as the movement of "critical regionalism"—as a reconfiguration of an ambivalence that is itself thoroughly modern and not a digression from the path of modernity.

The term *Heimat* makes these modern connotations of the imagination of place particularly explicit.[50] Yet even before this term became current, we can observe instances in which the vernacular was invoked as part of a strategy for reconstituting the public sphere of modernity. This strategy was an integral part of several political and cultural movements associated with the intellectual genealogy of modernism. The eighteenth century is a case in point. The Enlightenment saw a revival of the idea of the suburban Roman villa as the place from which a corrupt political and social regime could be challenged in the name of reason and morality. In England, the so-called "Country Party," an alliance of powerful aristocrats and Enlightenment writers, turned the country house into the site for launching their political critique of Walpole's "corrupt" regime and what they saw as the threat of emerging French-style absolutism at court.[51] They designed their neoclassical villas and estates, such as Chiswick and Stowe, in such a way as to give physical shape to this ideal, thereby turning the "English garden" into the most iconic space of modern Enlightenment culture, first in Britain and then throughout Europe and America.[52]

In the nineteenth century, clear oppositions turned into ambivalence. In criticizing the effects of industrialization, romantics idealized the countryside as a refuge in opposition to the "Satanic mills" of England's industrial

cities.[53] Yet they had no monopoly claim to the vernacular. While some linked it to social conservatism, paternalism, and agrarianism, others maintained a creative tension between the vernacular and the modern. The Arts and Crafts movement is a perfect example of this. Through its influence on industrial design, as well as the close connections with leading socialist reformers, the movement gave rise to a range of distinctly urban vernaculars that emancipated the notion of "homeliness" from the dichotomy of the evil city and an idyllic iconography of the rural.[54] In countries like Germany, where individual towns had long enjoyed political and cultural autonomy, the late nineteenth century saw a fusion of older particularistic styles with the qualities of Arts and Crafts–inspired vernaculars. A famous promoter of such a modern, urban vernacular was Hamburg's Building Commissioner Fritz Schumacher.[55]

After 1918, the vernacular even became the vehicle for a utopian project articulated by Ernst Bloch, among others.[56] To be sure, most writers of the European political left remained wary of any association with the local and the provincial. Bloch's positive appropriation of *Heimat* was exceptional. Theodor Adorno spoke for many when he associated *Heimat* with the politics of identity, which he called the "untruth." Bloch shared Adorno's indictment of the anti-modern, yet attempted to free the discourse of place from nostalgia and political reaction. For Bloch, *Heimat* is not a real place that can be rescued, reconstructed, or regained. It has no location in any particular past. Instead, it needed to be invented through imagination and dreaming and remains a mental sketch, an *Entwurf*. Reconstituted as an open and mobile space, Bloch believes, *Heimat* can be rescued from the parochialism of identity politics and fascist ideologies that (mis-)appropriate the term. Bloch's vernacular is defined through the metaphor of childhood: his notion of *Heimat* speaks to sentiments of security, trust, and happiness but avoids the solipsism of premodern communitarianism. Bloch diagnoses the existence of *hollow spaces* resulting from the collapse of metaphysical systems: these are spaces vacated by God and a Hegelian "spirit of history." These spaces now need to be defined in terms of material culture, without recourse to transcendence. Utopian as his construction is, Bloch contends that it cannot be invented "out of nothing": its elements come from lived experience, a reality disintegrated by a gaze that discovers traces of the new in banal spheres of live. This gaze elevates the vernacular, the narrow, and the concrete to the level of philosophical reflection.[57] And it also rescues it from political misappropriation. Bloch's *Heimat* does not designate an ontological state of being. It is continuously emerging and of-

fers no comfort for fundamentalists or prophets. As such, it resonates with the role of the vernacular in modernist literature. Jewish communities in the shtetels of Eastern Europe, for example, produced a literature based on a sense of place that used the vernacular as the semantics of ordinary people subjected to the whims of hegemonic regimes.[58] Kafka's fascination with the Yiddish theater was not entirely free from nostalgia, yet also drew upon the concrete utopianism the way Bloch conceived it.

Such readings allow us to appreciate the vernacular as a place of the imagination: none the less powerful for its imaginary qualities, yet fundamentally divorced from essentializing definitions of the "authenticity" of place. This perspective connects with recent anthropological research, which suggests that notions of *Heimat* assume cultural and political prominence precisely when conventional connections with place are disrupted or absent. Projects like the recent *New Heimat* exhibition have provided empirical evidence for the seemingly paradoxical contention that a sense of homeland is most important for nomadic communities.[59] Where a place-based identity cannot be taken for granted, the vernacular gains a special emotional, at times spiritual, significance that may propel it to center-stage of a particular culture. If we accept Gilles Deleuze's analysis of modernity, which he characterized as a state of nomadic deterritorialization,[60] such anthropological research sheds light on the phenomenon of vernacular modernism in general.

The Volume's Contributions to the Debate

Our contention that the vernacular functioned as a constitutive part of the modern connects with certain trends in the history of ideas, arguing that modernism was more pluralist, dialogical, open-ended, and tolerant than its critics suggest. In this vein, Stephen Toulmin proposed a genealogy of modernity that begins with sixteenth-century rhetorical humanism rather than with seventeenth-century Cartesian, scientific rationalism.[61] Similarly, Robert Pippin's *Modernism as a Philosophical Problem* suggested a nonfoundational reading of Hegel to prove that modern philosophy was in fact acutely sensitive to the "blindspots" unearthed by postmodernists.[62]

The contributions to this volume bring the perspectives of literary, intellectual, and, above all, architectural history to bear on this reevaluation. The volume begins with a symptomatic case study. The Museum of Modern Art in New York has long been seen as the institutional embodiment of classical modernism. Its agenda, notably the famous 1929 "International Style"

exhibition, defined the image of modernity as a place-defying movement toward abstraction. As Mardges Bacon's contribution reveals, such a reading distorts the real significance of modernism's prime institution. It attributes iconic status to one brief moment in the museum's history and downplays the importance of a concerted and much more prolonged effort to dismantle the agenda of heroic modernism, pushing, in its place, a movement best described as vernacular modernism. This second phase, Bacon suggests, started only a few years after the "International Style" exhibition and was motivated in part by a political response to the Great Depression. In the 1930s, the museum denounced classical modernism as elitist, overly abstract, and Eurocentric and staged a number of exhibitions shifting attention to native American developments and what it considered a grassroots vernacular in such exhibitions as *Housing* (1934), *Early Modern Architecture: Chicago 1870–1930* (1936), and *H. H. Richardson* (1936). What emerged from this political realignment was a fundamental paradigm shift in modernist discourse, from what Bacon calls "machine-centered" to "man-centered" concerns. In the latter category, the vernacular played a decisive role. For Bacon, the vernacular denotes a sensitivity to place, which operated both on the national and the local level. In political debates, the recourse to the vernacular promoted the emancipation of American modernism from its European models. But when it came to defining these American alternatives, region and locality provided a decisive impetus: the specificity of landscapes and even indigenous cultures were invoked to "ground" the aesthetics of American modernism in a concrete sense of place. Thus, the Museum of Modern Art in New York, conventionally regarded as the spearhead of abstract, universalizing modernism, emerges as a place where a new alliance of modernism and the vernacular was forged.

Taking this instance as their cue, Chapters 2 and 3 offer two distinct interpretations of how the vernacular was constituted in the discourse of modernity. Michael Saler brings a literary perspective to bear on the problem of vernacular modernism. Although in literary studies, the term "vernacular" is most frequently invoked as a linguistic category, designating a tradition of dialect literature, Saler's literary vernacular is just as much about a sense of place as Bacon's. Modernist literature, he argues, did not abolish vernacular sensibilities; rather, it reconstituted them, transferring them into the sphere of the "ironic imagination." At the center of Saler's investigation is a genre of popular science fiction literature that emerged in the decades around 1900. These texts exhibit key modernist characteristics, such as a fascination with science and the spirit of rational skepticism. Within these pa-

rameters, however, concrete geographical settings play a defining role. Detailed descriptions highlighted the particularism of place in a futurist universe; photographs, maps, appendices, and even footnotes were used to convey the "reality effect" of the novels' settings. Saler characterizes such places as secondary vernacular worlds, which readers came to inhabit like "homes," not in spite of but because of the scientific thoroughness with which their particular characteristics were conveyed. Ultimately, this argument transcends the boundaries of genre. In Saler's analysis, popular science fiction literature is just one example that offers us a new way of understanding the process by which self-consciously modernist techniques were used to redefine the vernacular of *Heimat* literature. In its concreteness, this sense of place revived classical attributes of the vernacular. Yet in its modernist reflexivity and playfulness, it transposed this sense of place into the sphere of the imagination: *Heimat* became virtual.

Chapter 3 examines a related process in German intellectual history but relates it to a specific geographical milieu in which such texts were produced. Bernd Hüppauf argues that the fragmented nature of German cultural and political life over centuries meant that German writers made a special contribution to the mediation between the vernacular and the modern. A sociopolitical structure that has been dubbed "individualized country" played the defining role in this development.[63] Its foremost representation was the German small town, which Mack Walker termed the "home town." Home towns blurred the binary opposition between the anonymous city and the local intimacy of the village. When the formation of modern nation-states led to the emergence of a unified public sphere structured around the metropolis, the continued territorial fragmentation of Germany obstructed such an unequivocal rationalization of space. In the hands of literary writers, this obstacle became an opportunity. Avoiding both the centralization of a metropolitan culture and the idealization of a pure agrarian countryside, the home town was perceived by German and foreign observers as a place of particular intellectual vibrancy. It is out of this tradition, Hüppauf suggests, that the vernacular utopianism of Ernst Bloch emerged. It was predicated on a sense of contrast between the particular place and the open space of the world. This vernacular is a modern state of mind, defined by the tension between *Heimat* and its opposite. In Bloch's own terms, happiness and hope, as a *principle*, are associated with space and a sense of belonging. Simultaneously, they create a sense of the freedom to leave: *Heimweh* and *Fernweh* condition and determine one another.[64]

The ensuing contributions—Chapters 4 to 6—focus on the role of architecture in mapping the vernacular agenda in modernity. Whereas the first three chapters were concerned with the representation of "place" in other media—from the architectural exhibition to the tree hut featured in Bloch's writings—in the following three chapters, the built environment of modernity is itself the object under analysis. Within these parameters, Maiken Umbach's contribution focuses on the genesis of modern material culture around 1900. She argues that reflections on the role of place in modernity were driven by political concerns. Then, as today, globalization, understood both as a threat and an opportunity, figured prominently in contemporaries' minds. There were, first of all, practical economic concerns about competition in the global marketplace. Yet the response was not purely defensive. A global market, many contemporaries believed, called for goods that embodied cultural distinctiveness, not only because this was a quality to be rescued from globalization, but because in a globalized world, cultural specificity would be a particular asset. The history of English goods from the days of Josiah Wedgwood was upheld as an example of the fact that what is distinctive and thus instantly recognizable is also more marketable. The Arts and Crafts movement was but one in a wave of reformist movements that revisited the vernacular as a platform from which a sense of place could be injected into modernity. And it quickly found imitators on the Continent. It was no coincidence that the final years of the nineteenth century saw the appropriation of the label "Made in Germany" as a positive marketing tool by German manufacturers.

Such economically driven concerns, centered on questions of industrial design, sparked off a more fundamental reevaluation of the meaning of place in the visual code of modernism, which we can best trace in architecture. The driving figures in the German *Werkbund*—ostensibly an association to promote better industrial design—were in fact architects, not designers. In Umbach's view, architecture, as a practice that interprets spaces and makes them culturally legible, became the primary field in which new articulations of the vernacular were realized. The decades around 1900 were much more than a springboard for the development of "modernism proper." The housing and urban development programs initiated by men such as Hermann Muthesius, Fritz Schumacher, and Richard Riemerschmid created decisive precedents for integrating vernacular sensibilities into the modern city. If these experiments came under attack from more radical modernists in the 1920s, as well as reactionary nostalgics in the

1930s, this was a result of the political polarization of the Weimar years, but not a symptom of some inevitable march toward spatial abstraction.

Francesco Passanti's contribution picks up this thread, and argues that the vernacular lived on in the oeuvre of seminal figures of classical modernism. The Swiss-born French architect Le Corbusier is typically regarded as the epitome of everything that was problematic about abstraction and the "International Style." In the years immediately after World War I, he attacked regionalism, proposed to raze much of downtown Paris to make room for rows of functional skyscrapers, and declared that the house should be a "dwelling machine as practical as a typewriter." Through a careful reexamination of both written and visual evidence, Passanti argues that, contrary to the received view, the vernacular played an essential role in the conception of Le Corbusier's modernist architecture. Le Corbusier's extensive study of various indigenous architectures provided a model for a notion of *modern vernacular*—one that issued as naturally from modern industrial society, and was as representative of it, as the traditional vernacular of common parlance had been of earlier societies. Le Corbusier arrived at this notion by layering upon each other several discourses concerning regionalism, folklore, and the more complex concept of *Sachlichkeit* (sobriety), as developed by the Arts and Crafts reformers discussed in Umbach's chapter.

Passanti's contribution also reveals a distinctive and telling difference in the way in which different academic disciplines approach the problem of the vernacular. The pattern of national variations in definitions of the vernacular outlined in this Introduction finds its analytical equivalent here. For architectural historians have largely internalized the transition initiated by Le Corbusier: they detect the "vernacular" in allusions to the everyday environment, where the sense of place is no longer made explicit but merely implied. Whereas literary and philosophical discourses "name" the vernacular and represent it as a narrative of place, in architecture, the vernacular is often embedded in particular attitudes to material, practicality, and social context. Its temporality is not one that is told in story form. It has to be carefully unearthed by using the analytical tools of the architectural critic. Such is the task performed by Stanford Anderson in his contribution to this volume. Invoking the example of traditional Dutch town houses, he decodes vernacular architecture as a carrier of certain social memories and meanings. Much modernist architecture invokes these memories. The sense of place and the sense of the past emerge as closely intertwined. Yet memory does not preclude development. Properly used, Anderson suggests, in

modern architecture, the vernacular adds a temporal dimension without denying the ideas of change and, indeed, self-conscious modernism. This is evident in the work of current practitioners such as Dimitris Antonakakis, Marlon Blackwell, Will Bruder, David Chipperfield, Sverre Fehn, Rick Joy, Ricardo Legoretta, Donlyn Lyndon, the late Samuel Mockbee, Glenn Murcutt, John and Patricia Patkau, Antoine Predock, and Maurice Smith, to name but a few. Although operating in the intellectual context of postmodernism, none of these architects can be dubbed stylistically "postmodern." They do, it is true, employ a certain narrativity, which distinguishes their work from, say, Le Corbusier's. Yet they combine this with a formal rationality that is undisputedly modern. In such work, the vernacular features as a trope around which an alternative modern sensitivity is built—but not as a polemical platform for the rejection of the modern condition.

In the light of Umbach's and Passanti's contributions, we can appreciate such efforts as a much less radical departure from twentieth-century developments than had often been assumed. Yet while we recover this "other history" of modernity, we must not forget that radical ruptures existed as well. In the name of modernization, and under the cultural hegemony of heroic modernism, local cultures were destroyed and irreparable physical and psychological damage was done. The Stalinist version of modernity is a clear case in point. While it cannot be equated with modernism per se, it would also be naïve to treat it as a mere aberration. Programs of forceful industrialization, and the dehumanizing town planning that accompanied them, were widespread in the Soviet empire, but by no means confined to it. When confronted with such a legacy, the vernacular often takes on a seemingly anti-modern subtext. The reconstruction of a sense of place in eastern European cities, which is the topic of John Czaplicka's contribution in this volume, is clearly driven by an association of modernity with Soviet-style modernization. Vernacular revivalism in the former Eastern bloc thus often harks back to the pre-Soviet past and is predicated on a total rejection of the past sixty years or so. Even this, however, does not make such reconstructive efforts purely backward-looking. Czaplicka suggests that in post-Soviet cities, the local mode of expression is dynamic in that it relates to an imagination of ethnic or national characters, which in itself is a thoroughly modern phenomenon. De facto, any sense of the vernacular here is inherently unstable, contingent on demographic, material, social, and economic relationships in places that change and evolve all the time. Moreover, the neovernaculars that are now being "re-"constructed often simply replace

one historical myth with another, substituting politically useful central European idioms—such as art deco—for styles reminiscent of Russian predominance.

In recent years, the debate about the role of the vernacular in the built environment has been shaped by the notion of "critical regionalism."[65] In his Epilogue to this volume, Kenneth Frampton, who has played the key role in introducing the term, provides some thoughts on this debate's outcomes to date. "Critical regionalism" inspired both applause and criticism well beyond specialist architectural circles. Frederic Jameson, a theorist of postmodernity, described critical regionalism as a "retro" position, aspiring to negate the negations of postmodernism.[66] This position can lead to a paradoxical rehabilitation of classical modernism in a postmodern context. The late Ignasi Sola, who was responsible for the recent reconstruction of Mies van de Rohe's famous Barcelona pavilion, argued that in an age of globalization, architecture's purpose has to be politically subversive. This subversive power can only be derived, according to Sola, from the autonomy of the pure work of art. Only the neo-Kantian idealism that he sees in Mies van de Rohe's language of forms, Sola believed, has the potential to act as a subversive force capable of countering the political corruption with which globalization is associated. Confidence in the power of resistance vested in the autonomous work of art was symptomatic of critical theories of modernity. Yet even Theodor W. Adorno, arguably the strongest advocate of modern art as a technique of subversion, had significant doubts. Against theories of the radical autonomy of art, Frampton posits the notion of a dialogue with the past, one that is essentially critical of the past, that questions authority but nevertheless insists that architecture engage with its historical and geographical contexts, rather than assert its total autonomy.

In summary, then, all our contributions make the case for the presence of the vernacular within the modern. In coining the phrase "vernacular modernism," we do not presume to advance a new theory of modernity. Modernity, we contend, is by definition heterogeneous, and no single theoretical model can capture its intrinsic oppositions. We are approaching it, instead, by focusing on praxis, exemplified here by a set of characteristic moments in its historical evolution that are subjected to a close analysis. In keeping with this approach, we have not attempted to synthesize different disciplinary perspectives into a single meta-concept. We hope, rather, that the contributions in this volume can serve as exemplars for the way in which distinct approaches elucidate a single phenomenon—vernacular modernism—while preserving the unique methods and sensitivities that de-

fine the authors' respective intellectual disciplines. What emerges from these chapters is a flexible framework that makes it possible to conceive of the vernacular as a constitutive part of the modern. It can be described as an imaginary place, evoking a sense of locality or *Heimat* in the face of modern anomie, and also invites a language of aesthetic forms used to transform an imagined place into concrete reality. In this synthetic character, mediating between imagined realms and real communities, lies what is perhaps the most enduring contribution of the vernacular to modernity.

CHAPTER ONE

Modernism and the Vernacular at the Museum of Modern Art, New York

MARDGES BACON

With its founding in 1929, the Museum of Modern Art in New York provided a principal site of modern visual culture in the United States.[1] To the leadership of the Modern, and especially its first director, Alfred H. Barr Jr., modernism was inextricably associated with the European avant-garde but held a global destiny. By establishing the museum as a locus of modernism in the New World, Barr and his colleagues confirmed the teleology of the movement to be international. As a cross-cultural and interdisciplinary enterprise, modernism shared a set of values that sought to give artistic expression to modern times. Thus, a concept of the "present" infused an international language of the avant-garde.[2] Working against the dominance of the European project as well as the homogenizing currents of internationalism, like warp against woof, a local vernacular associated with regional and cultural identity entered the American discourse on modernism: the vernacular of authenticity that could plumb native sources of modern art within an academic tradition, the vernacular of folk art, the vernacular of indigenous traditions and ethnography, the vernacular of the everyday, and the vernacular of regional artists, photographers, and filmmakers giving expression to national consciousness during the lean years of the Great Depression. In architecture, modernism looked to the vernacular in its search for cultural authenticity and models of utilitarian urban building, through an "Americanization" of the "International Style" synthesizing received traditions from Europe and native ones associated with place, and in its commitment to social housing.

During the 1930s, modernism on both sides of the Atlantic continued to embrace machine-centered imagery and symbolism, long associated with

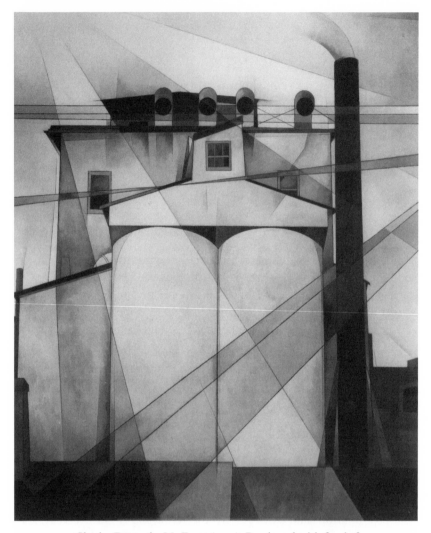

FIG. 1.1. Charles Demuth, *My Egypt* (1927). Purchased with funds from Gertrude Vanderbilt Whitney, 31.172. Reproduced by kind permission of the Whitney Museum of American Art.

European production, while it turned increasingly to representations of human-centered concerns where the touchstone was vernacular and regional expression. Promoting modernism as both a transatlantic and interdisciplinary project, the Museum of Modern Art engaged both cultures—mechanical and human—in forging its identity as an avant-garde American institution. This dichotomy entered into the Modern's early art and architecture

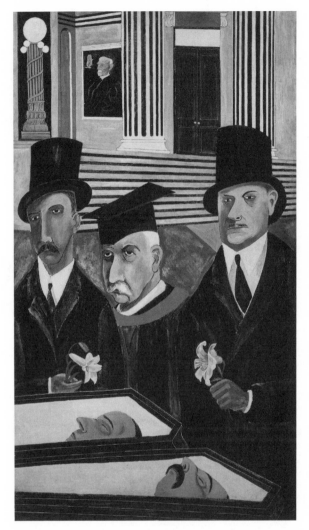

FIG. 1.2. Ben Shahn, *The Passion of Sacco and Vanzetti* (1931–32). Large panel, tempera on canvas. Gift of Mr. and Mrs. Milton Lowenthal in memory of Juliana Force, 49.22. Reproduced by kind permission of the Whitney Museum of American Art.

exhibitions. For example, in exhibitions of American painting, Charles Demuth's *My Egypt* (1927; fig. 1.1) presented a precisionist image of American technology, while Ben Shahn's *The Passion of Sacco and Vanzetti* (1931–32; fig. 1.2) invoked social injustice.[3] In architectural exhibitions, a shift of axis toward more explicit references to the vernacular was evident, for example,

FIG. 1.3. Le Corbusier, de Mandrot House, Le Pradet, near Toulon, France (1929–31). From Le Corbusier and P[ierre] Jeanneret, *Oeuvre complète de 1929–1934*, vol. 2, ed. Willy Boesiger (Zurich: Girsberger, 1934; reprint 1964), p. 58.

in the trajectory within Le Corbusier's work from the Villa Savoye, Poissy, France (1928–31; see fig. 5.3), emphasizing purist forms and metaphors associated with the machine, to his design of the de Mandrot House at Le Pradet near Toulon, France (1929–31; fig. 1.3) whose rubble walls suggested a pre-industrial artisan culture.[4]

My contention is that in its mission to acquire, display, and educate, the Museum of Modern Art was confronted with an ideological conflict that emerged in conjunction with the Depression: to introduce European avant-garde developments and yet also be both "American," and "democratic." On the one hand, Barr and his mentor and founding trustee Paul Sachs shared an elite vision of "exacting standards."[5] On the other hand, the museum's charter underscored its educational mission of "encouraging and developing the study of modern arts and the application of such arts to manufacture and practical life, and furnishing popular instruction," but intentionally left "modern" undefined.[6] Reluctant to circumscribe modern art "with any degree of finality either in time or in character," Barr eventually characterized it as an "an elastic term that serves conveniently to designate painting,

sculpture, moving pictures, architecture, and the lesser visual arts, original and progressive in character, produced within the last three decades but including also 'pioneer ancestors' of the 19th century."[7] Many of the museum's early exhibitions bring into sharp relief, sometimes in a tensional relationship, the dual commitment to the formal search for quality and the institutional mission to democratize an appreciation of modern art. Among the competing voices and agendas of the leadership, Barr, Holger Cahill, Sachs, Abby Aldrich Rockefeller, and other trustees pursued these objectives to varying degrees. In architecture and design, Barr, Henry-Russell Hitchcock, and Philip Johnson advanced a set of formal principles based on aesthetic standards, while Lewis Mumford and others advocated a social program. With little established museum policy, the Modern took no formal position on resolving any variance between an elite vision and a democratizing mandate. Indeed, its organizational structure decentralized power through a series of trustee-curatorial committees, initially giving Barr more influence than actual power.[8] Moreover, although Barr felt that art performed an important role in helping modern democracies understand "that which is different from us," there was resistance to his Eurocentric persuasion.[9] Rather, what emerged during the Modern's path to institutional maturity was a discourse on modernism that incorporated the received tradition of European abstraction, American traditions of realism and romanticism as well as abstraction, American folk art, the indigenous art of both Africa and the pre-Columbian New World, contemporary American art, and other forms of visual culture. In addressing a field of modernism from international to local and from "high" to "low," the museum engaged a range of vernacular expression. Although the term "vernacular" was rarely employed until the late 1930s, early advocates of modernism implicitly understood it as a language native to a country or region that could be communicated across disciplines, particularly at the level of the everyday.

The founding of the Museum of Modern Art by a trio of collectors—Abby Aldrich Rockefeller, Lillie P. Bliss, and Mary Sullivan—and its subsequent transformation into a chartered institution, has been well documented. It is significant to emphasize that all three were women; all had been drawn into the circle of Arthur B. Davies, the artist and creative force behind the Armory Show of 1913. The families of Rockefeller and Bliss derived their fortunes from American industry, while Sullivan was married to an attorney.[10] Of the three collectors, Rockefeller held the dominant vision of modern art, which encompassed the European avant-garde as well as both American academic art and vernacular expressions. The museum's

view of modernism was influenced by not only Rockefeller's vision but also her preferences as a collector. In addition to Davies, her advisers were William R. Valentiner, director of the Detroit Museum of Art; Holger Cahill, who curated exhibitions at the Newark Art Museum and also worked for Rockefeller; and the New York art dealer Edith Halpert.[11] From the mid 1920s, Valentiner served as Rockefeller's principal mentor in matters of connoisseurship and the acquisition of contemporary European art, especially the work of German expressionists from the groups called Die Brücke and Der Blaue Reiter that looked to the art of peasants and children, an interest that drew her to folk art. Davies also helped to shape her collection of modern European paintings. Cahill and Halpert, both authorities on American folk art, were instrumental in the formation of her folk art collection. Duncan Candler, a New York architect who designed the seventh-floor gallery (with Donald Deskey) in her house at 10 West 54th Street, encouraged her to acquire work by a wide range of young American artists, including Demuth, John Marin, Max Weber, and William Zorach, many of whom were foreign-born.[12] Lillie Bliss made her impact on modernism through her efforts to involve the Metropolitan Museum of Art in it and through her collection of postimpressionist, cubist, expressionist, and fauve paintings. Bliss's bequest of a major portion of her collection to the Modern in 1931 and the trustees' success in raising an endowment laid the foundation for its permanent collection. Mary Sullivan, an art educator who had studied impressionism and postimpressionism in Europe, formed an important modern art collection, which included works by Cézanne, Braque, and Picasso. Sullivan assisted the museum in locating rental space for its early exhibitions on the twelfth floor of the Heckscher Building at Fifth Avenue and 57th Street. Later she joined with Barr to promote the Modern's outreach program for students and teachers.[13]

Barr's Vision of Modernism

The Museum of Modern Art opened its doors on November 8, 1929, little more than a week after the Wall Street stock market crash. To conservative elements in the public at large, to isolationists, and to leftist social commentators, a museum under the banner of the Rockefellers promoting the cause of avant-garde art was suspect. But Alfred Barr's approach to modernism, which dominated the institutional vision during its first decade, was intellectually complex and purposely open-ended. Although predisposed to European modernism, Barr embraced contemporary develop-

ments on both sides of the Atlantic with sufficient vigor to reach a broad spectrum of the American public.

As Sybil Kantor suggests, both Barr's intellectual formation and the organizational structure he crafted for the Modern were grounded in traditions at Harvard University, where he had been a graduate student and instructor.[14] For Barr was immersed in formalism—a critical perspective based on the formal qualities of a work rather than its meaning, symbolism, or content—and aestheticism, both of which were drawn from Barr's experiences in two intellectual circles at Harvard.[15] The first was a group of students in a seminar at the Fogg Art Museum taught by its associate director Paul Sachs, with whom Barr had studied.[16] In 1926–27 the group included Hitchcock, A. Everett ("Chick") Austin, James Rorimer, and Kirk Askew, all of whom were early supporters of the Modern. Sachs's museum course stressed connoisseurship based on the empirical study of objects in a tradition going back to Giovanni Morelli and Bernard Berenson. Additionally at Harvard, Barr fell heir to the aesthetic tradition of George Santayana. Under Sachs's mentorship, and also influenced by his earlier studies with Charles Rufus Morey at Princeton, Barr developed a method of mapping complex artistic developments by means of diagrams, one he would later employ at the Modern. Like Sachs's study model, Barr's diagram seemed to offer a "scientific" method of analysis that would help to define his mature scholarship.

The second intellectual circle was an avant-garde student organization, the Harvard Society for Contemporary Art (HSCA), many of whose members were already associated with the arts and letters journal *Hound & Horn*. Both were founded and directed by Lincoln Kirstein, whose family supported them.[17] Many of the exhibitions organized by the HSCA from 1929 to 1932 served as models for the Modern. HSCA member Edward Warburg later recalled that on visiting its Cambridge gallery, which occupied two rooms above the Harvard Coop, Rockefeller told Sachs that she thought New York should emulate "*en gros* what they were doing."[18] In the orbit of the Harvard Society for Contemporary Art, and also writing for *Hound & Horn*, were not only Barr and Hitchcock but also Jere Abbott (later Barr's assistant and associate director at the Modern) and Philip Johnson.

In constructing the Museum of Modern Art's view of modernism, Barr promoted his formalist agenda and drew upon his expertise in European modernism and its sources. Barr and his colleagues were mindful of the Modern's fragile position as a new institution among such venerable ones

as the Metropolitan Museum of Art, which had only recently endorsed modern French art in its exhibition of "Impressionist and Post-Impressionist Painting."[19] In effect, Barr's plans for the Modern were bound up with his aspirations for the United States and more particularly New York City. They emphasized cultural objectives over sociopolitical ones. As an American site of an international movement, the Modern would become a major vehicle of transatlantic exchange and help to overcome the European perception of New York as a city of unbridled capitalism with few institutions of art and culture. "New York is the most influential center of activity in modern art," Barr maintained, "its modernity, its function as a double-ended funnel through which Europe and America exchange ideas as well as merchandise, make it the artistic as well as the commercial and financial capital of America."[20] Under the influence of its president, A. Conger Goodyear, and a group of trustees, the Modern directed its efforts toward both connoisseurship and didactic programs employing the rhetoric of capitalism and consumerism. In a confidential report of 1933 to the museum's executive committee, its secretary Alan Blackburn defined a dual institutional mission: first, to form "taste" and promote "production" through scholarship and criticism; and second, to democratize an appreciation of modern art for public consumption through channels of "distribution" including exhibitions, traveling exhibitions, catalogues, radio programs, and other forms of "publicity." The report also defined six groups that comprised a broad constituency for the Modern: intellectuals and the avant-garde identified as "a small but powerful minority of professionals and amateurs, critics, collectors, scholars, dealers who know about modern art," the socially prominent or "social group"—assumed to be the "majority" of the members—businessmen and industrialists called the "action group," students and their teachers, the public, and trustees.[21]

In one sense, Barr viewed modernism as a critical term associated with European avant-garde developments. In another sense, he understood that the essence of modernism was its open-ended and pluralistic character, embracing realism as well as abstraction.[22] Toward the objective of forming a permanent museum collection, Barr advanced his concept of modernism as a "torpedo moving through time." In 1933, he represented it graphically as a diagram, "its nose the ever advancing present, its tail the ever receding past of fifty to a hundred years ago" (fig. 1.4).[23] From that vantage point, "modern" extended back to the early 1880s; it included the work of "living artists," native as well as foreign-born. Barr's concept of modernism also extended to American folk art, although it was excluded from his diagrams of academic art movements.

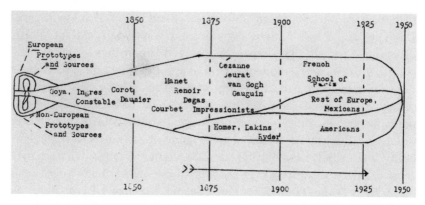

FIG. 1.4. Alfred H. Barr Jr., "Torpedo Moving Through Time" (1933). Diagram representing the ideal permanent collection for the Museum of Modern Art (1933). Alfred H. Barr Papers,. Digital Image © The Museum of Modern Art / Licensed by SCALA / Art Resource, NY. Reproduced by kind permission of the Museum of Modern Art, New York.

In sync with his concept of modernism, Barr, together with his museum colleagues, sought to respond to the needs of contemporary American artists and, as the institution matured, to ongoing criticism that it did not do enough to represent them in a time of economic uncertainty. These concerns surfaced in preparations for the Modern's inaugural exhibition, producing an internal debate between European modernism and American contemporary art, as well as questions about the democratic nature of the institution. Barr and Sachs preferred a first show dedicated to contemporary American art, while Rockefeller, Bliss, and Sullivan advocated French postimpressionism. Deferring to its founders, the Modern opened its first season in 1929–30 with a loan exhibition of works by Cézanne, Gauguin, Seurat, and van Gogh, considered "ancestors" to twentieth-century European modernism based largely on affinities of style.[24] Its second exhibition, "Paintings by Nineteen Living Americans," was modeled in part on the annual contemporary art exhibitions of Gertrude Vanderbilt Whitney, who would found the Whitney Museum of American Art in 1931.[25] With little formal museum policy, and cautious about any charge of favoritism, the trustees of the Modern devised a selection process they considered democratic. Barr described their method based on consensus: ballots listing over 100 contemporary artists were distributed among the trustees, who were each asked to select 15. The show that emerged from the tabulated responses, Barr explained, included 19 American painters: some, such as Rockwell Kent and Ernest Lawson who were considered so "'conservative'

that they are out of fashion" and others like Charles Demuth, Lyonel Feininger, and Yasuo Kuniyoshi who were considered so "'advanced' that they are not yet generally accepted."[26] It was an opportunity for Barr to emphasize the diversity of modern American art, including both a native predisposition to realism and European-inspired abstraction, and thereby to distinguish the show from Whitney's well-exhibited collection of realist and figurative art.[27] However, some critics charged that the Modern's exhibition was not sufficiently American, because many of the artists were foreign-born; other critics claimed that it was incoherent.[28] Exhibited in a separate room, along with other works the *New Yorker* called "Left Wing," such paintings as Demuth's *My Egypt* (1927; see fig. 1.1) engaged a machine-age metaphor associated with an American vernacular structure, while combining representation with abstraction.[29]

Over the next two years, Barr played his strong suit, organizing such group shows as "Painting in Paris from American Collections" (1930), which presented works by the fauves Henri Matisse and André Derain, the cubists Pablo Picasso and Georges Braque, and the surrealists Giorgio de Chirico and Joan Miró. Barr also exhibited paintings by such artists as Fernand Léger, which offered a mechanized view of modern life.[30] Indeed, in another Barr diagram, captioned "The Development of Abstract Art," which appeared on the dust jacket of his 1936 exhibition catalogue *Cubism and Abstract Art*, "Machine Aesthetic" assumed a central position during the period from 1910 to 1925.[31] Barr deployed the diagram as an analytical tool, paralleling its pervasive use in architectural publications after World War I, to establish not only chronologies but also discursive relationships among art movements and influences upon them.[32] Following the "Painting in Paris" show, Barr gave solo exhibitions to the European modernist painters Paul Klee (1930) and Henri Matisse (1931), as well as to the sculptors Wilhelm Lehmbruck and Aristide Maillol (1930). At the same time, he continued to promote contemporary American art through such shows as "An Exhibition of Work of 46 Painters and Sculptors under 35 Years of Age" (1930), devoted to the work of emerging artists, many of whom would be little known today.[33] He also organized an exhibition of the Bliss collection (1934), which emphasized modern French painting but included the figurative art of the Americans Arthur Davies and Walt Kuhn.

If, under Barr's direction, the Modern sponsored European abstract painting and sculpture, including machine-centered imagery of the 1910s and 1920s, how did it construct a comprehensive view of modernism in the 1930s that also supported the increasing emphasis on human-centered artis-

tic production? Moreover, as the decade 1929–39 unfolded, what cast of modernism could explain the diversity of the Modern's exhibitions on topics ranging from European modernism to American folk art (1932, 1938), pre-Columbian art (1933), theater art (1934), machine art (1934), low-cost housing (1934, 1936), American rugs (1937), subway art (1938), and useful household objects under $5 (1938)? To account for the pluralism of the Museum's early vision, I propose to consider ways in which Barr and his colleagues engaged the vernacular, even though they did not necessarily pursue an intentional search for it. Viewing modernism through the lens of the vernacular allows us to understand the ways in which it embraced social concerns and shaped both Barr's approach and the museum's early discourse on modern visual culture.

In Barr's worldview, modernism and the vernacular lay at the crossroads of a tensional relationship that could be reconciled. As the product of an academic tradition that sought to express a culture of the present, modernism shared a transnational and interdisciplinary language of the avant-garde.[34] In common with popular art, modernism spoke a lingua franca across borders but was subject to change over time. By contrast, vernacular and folk expressions were circumscribed within a region. Geographically limited, therefore, vernacular traditions resisted change and remained relatively constant over time.[35] Notwithstanding a critical position governed by formalism and aestheticism, Barr endorsed a culturally based view of modernism that could connect with the vernacular. He held that "Modern Art is almost as varied and complex as modern life."[36] Kirstein recognized the way in which Barr "judged art as anthropology[,] for whatever the object, he judged its essence as that of genus, species or order."[37]

Evidence of Barr's early search for artistic expressions of modern life across cultures and disciplines is found in his intellectual formation at Princeton, his earliest lecture course on modern art at Wellesley College (perhaps the first modern art course in the United States), and his subsequent study tour to Europe and Russia. Early on Barr's cultural construction of modernism was shaped by Morey's comprehensive view of medieval arts at Princeton, which examined folk, craft, religious, and cultural traditions to understand the evolution of style. In this way, cultural considerations provided the means to achieve a formalist perspective, a method that Barr adopted.[38] The value Barr placed on a cross-cultural and interdisciplinary approach to modernism is confirmed in the "Modern Art Questionnaire" he prepared for his Wellesley students to assess their general knowledge of the significance of "modern artistic expression." The list specified a

diverse range of modernism from "Max Reinhardt" to "James Joyce," "John Marin," "The Zoning Law," "Oswald Spengler," and "The Barnes Foundation," among others.[39]

Barr's search for expressions of modern culture also dominated his study tour to Europe and Russia in 1927–28 with Jere Abbott.[40] Among their visits to London, Holland, Dessau, Berlin, Moscow, Leningrad, Czechoslovakia, Vienna, Stuttgart, Munich, and Paris, three cultures were significant in the formation of Barr's vision of modernism. His tours of housing estates, notably J. J. P. Oud's low-cost housing at the Hook of Holland and the Weissenhofsiedlung in Stuttgart by Mies van der Rohe, Le Corbusier, and others, helped to refine his formalist and transnational approach to the "International Style," which would later inform the 1932 "Modern Architecture: International Exhibition."[41] Barr's four-day visit to the Bauhaus in Dessau and ten-week trip to Russia confirmed that these cultures interpreted modernism as an interdisciplinary project. At the Bauhaus, he absorbed the idea of a "unity of style" among the fine and applied arts, including architecture and industrial design, which Kantor has called "the single most important idea governing the founding of the new museum."[42] In Russia, Barr saw further expressions of modern culture. His "Russian Diary" documents an infusion of modernism, especially constructivism and suprematism in the art, theater, film, music, and especially architecture that he and Abbott encountered.[43] Barr also recognized the emergence in Russia of what Konstantin Umansky, director of the foreign news agency TASS, called a "proletarian style" found in wall newspapers, an assemblage of text, poster, and photomontage.[44]

Five Approaches to Modernism and Vernacular Expression

Guided by the vision of Barr and others during its first decade, the Museum of Modern Art entered into a discourse on modernism that explicitly or implicitly addressed five interrelated approaches to vernacular expression. The first is a search for authenticity to modern art. Toward that objective, the museum leadership sought to identify its ancestral roots—from shallow to deep, both stylistic and cultural. In pursuit of a genealogy for modern art, Barr organized exhibitions of works by postimpressionists as well as Corot and Daumier (1930), which situated these artists as antecedents of French modernism. Barr sought to establish a similar genealogy of modern American art. Although he professed no scholarly expertise in the field (after 1934 relying on that of his assistant Dorothy Miller, who

served as curator of American painting from 1942 to 1963), he wrote frequently on American art and held critical positions on it.[45] For the Modern's sixth loan exhibition, Barr organized the "Homer Ryder Eakins" show (1930). He considered these artists pioneers of American modernism, as the postimpressionists had been the pioneers of European modernism. For its catalogue, Barr commissioned essays by Frank Jewett Mather, Bryson Burroughs, and Lloyd Goodrich—all scholars of American art. In his prefatory essay, Barr suggested that the new generation of American painters transcended the "doctrine of art for form's sake." He endorsed Homer and Eakins's "objective observation," on the one hand, and Ryder's "expressionism," on the other.[46] More than just "good artists," he maintained elsewhere, the trio also ranked in importance because they were "practically independent of European influence," a view not supported by recent scholarship.[47] Thus, what Barr valued in American art was its independence from, rather than imitation of, European modernism, a position grounded in cultural identity and place.[48] At the same time, he recognized that neither "aggressive nationalism" nor foreign influences or internationalism could predict the path to great art. In his essay for the "Edward Hopper Retrospective Exhibition" in 1933, Barr proposed that the artist's mature work showed little sign of his early studies in Paris. Rather than rich and sensuous surfaces, those canvases used intensity of light and "matter-of-factness" to create realism and "pictorial drama." Barr understood that much of Hopper's greatness lay in his ability to render the platform for human events in streets, houses, and interiors. From formal comparisons, Barr drew insightful stylistic and cultural parallels. Such interiors as *Room in Brooklyn* (1932) suggested at once the city's ancestry and Hopper's own Dutch ancestors: "The delight in the clean and precise pattern of empty sunlit rooms calls to mind Dutchmen like de Hooch and Janssens."[49]

When Barr searched for cultural authenticity in modern American art, he sought to mine its essence, one that would distinguish it from European modernism. Although he did not regard either abstraction or realism as a formal property exclusive to any one school, he tended to emphasize abstraction in European modernism and realism in American art. In his two major exhibitions of European modernism, "Cubism and Abstract Art" and "Fantastic Art, Dada, and Surrealism," both in 1936, he advanced abstraction and the ideal. By contrast, the exhibitions he sponsored on American art followed the path of the "Homer Ryder Eakins" and "Hopper" shows by emphasizing the real, nowhere more so than "American Realists and Magic Realists" in 1943, the year he stepped down as director. Barr used the

term "magic realism" to signify the "work of painters who by means of an exact realistic technique try to make plausible and convincing their improbable, dreamlike or fantastic visions."[50]

In seeking authenticity and the essence of American art, Barr further recognized the importance of multiculturalism, evidence of the international diffusion of modern art in the Americas, with its regional roots. In 1930, he exhibited the work of Hispanic and Native American artists in "An Exhibition of Work of 46 Painters and Sculptors under 35 Years of Age."[51] The following year, he organized a solo exhibition of the work of the Mexican muralist painter Diego Rivera, whom he had met in Moscow during the winter of 1927–28.[52] Frances Flynn Paine wrote the catalogue and the Rivera show became the Modern's first traveling exhibition.[53] But in spite of such multicultural projects, Barr lent little support to African-American artists, although he did exhibit painting and sculpture devoted to African and African-American subjects. It was not until 1938 that the Modern exhibited the work of the African-American artist Horace Pippin in an exhibition called, "Masters of Popular Painting: Modern Primitives of Europe and America."[54] Under Barr's directorship, the Modern generally ignored the intersection of art and race in the United States, deferring to both the Whitney Museum of American Art and more politically engaged critics, including such leftist scholars as Meyer Schapiro.[55]

The second expression of the vernacular is folk art, which Lincoln Kirstein defined as a social art "springing from the common people . . . in essence unacademic . . . generally speaking, anonymous." Barr understood that the craft tradition of folk art and artifacts shared, in Kirstein's words, "a direct quality" with American modernism. Barr had been impressed by John Cotton Dana and Holger Cahill's successful exhibitions of American primitive and folk art at the Newark Art Museum in the 1920s and Kirstein's exhibition of "American Folk Painting of Three Centuries" at the Harvard Society for Contemporary Art in 1930.[56] In the spring of 1932, Barr envisioned two future exhibitions on American art.[57] But he would not be their curator. Having mounted seventeen exhibitions in the Modern's first three years, Barr experienced what was generally referred to as a "nervous breakdown" and was granted a one-year leave of absence to study in Europe.[58] In his place, Holger Cahill was appointed director of exhibitions for the coming year. Barr retained his position as director but Cahill was, in effect, the institution's acting director.[59] With the accent now on American, Cahill curated first an exhibition of "American Painting and Sculpture,

1862–1932" and then "American Folk Art: The Art of the Common Man in America, 1750–1900," which consisted of 174 works from Rockefeller's own collection.[60] Barr and Cahill's philosophical approaches to art were fundamentally different. Barr's formalism flowed from the legacies of Sachs's connoisseurship tradition and Santayana's aesthetics. By contrast, Cahill considered art—especially folk art—a representation of experience, suggestive of John Dewey's ideas on pragmatism. Dewey held that American artists must derive their subject matter from human experience and that art was essential to democratic culture, a position endorsed by New Deal advocates. During the 1930s, the production of art in America was important for Cahill, as for Dewey, the pragmatists, and New Dealers because the process of making art within a community served a social function that could be shared in a democracy.[61]

On another tack, Cahill's appointment enabled the Modern not only to tap an expertise that Barr did not have but also to respond to external events. Not immune to the effects of the Depression and criticism that the Modern served only an elite, its trustees hoped that under Cahill's direction and the American exhibitions he organized, the institution would effectively counter the perception that it was, in the words of a critic for the *Nation*, "the phantom of a narrow aesthetic preoccupation, given to moonraking among splendid objects" when there were "gray bread lines wound about city blocks."[62] Cahill's curatorial leadership at the Modern marked an important episode in bringing a wider range of American art to public attention and creating a broader constituency for the Museum.

A search for the origins of modernism in indigenous traditions and ethnography suggests a third form of vernacular enterprise. Barr himself had intended to write his dissertation on "the influence of primitive and e[x]otic forms upon modern European painting."[63] In his foreword to the first loan exhibition, "Cézanne, Gauguin, Seurat, and van Gogh," Barr had said that "the genealogy of contemporary painting extends far beyond this 19th century European group to almost every preceding period and almost every exotic culture."[64] If Barr endorsed the view that the distant roots of European modernism lay in African art and the "primitive," Cahill believed that American modernism had been influenced by the precolonial art of the Americas. During Barr's absence from the museum in the spring of 1933, Cahill also curated a groundbreaking exhibition of Aztec, Mayan, and Incan art called "American Sources of Modern Art."[65] Notwithstanding his advocacy of ancient American sources, Cahill understood that Rivera and

FIG. 1.5. John B. Flannagan, *Alligator* (1932). Alfred H. Barr Jr., *Modern Works of Art* (New York: Museum of Modern Art, 1934), p. 19, cat. no. 167. Digital Image © The Museum of Modern Art / Licensed by SCALA / Art Resource, NY.

other Mexican modernists could not have recognized the importance of their pre-Columbian artistic ancestry without the formal intermediary of Parisian modernism.[66]

After his return to the Modern in the fall of 1933, Barr continued Cahill's project while he was also more responsive to criticism that the institution was merely an agent of European modernism. In *Modern Works of Art*, the catalogue he edited for the Fifth Anniversary Exhibition the following year, Barr proposed early sources for modern art beyond the European tradition, including both Africa and the New World: "Matisse's *Standing Woman* may well have been suggested by primitive African sculpture . . . the concentric compactness of Flannagan's *Alligator* by Aztec stone serpents."[67] The latter were references to a sculpture by John B. Flannagan (1932; fig. 1.5) and to pre-Columbian works similar to those in Cahill's "American Sources of Modern Art" exhibition, including the Mayan sculpture *Serpent Head in*

FIG. 1.6. *Two-Toned Drum of Wood in Form of Tiger.* Aztec sculpture from the Valley of Mexico shown in the Museum of Modern Art exhibition "American Sources of Modern Art" (1933). Holger Cahill, *American Sources of Modern Art* (New York: Museum of Modern Art, 1933), 30, cat. no. 21, Digital Image © The Museum of Modern Art / Licensed by SCALA / Art Resource, NY.

Trachyte (c. 525 C.E.) and the Aztec *Drum of Wood in Form of Tiger* (fig. 1.6).[68] Like ancient animal sculpture, Flannagan's *Alligator* seems to emerge from the stone block. In 1935, James Johnson Sweeney organized a seminal exhibition "African Negro Art," which advanced its "basic plastic integrity" and "vitality of forms," as well as its influence on European art.[69] Two years later, the museum mined even earlier sources of artistic and cultural expression in its exhibition of "Prehistoric Rock Pictures in Europe and Africa."[70]

A fourth approach to the vernacular at the Museum of Modern Art engaged everyday forms of art including film and photography, as well as industrially produced and commercially available objects. This everyday modernism derived from the programmatic structure and pedagogy of the Bauhaus, which Barr had experienced during his visit to Dessau in 1927 and whose legacy he encouraged in the Modern's 1938 exhibition, "Bauhaus 1919–1928."[71] From the beginning, Barr had envisioned a plan for separate departments based on the Bauhaus model, but A. Conger Goodyear and others deferred its execution.[72] After the success of its "Modern Architecture: International Exhibition" the museum established architecture as a department in 1932, followed by industrial arts in 1933, film in 1935, and later by departments of drawings, prints, and photography. Film and photography were considered democratic forms of expression and popular arts because of their association with mass culture and communication. However,

they had the capacity to evoke local culture and national expression, which could place them at the intersection of modern and vernacular. For example, Ernst Kirchner's painting *The Street* (1913) shared with Robert Wiene's film *The Cabinet of Dr. Caligari* (1919) gestural forms, tilting perspectives, and affective responses, identifying them as exemplars of German expressionism.[73] In 1933, the Modern hired Iris Barry to establish a film library and appointed her curator, offered a popular column "Film Comments" in its *Bulletin*, and sponsored screenings of both commercial and avant-garde films by such directors as John Ford, D. W. Griffith, G. W. Pabst, and Sergei Eisenstein. In 1936, the Modern launched a new initiative to circulate two film programs to colleges and museums: "A Short Survey of the Film in America, 1895–1932" and "Some Memorable American Films, 1896–1934."[74] The following year, it held two film exhibitions: "A Brief Survey of American Film" and "The Making of a Contemporary Film." Indeed, Barr supported these efforts because he regarded American film and photography as artistically superior to either their European counterparts or American painting and sculpture. Similarly, he sponsored the Modern's early exhibitions of photographs by Walker Evans (1933; 1938), Edward Steichen (1936), and Charles Sheeler (1939), as well as the retrospective exhibition "Photography, 1839–1937" (1937).

With early exhibitions devoted to industrially produced objects, the Modern continued to endorse the Bauhaus model of blurring distinctions between "high" and "low." In his exhibition "Machine Art" (1934), Johnson proposed that everyday useful objects, mass-produced and sold in America, combined beauty with utility. Barr further called for an assimilation of the machine, "aesthetically as well as economically," to eliminate the divide between art and industry.[75] Johnson and Barr's conjunction of aesthetics and function suggested the theoretical positions of Horatio Greenough and Edward Lacy Garbett more than that of John Ruskin. The Modern's alliance of art with industry also recalled the more recent German discourse on the *neue Sachlichkeit*, literally, "new factualness," advanced by Herman Muthesius, partisans of the Deutscher Werkbund, and the Bauhaus.[76] A number of other exhibitions at the Modern also focused on quotidian art, namely, well-designed inexpensive commercial household objects.[77]

A fifth expression of the vernacular is embodied in what the architectural and cultural historian William Jordy has called the search for a "deepened national consciousness" in contemporary American culture of the 1930s.[78] In some respects, it evoked earlier German expressions of nationalism in its visual culture. Regionalist painters and photographers as well as filmmak-

ers and directors in the United States gave voice to this national feeling. Interpreted as a counterpoint to the influence of the European avant-garde through "separatist" expressions of the native and local, regionalists painters such as Thomas Hart Benton made their first appearance at the Modern in 1932 with the opening of Cahill's "American Painting and Sculpture, 1862–1932" exhibition, followed by Barr's "Painting and Sculpture from Sixteen American Cities" exhibition in 1933 and the Fifth Anniversary Exhibition "Modern Works of Art" in the winter of 1934–35. Barr admired the "vigorous nationalistic feeling" in Benton's art and had invited him to show his work at the Modern as early as 1930. But he was less sympathetic to the narrow range of Benton's subject matter, which, he said, depicted "the American scene . . . to the point of excess."[79] In the end, the Whitney Museum of American Art became the principal sponsor of contemporary regionalist painters. But Barr did lend more support to regionalism as a significant historical development in American painting with the exhibition "George Caleb Bingham, the Missouri Artist, 1811–1879" (1935). Later in 1941, the Modern would exhibit photographs of the Tennessee Valley Authority, a federal project dedicated to regional concerns.[80]

Like their counterparts in the city, Depression-era painters, photographers, and filmmakers in rural America sought to mine its culture at the "moment of impending change."[81] Thus the need for documentation, coupled with a search for authenticity and national awareness, suggested an obsession with the real and factual to counteract evanescence and loss, which pervaded an era of insecurity. Across disciplines, John Steinbeck's novel *The Grapes of Wrath* (1939) and its film version by John Ford (1940) shared with Works Progress Administration photographs of the 1930s by Walker Evans and Dorothea Lange an approach to realism (whether documentary or fictional) and a set of social concerns.[82] Institutions such as the Modern set about recording and cataloguing "things," then "fixing" them in a museum setting, as if curators could "fix" a culture. Kirstein expressed these thoughts in his description of the Modern's first solo exhibition of photography in 1933, "Walker Evans: Photographs of Nineteenth Century American Houses." He drew attention to photography's "stationary magic that fixes a second from time's passage on a single plane," all the more poignant when the American Federal and Victorian wooden houses Evans depicted "disintegrate, almost, between snaps of the lens."[83] At the institutional level, Barr's concern for didactic documentation and mass communication suggests an American predisposition to the pragmatic and factual. He introduced comprehensive wall texts at the Modern, a practice that Sachs had advocated,

but that was more directly inspired by those he had seen in Russia in 1927–28, to accompany and explain works on exhibit. Moreover, toward the democratization of modern art for public consumption, the museum produced press releases, posters, radio broadcasts, traveling exhibitions, and inexpensive paperback exhibition catalogues.[84] Thus, like curators from earlier periods, Barr wanted to "fix" modern art. But as his metaphor of a "torpedo" in motion affirmed, this was an oxymoron, because flux and evanescence were qualities that defined the essence of modern art, drawn from modern life and especially urban culture.

Modernism and the Vernacular in Architecture

The museum's discourse on modernism governed its early architectural exhibitions. The 1932 "Modern Architecture: International Exhibition" advanced the idea of a unified contemporary "style" without borders known as the "International Style," a term shown to have been used liberally from the late 1920s by Barr, Jere Abbott, Hitchcock, and others within the HSCA circle. In his foreword to the catalogue *Modern Architecture: International Exhibition,* Barr laid out the aesthetic principles that would later dominate the more famous publication *The International Style* by curators Hitchcock and Johnson. There, Barr conceptualized his notion of a transnational style based on a set of formal properties—volume rather than mass; structural supports that encouraged regularity rather than Beaux-Arts symmetry; and fine proportions, technique, and elegant materials rather than applied decoration. But the new "style" also conveyed a range of personal expression, especially in the work of its four masters: Gropius, Le Corbusier, Oud, and Mies van der Rohe.[85] To the curators, Le Corbusier's Villa Savoye at Poissy (1928–31; see fig. 5.3), which figured prominently in the exhibition, embodied its principles. Such an international consensus of architects responding to modern life even received the endorsement of Lewis Mumford, who contributed a section on housing to the exhibition. Mumford had been reluctant to collaborate on an exhibition devoted to the idea of an "International Style" with a European bias. In a letter to Frank Lloyd Wright, Mumford expressed his opposition to the "dreadful phrase, since architecture is architecture and never; except in a bastard form, a style." Notwithstanding his resistance to such formalism, Mumford supported the new awakening across cultures. "While the phrase international style emphasizes all the wrong things architecturally," he conceded to Wright, "I think it is a fine sign that men o[f] good will all over the world are begin-

ning to face life in the same way, and to seek similar means of expressing it."[86]

Vernacular expression entered the museum's discourse on modern architecture in two ways: first, a search for cultural authenticity resulted in a wider recognition of its sources in the work of American architects, engineers, and builders; second, a local acculturation or Americanization of the "International Style" responded to human-centered concerns of the period. In seeking cultural authenticity and antecedents for modern architecture, Barr constructed a genealogy based on formal principles. Barr situated Wright as a "pioneer ancestor" of "International Style" practitioners, as he had recently cast Homer, Ryder, and Eakins as pioneers of modern art.[87] In their book *The International Style,* Hitchcock and Johnson expanded the list of architect pioneers into a family tree. It was undoubtedly a belated response to Mumford, who had unsuccessfully lobbied Johnson to dedicate a section of the exhibition to the history of modern architecture. It was needed, Mumford explained, "so that no one would think it was invented by Norman Bel Geddes and the Bowman Brothers . . . the day before yesterday."[88] Under the influence of Mumford's *Sticks and Stones* (1924) and *The Brown Decades* (1931), Hitchcock joined with Barr to promote American sources of modern architecture in other exhibitions.[89] At the Modern, Hitchcock organized a didactic exhibition in 1933, "Early Modern Architecture: Chicago 1870–1910," focusing on the technical, aesthetic, and pragmatic developments associated with the skyscraper, which he called "the conspicuous achievement of American architecture" after 1850. In his catalogue, he emphasized the "originality" of such architects as William Le Baron Jenney ("the first to use steel skeleton construction"), Henry Hobson Richardson ("based on the integrity of his use of traditional construction" and "formative spirit"), Louis Sullivan (who "alone made of the early skyscraper an aesthetic invention"), Wright (who developed a "new type of domestic design"), and Burnham & Root ("responsible for the development of the highly organized and specialized American architectural office and methods of practice").[90] In the museum-sponsored publication *Art in America in Modern Times* (1934), Hitchcock designated Richardson's "simplification of design" and "direct expression of structure" as antecedents to both the "International Style" and the skyscraper.[91] In his monograph for a subsequent exhibition at the Modern, "The Architecture of Henry Hobson Richardson" (1936), Hitchcock continued to uphold Richardson's work as an ancestor of contemporary architecture. In the Cheney Building in Hartford (1875–76), for example, Richardson approached "modern problems in

a spirit not wholly dissimilar to that of the men of the twelfth century."[92] To Hitchcock, it meant that the American architect shared with medieval builders a common approach to style, as well as technical innovation.

But the link that Hitchcock forged between Richardson and twelfth-century builders entered into the discourse on modernism and the vernacular in another way. It recalled the European modernists' admiration for American utilitarian and vernacular buildings as sources for modern architecture. In their early writings, Walter Gropius and Le Corbusier appropriated and manipulated images of American technology: grain elevators, daylight factories, and skyscrapers. For example, in his polemical *Vers une architecture* (1923), Le Corbusier used the image of an American skyscraper both to denounce the academic classicism of its masonry cladding and to praise the "anonymous" engineering of its skeletal frame, an object lesson for contemporary architects.[93] Early on, Hitchcock and Barr appreciated the role assigned to American technology and vernacular buildings within European modernism. Inspired by modernist theory, *Hound & Horn* editors reproduced a quartet of Jere Abbott's photographs of the Necco candy factory in Cambridge, Massachusetts (1927), which Hitchcock captioned "the finest fragments of contemporary building."[94] Barr followed with an essay on "The Necco Factory" for *Arts* (1928), illustrated with Abbott's photographs (fig. 1.7). It was Barr's homage to a local industrial building that was at once modern and vernacular; he called it a "document in the growth of a new style."[95]

Hitchcock drew further comparisons between the modern and the vernacular. He proposed that the "International Style" recalled an earlier episode in American city building, which had produced a local language. In 1934, he curated an exhibition at Wesleyan University, "The Urban Vernacular of the Thirties, Forties and Fifties: American Cities before the Civil War." It consisted of fifty photographs by Berenice Abbott, a photographer predisposed to modernism, as well as to both vernacular and urban architecture.[96] Hitchcock's thesis advanced the idea that formal elements in the unadorned but well-proportioned row houses, warehouses, and other utilitarian buildings in American port cities during the Antebellum period were analogous to those of the "International Style": "extreme rationalist discipline," "the sense of fine proportions," and "simple expanses of the best obtainable materials." Alexander Parris's granite structures on North Market Street (Quincy Market) in Boston (1823; fig. 1.8), along with Richardson's Cheney Building, were among the many examples that confirmed the "communal ordering of design" and "high general level of excellence" of

FIG. 1.7. Jere Abbott, photograph of the Necco Factory, Cambridge, Massachusetts (1927). From Jere Abbott, "Four Photographs," *Hound & Horn* 1 (September 1927), opposite page 36.

American urban building. They compared favorably with their counterparts in European cities. Both the "International Style" and the American urban vernacular of the previous century could, therefore, provide models to the present generation. "The real architectural quality of a fine city," Hitchcock emphasized, did not reside in individual monuments but "in the general consistency and order of its vernacular building."[97]

The vernacular also assumed a seminal role in the Americanization of modern architecture. Although the "Modern Architecture: International Exhibition" promoted an "International Style" of European extraction, its popular diffusion and widespread acculturation on this side of the Atlantic predisposed its "Americanization." Because the "International Style" embodied a set of aesthetic principles based on formal properties, American architects could appropriate certain elements without reference to the sociopolitical issues that had informed European modernism. By 1937, even

FIG. 1.8. Alexander Parris, North Market Street (Quincy Market), Boston (1823). Photograph by Berenice Abbott. Reproduced by kind permission, Davison Art Center, Wesleyan University.

Hitchcock distanced himself from the "International Style" in the United States, calling it "aesthetically second rate."[98] As he predicted, some architects would continue to adhere to its narrowly defined aesthetic parameters. For example, Philip Goodwin and Edward Durell Stone's design for the Museum of Modern Art (1936–39) relied largely on formal pastiche.[99] However, it was not the formal elements but the technological advances that distinguished American modernism in the late 1930s, because dependable heating and air-conditioning systems made glass walls viable and prefabricated building supplies fulfilled the promise of machine-age metaphors.[100] Lack of advanced building technology had been one of the conspicuous defects of Russian modernism, which Barr and Jere Abbott had experienced during the winter of 1927–28 when they visited a Moscow apartment house designed by the constructivist architect Moisei Ginzburg.[101]

During the 1930s, architects sought to localize modernism through associations with place and native building traditions. Their emphasis on local conditions and region meant that buildings could respond directly to

such environmental conditions as site contours, views, and access to sunlight. Architects employed more earth-bound materials and often used curvilinear forms. From an American perspective, the "International Style" was gravitating toward a synthesis of the machine-inspired forms of European modernism, native technical proficiency, human-centered forms recalling the organic tradition of Frank Lloyd Wright, and vernacular expressions of both materials and building methods. Curators of the 1932 exhibition had already observed the possibilities of a new synthesis in the correspondence they perceived between the work of European modernists and Wright, notwithstanding the latter's individualism that checked any consensus based merely on "style." In his catalogue essay, Hitchcock suggested that Le Corbusier's de Mandrot House at Le Pradet (see fig. 1.3) and Wright's R. L. Jones House in Tulsa (1931) shared in common a new sense of plasticity and economy of ornament.[102] A partisan of Wright, Mumford observed in his review of the 1932 exhibition that the architect's importance should not be restricted to that of mere pioneer. Like Mies van der Rohe's and J. J. P. Oud's designs for country houses, Mumford argued, Wright's could be "intellectually grasped, humanly embodied, architecturally expressed." Wright's "love for natural materials, his interest in the site and the landscape, his feeling for the region," Mumford concluded, made him a new source of interest to European modernists.[103]

The transatlantic synthesis, which engaged modern and vernacular in contemporary architecture, had even deeper historical precedents. In 1938, the Museum of Modern Art organized an exhibition, "Trois siècles d'art aux États-Unis," at the Musée du Jeu de Paume in Paris, in which the play between Europe and America dominated the architecture section. In his catalogue essay "Architecture in the United States," curator John McAndrew sketched a brief history of European-inspired American architecture modified through local tradition. He mapped the terrain from forts and meetinghouses of the colonial period, when "honest vernacular" became a "serious rival of the elegant importations," to more recent commercial and utilitarian buildings, which had solved problems of function and structure with "unconscious candor" and "technical efficiency." The more recent assimilation, McAndrew concurred with Mumford, resulted in a "naturalization" or Americanization through a repatriation of Wright and native utilitarian structures, in addition to vernacular and regional expressions, including the use of ordinary materials, such as cinder blocks, as well as open plans and glassed-in porches, adjusted to American living patterns.[104]

By World War II, American critics continued to endorse the synthesis of

European and American modernism with vernacular and regional expressions. In her catalogue for the Museum of Modern Art exhibition "Built in USA—1932–1944," Elizabeth Mock observed that the new architecture had undergone a "process of humanization," shedding its "romantization of the machine which had produced . . . cold abstractions." She argued that American architecture had undergone the transformation through a fusion of influences: Wright, vernacular building, and Le Corbusier's use of natural materials, evinced in his de Mandrot House at Le Pradet (see fig. 1.3) and Swiss Dormitory at the Cité universitaire in Paris (1930–31). Both Wright and Le Corbusier, Mock suggested, had encouraged Americans to appreciate their native folk architecture, including California redwood houses of the late nineteenth century and Pennsylvania stone and timber barns for "their straightforward use of material and their subtle adaptation to climate and topography." Sharing similar design objectives, Americans and Europeans together could provide "local encouragement for the growing international movement towards a friendlier, more differentiated contemporary architecture."[105] This synthesis had become increasingly evident in the work of European émigrés such as William Lescaze, Walter Gropius, and Marcel Breuer, as well as of the Americans Wallace Harrison and Edward Durell Stone and San Francisco "Bay Area Regionalists." Museum curators promoted the new regionalism. In the 1932 exhibition, Hitchcock recognized the way in which Richard Neutra's California houses and garden apartments adapted European modernism to local climate though the use of balconies and roof terraces.[106] The Modern continued to endorse the response to local conditions when it featured the work of Neutra and other West Coast modernists, including William Wurster's Colby House (Berkeley, 1931), in its subsequent exhibition "Modern Architecture in California" (1935).[107] In 1938, the museum gave a solo exhibition to Wright's Fallingwater (Kaufmann House) in Mill Run, Pennsylvania (1934–37).[108] That year it also advanced the European synthesis of modern and vernacular in its exhibition "Alvar Aalto: Architecture and Furniture," which underscored the ways in which organic forms, local materials, and sensitivity to both site and region joined with personal invention and proficient technical means.[109] As regionalist artists turned to local traditions in an anxious effort to counter loss, so architects of the period engaged vernacular culture and local traditions to counter the consumerism of modern culture, thereby anticipating what in recent times has been called "critical regionalism."[110]

As the social and economic deficit of the Depression affected architectural practice during the 1930s, modernists turned increasingly to vernacu-

lar expression. The Museum of Modern Art responded with a new emphasis on the everyday necessity of low-cost housing adjusted to regions. Mumford's housing section of the 1932 "Modern Architecture: International Exhibition" informed the general public on both European and American models, while his catalogue essay emphasized the need for new social housing in the context of community planning. Two years later, Carol Aronovici, director of the Housing Research Bureau of New York City, organized the "Housing Exhibition of the City of New York," at the Modern in conjunction with the New York City Housing Authority (NYCHA) and other agencies in both the public and private sectors. Charged with a pragmatic agenda, the exhibition showed existing housing conditions in the city, identified impediments to reform, and endorsed new housing models in both Europe and America. It featured Williamsburg Houses, a NYCHA project designed by the Swiss-born Lescaze and a team headed by Richmond H. Shreve (1934–37). Philip Johnson even planned full-scale models of rooms intended to contrast a modern low-cost apartment, furnished by Macy's, with an existing old-law tenement unit. To accompany the exhibition, Aronovici published an influential collection of essays by leading European and American housing specialists bearing the provocative title *America Can't Have Housing*.[111] In the fall of 1934, the Museum also sponsored a radio program "Art in America" and published *Art in America in Modern Times*, with didactic essays on architecture and other forms of visual culture. For an essay on "House and Cities," the editors, Barr and Cahill, brought in the housing expert Catherine Bauer who proffered a sociopolitical response to the urban housing crisis. Following the housing models of Rotterdam and Frankfurt, she advised, Americans would need to "plan for *use* and not for profit."[112] The Modern sustained its social commitment to public housing when it showed work being produced under the Public Works Administration and the Resettlement Administration in its exhibition "Architecture in Government Housing" (1936), followed by McAndrew's architecture section of the 1938 "Trois siècles" exhibition, and the "Houses and Housing" section of its landmark "Art in Our Time: Tenth Anniversary Exhibition" (1939), prepared in collaboration with the United States Housing Authority.[113] By the late 1930s, McAndrew argued that structural, functional, and aesthetic issues were not as important as humanitarian and social ones. The Modern had taken the lead in promoting urban low-cost housing as the nation's critical challenge.[114]

In establishing the Museum of Modern Art in New York as a principal site for modernism in North America, its founders validated the interna-

tionalism of modern art and architecture across cultures. As the museum searched for identity during its first decade, Barr, Cahill, Hitchcock, Johnson, Mumford, McAndrew, and others constructed an archaeology of modernism that embraced vernacular expression. At once sponsoring the avant-garde but also mining historical as well as folk sources and anonymous building traditions, increasingly human-centered but still connected to the machine age, supporting realism and figurative art—particularly in American art—while still an outpost of European abstraction, the new museum sought to project a complex view of modernism that was sufficiently pluralistic and open-ended to respond to a democratic mandate and secure a broad audience in a time of economic and social uncertainty. Its governance was not the result of a conscious strategy as much as a pragmatic response to a set of competing voices and agendas within the institutional leadership and among its constituency. Thus, as the Museum of Modern Art increasingly explored both the vernacular dimensions of modernism and an interdisciplinary agenda, it arrived at a more deeply examined expression of visual culture that oscillated between the local and the global.

CHAPTER TWO

At Home in the Ironic Imagination: The Rational Vernacular and Spectacular Texts

MICHAEL SALER

Modern Enchantment via the "Rational Vernacular" and the "Ironic Imagination"

As the chapters in this volume reveal, the "vernacular" is a complex concept: at once an imaginary space evoking a sense of native place, or *Heimat,* in the face of modern anomie, and a language of aesthetic forms used by individuals to translate that imagined space into concrete reality. The term "vernacular" can also refer to a specific type of linguistic discourse shared by a community. When we speak "in the vernacular," we imbue abstract terms with particular associations and emotional resonances. Literature, of course, is one important source of the vernacular, and this essay examines the ways in which many of the universal and seemingly impersonal attributes ascribed to modernity were domesticated in the late nineteenth and early twentieth centuries through new genres of fiction and new concepts of the imagination as a space of habitation.

Standard tropes used to define the modern, such as rationality, science, secularism, and consumerism, are often understood as the antithesis of the vernacular: when the two terms are paired, modernity can be seen as being alienating and isolating, in contrast to the embracing and familiar connotations represented by the vernacular. But during the fin de siècle in Britain and America, such tropes of modernity were used to create imaginary "secondary worlds" that readers came to inhabit both individually and communally; in this fashion, a discourse of modernity became a way to create imaginary spaces that were themselves vernacular "homes" of modernity. The habitation of such imaginary worlds should not be dismissed as mere

escapism: these worlds enabled individuals to conceive of modernity as alive with possibilities that might be attained through the exercise of reason as well as desire. Thus the modern tropes that seemed to oppose the vernacular became themselves a "rational vernacular" used to render the modern entrancing rather than alienating. The built environments I discuss are those created in the imagination, intentionally formulated through a rational vernacular for the purpose of replacing modern anomie with modern enchantment.

This association between modernity and enchantment may at first seem implausible, however. According to an influential strand of European thought, one of the most alienating aspects of modernity has been its emphasis on reason at the expense of magic or "enchantment." The wonders, marvels, and spiritual correspondences that had allegedly made the premodern world nurturing seemed to be banished, in principle, by the secular faith in instrumental rationality. Modernity had become "disenchanted," as Max Weber famously argued, and while this brought certain corresponding benefits, it also stripped existence of overarching purposes or foundational meanings: the existential habitat of humanity, according to him, threatened to become a constricting "iron cage of reason."[1] Weber's gloomy phrases echoed the critiques of modernity advanced by the romantics in the late eighteenth century; by the late nineteenth century, the association between modernity and disenchantment had become common in western Europe and America. The negative effects of industrialization, urbanization, mass politics, and mass culture were widely discussed, and the triumph of scientific naturalism in the wake of Darwin's theory of evolution seemed to rule out any divine purpose or legible meaning to existence. Adherents of positivism, materialism, and literary realism in the latter half of the century often presented a bleak picture of human existence, governed by bestial instincts that were themselves reducible to mere chemical and physical processes. The discourse of disenchantment was pronounced in the writings of cultural pessimists ranging from Arthur Schopenhauer in the early nineteenth century to Max Nordau, the author of *Degeneration*, at the end of the century. Perhaps proving that you can never get too much of a bad thing, the discourse continued into the new century in the writings of Toynbee, Spengler, Freud, and many others. As Georges Bataille observed in 1955, "It generally seems to me that the present world scorns the nostalgia people have for the marvelous. The present world tends to neglect the marvelous."[2]

Indeed, during the fin de siècle, the discourse of disenchantment pro-

voked many to seek alternatives to the rational, secular, and consumerist tenets of Western modernity.[3] This widespread "revolt against positivism" led individuals to embrace aestheticism, Eastern religions, the occult, spiritualism, and the instinctual "will." But it would be a mistake to see modernity and enchantment as inherently incompatible, despite the polarities of the received debate.[4] Just as the modern and the vernacular can be shown to be compatible in interesting ways, so too can modernity and enchantment.

Thus I hope to show that one way in which modernity and enchantment were reconciled was through the vernacular of modernity itself. Beginning in the fin de siècle, tropes of rationality, objectivity, empiricism, and skepticism—the "rational vernacular" of nineteenth-century Western modernity—were used in works of fantastic fiction to create convincing worlds of enchantment and wonder that readers could inhabit imaginatively. The genre of the "New Romance" originated in Britain in the 1880s as a concerted attempt by its authors to restore enchantment to literature without abandoning the verisimilitude established by the reigning genre of realism.[5] The New Romance was, in part, a reaction to the perceived pessimism of literary realism, yet incorporated the realists' fidelity to modern life as well as their pretensions to scientific objectivity. In works by Robert Louis Stevenson, H. Rider Haggard, Arthur Conan Doyle, Rudyard Kipling, and many others, readers were presented with marvels whose plausibility depended on their being framed in the rational vernacular of scientific naturalism. These texts were often presented as if they were objective, factual accounts, and their putative veracity was increased through the use of footnotes, appendices, maps, glossaries, and other paratextual apparatus more often associated with nonfiction than with fiction. Such paratexts did more than render fictional marvels palatable in a scientific age: they provided adult readers with sufficient information to construct coherent "secondary worlds" of the imagination that could be revisited and augmented over time.[6] New printing techniques developed during the fin de siècle, such as halftone lithography, enabled these texts to include photographs and other lifelike forms of reproduction, heightening their "reality effect."[7] Many New Romance works were "spectacular texts" for the new age of the spectacle, pairing the visual and the verbal synergistically to enhance the imaginative immersion of their beholders. As we shall see, a number of the detailed worlds they constructed became enduring habitations of the mind for adults, made possible in part by the rational vernacular.

The philosopher Richard Rorty has argued that the progressive disen-

chantment of the world through science "force[s] us to the conclusion that the human imagination is the only source of enchantment."[8] This was certainly the approach taken by the romantics beginning in the late eighteenth century, and the New Romance of the late nineteenth century is one further instantiation of this romantic turn toward the imagination as a source of enchantment in the modern world—but with an important difference. During the final third of the nineteenth century, the play of this imagination was at once immersive and, paradoxically, detached and self-undermining; it deserves to be distinguished as an "ironic imagination." The ironic imagination is related to Coleridge's contention that we experience fiction in an enlightened age through "the willing suspension of disbelief."[9] But those who use the ironic imagination do not so much willingly suspend their disbelief in fictional characters or worlds, as willingly believe in them with the double-minded awareness that they are engaging in pretense.[10] The ironic imagination is a form of the modernist "double consciousness" that is found not only in the high modernist works of the late nineteenth and early twentieth centuries but also in the mass culture of the same period, including the New Romance. As the literary critic Michael North has observed, "Even by the turn of the century, irony had become less a defense against commercialized modernity and more a way of participating in it. . . . As society becomes progressively aestheticized . . . as audiences begin to consume imaginative and symbolic materials as they had previously consumed material goods, then everyday life acquires an inherent ironic distance from itself."[11]

While often ironic, the texts of the New Romance tend not to be metafictions—that is, they don't call attention to their artifactual nature to such an extent that imaginative immersion is lost.[12] Instead, they are similar to hoaxes, a term used by the American author H. P. Lovecraft to describe his realistically detailed tales of frightening yet wondrous creatures who invade our world from other dimensions of time and space. In the early twentieth century, Lovecraft used the rational vernacular to recast "supernatural fiction," which he felt had been discredited by modern science, into the literature of "cosmic fear," which he felt was compatible with scientific rationality. Lovecraft described how what I am calling the ironic imagination enabled him to write and to read stories of the marvelous in a rationalistic age: "[I get a] big kick . . . from *taking reality just as it is*—accepting all the limitations of the most orthodox science—and then permitting my symbolizing faculty to *build outward* from the existing facts; rearing a structure of *indefinite promise and possibility*. . . . But the whole secret of the

kick is *that I know damn well it isn't so.* I'm probably trying to have my cake and eat it at the same time—to get the intoxication of a sense of cosmic contact and significance as the theists do, and yet to avoid the ignorant ostrichact whereby they cripple their vision and secure the desiderate results." Here we see an example of the conjunction of enchantment and modernity within the ironic imagination, via the rational vernacular. Lovecraft's own fictional universe of New England towns menaced by aliens from beyond the known dimensions of time and space was so memorably detailed and ironically "plausible" that it has formed the basis for works by other authors, films, pastiches, and role-playing games. (The *Necronomicon*, his invented tome of "forbidden lore" recording past visitations by these aliens and the means whereby they might be summoned again, has assumed a virtual reality of its own; although during his lifetime Lovecraft only quoted brief passages from this nonexistent work in a few of his stories, at the present moment there are at least two editions available in paperback.)[13] Like other fictional worlds of the late nineteenth and twentieth centuries, including those of Sherlock Holmes, the *Lord of the Rings*, Star Trek, and Star Wars, rational adults have come to inhabit the imaginative space Lovecraft created as a way to reconcile enchantment with modernity.

Thus, while the ironic imagination is related to the early romantics' attempts to redress a seemingly disenchanted world through the imagination, it is also different from the romanticist project in important respects. First, the romantics tended to define the imagination in metaphysical terms, even when they were dealing with irony, whereas the ironic imagination is not metaphysical; it emphasizes the provisional, the contingent, and the artificial.[14] A second distinction follows from this: whereas the romantics stressed sincerity and authenticity, the ironic imagination is comfortable with the artifices of mass culture, and the phantasmagoria of symbols and representations that accompany a capitalist economic order. Finally, the ironic imagination of the late nineteenth century was accepted by the public in a way that had not been the case for the imagination extolled by the romantics in the early nineteenth century. At that time, the majority of the middle classes did not share the romantics' enthusiasm for the imagination as an equal or superior partner to reason. Middle-class culture in Europe and America through the mid-century was influenced by religious and utilitarian strictures; for most, the imagination was understood to be subordinate to reason and in need of surveillance to prevent dangerous expressions of desire.[15] While vogues for certain fictional characters extended back to the eighteenth century (notable examples of such characters include Rich-

ardson's Pamela, Goethe's Werther, and Dickens's Little Nell), these amounted to brief fads and were not comparable to the ongoing imaginative immersion in the fictional universes created by Doyle, Lovecraft, and many others beginning in the late nineteenth century and continuing through the present.[16] (Indeed, Sherlock Holmes was the first fictional character to be widely written about as if he were real and his creator fictitious, and the numerous articles and books about his "life" that began to appear in the 1890s inspired similar quasi-scholastic approaches to many other fictional worlds and characters.)[17] Many adults would have frowned upon such extended forays into imaginative worlds during the early nineteenth century; luxuriating in the imagination was a trait usually associated with those who tended to be less rational and responsible (children, women, "primitives," etc.).

These early Victorian inhibitions concerning the imagination began to erode by mid-century, however, owing to the gradual spread of secularism, a greater diffusion of economic prosperity, an increase in leisure time, and the irresistible enticements of the new mass culture. By the end of the nineteenth century, there were more venues available for people to exercise their imaginations, including mass-circulation newspapers and magazines, museums, circulating libraries, music halls, and even films in their nascent form. These new attractions helped to circumvent residual Victorian emphases on "rational recreation"[18] and gave wider latitude to the free play of the imagination.

One important sign of this new tolerance for a less inhibited imagination was the emergence of children's literature as a genre in the 1860s.[19] Before this, children's literature tended to be didactic and highly moralistic or, in the case of "penny dreadfuls," proscribed by the middle classes; the children's literature of the 1860s was more accepting of the whimsical free play of a child's imagination. I stress this change in children's literature because many of the popular authors of the New Romance stated that they wanted to recover the autonomous worlds of enchantment they had experienced as children. The spirit of play and make-believe encouraged by the new children's literature sowed the seeds for fantastic texts written for adults starting in the 1880s.

This less inhibited imagination often took on an ironic cast. Scientific skepticism was part of the tenor of the times, but the sheer profusion of visual representations found in mass culture, abetted by the concomitant rise of professional advertising at the end of the century, inculcated an awareness of artifice among the public. This in turn imparted an enhanced mo-

mentum to the skeptical, ironic attitude toward this new society of the spectacle that had been developing for decades—an ironic imagination.[20] Many postmodern theorists have simply asserted that the public remained passively in thrall to the blandishments of mass culture, but more recent research suggests that the public enjoyed playing with these "artful deceptions," even when they knew or suspected fakery. This was recognized by P. T. Barnum, who wrote in his autobiography: "The public appears to be disposed to be amused even when they are conscious of being deceived."[21]

By the late nineteenth century, this freer and more ironic use of the imagination was being legitimated by the findings of psychologists, scientists, and philosophers, who stressed the great extent to which perceptions of the "real" were indebted to the imagination and other subjective factors. In the wake of Darwinian evolutionary theory, many writers turned to the imagination as the source for existential meaning and spiritual sustenance. Friedrich Nietzsche, Oscar Wilde, and Stéphane Mallarmé extolled the fictive aspects of existence, and in 1911 the philosopher Hans Vaihinger published a manifesto of "fictionalism" entitled *Die Philosophie des als ob* (translated by C. K. Ogden as *The Philosophy of 'As If'*), in which he discussed the prevalence and utility of fictions in science and in everyday life. (The ironic imagination is very much an "as if" imagination.) Thus, by the turn of the century, a more widespread recognition that perceived reality was to some extent an imaginative construct, and that rationality itself was beholden to imaginative insights and desires, made indulgence in the imagination more permissible for adults: one could actively believe, albeit ironically, in marvels and wonders, without compromising one's standing as a rational and responsible adult.

During the fin de siècle fantastic and autonomous worlds of the imagination appeared in popular fiction as well as in more recondite works by symbolists and aesthetes. These two branches of fiction, mass and elite, often defined themselves against one another, but in one respect they shared the same end: the creation of autotelic worlds of wonder for a modern age.[22] One popular New Romance author, Robert Louis Stevenson, used terms similar to contemporary aesthetes in his description of how reading popular fiction can transport readers into a separate sphere of consciousness: "The process itself should be absorbing and voluptuous; we should gloat over a book, be wrapt clear out of ourselves, and rise from the perusal, our mind filled with the busiest, kaleidoscopic dance of images, incapable of sleep or of continuous thought. The words, if the book be eloquent, should run thenceforward in our ears like the noise of breakers, or the story,

if it be a story, repeat itself in a thousand coloured pictures to the eye. It was for this last pleasure that we read so closely and loved our books so dearly in the bright troubled period of our boyhood."[23]

However, while many of the works produced by the aesthetes repudiated the rational vernacular of empiricism, positivism, and scientism, New Romance authors worked within these tenets of modernity to facilitate their readers' immersive experience.[24] Their examples became formalized when "science fiction" emerged as a distinct literary genre in the 1920s, but the rational vernacular was not restricted to this genre. The contemporary mystery genre also embraced it, and even a genre like fantasy, which would seem to reject modernity, in its modern form often accepts the rational vernacular. For example, in his 1938 discussion of fantastic literature, J. R. R. Tolkien argued that modern readers would accept secondary worlds of "arresting strangeness" provided that these worlds were also logically and internally consistent. Like New Romance works, Tolkien's *The Lord of the Rings* combined the rationalist and aestheticist outlooks. (He also outdid his predecessors when it came to the incorporation of maps, glossaries, and other paratexts signifying the rational vernacular.) Tolkien insisted that "fantasy is a rational not an irrational activity" and that "it does not either blunt the appetite for, nor obscure the perception of, scientific verity. On the contrary. The keener and the clearer is the reason, the better fantasy will it make." While rational, the modern enchantments of fantastic literature are also allied to the formalist creations of the aesthetes, for both evoke autonomous worlds of wonder intended to transcend the everyday: "Enchantment produces a Secondary World into which both designer and spectator can enter, to the satisfaction of their senses while they are inside; but in its purity it is artistic in desire and purpose," Tolkien asserted.[25] Tolkien's creation, like those of the earlier New Romance authors, was at once marked as an aesthetic artifact—an object of ironic, adult play—and a convincing and captivating secondary world, a "virtual" built environment that adults could actively believe in and inhabit imaginatively: as he also acknowledged, "I wanted people simply to get inside this story and take it (in a sense) as actual history."[26]

Thus, from New Romance through such modern genres as science fiction, fantasy, and mystery, the rational vernacular of modernity has been used to reenchant modernity. And the habit of juxtaposing the real and the fantastic, which became established during the fin de siècle, has gained even greater prominence during our own time. For example, the British *Dictionary of National Biography*, in the edition published in 2004, contains en-

tries for John Bull, Springheel Jack, and Robin Hood.[27] Such entries would have been inconceivable in the original Victorian edition of the sober *DNB*, but are entirely congruent with the post-Victorian world of the ironic imagination: as the *New York Times* observed recently, "today there are hundreds of thousands, perhaps millions of people whose grasp of the history, politics and mythological traditions of entirely imaginary places could surely qualify them for an advanced degree."[28] And these secondary worlds of the imagination, no less than actual built environments, can have determinate social consequences. They ought not to be dismissed as a form of escapism, for, as the anthropologist Arjun Appadurai notes,

> Until recently, whatever the force of social change, a case could be made that social life was largely inertial . . . and that fantasy and imagination were residual practices, confined to special moments or places. In general, imagination and fantasy were antidotes to the finitude of social experience. . . . [A]s the deterritorialization of persons, images, and ideas has taken on a new force, this weight has imperceptibly shifted. More persons throughout the world see their lives through the prisms of possible lives offered by the mass media in all their forms. That is, fantasy is now a social practice; it enters, in a host of ways, into the fabrication of social lives for many people in many societies.[29]

The historically specific ways in which these enchanted secondary worlds have intersected with the real world are beyond the limited scope of this essay, which is to trace how such worlds emerged to address the discourse of disenchantment by associating wonders and marvels with the rational vernacular of modernity. It is true that many of these texts reflected the prevailing prejudices of their day and may have exacerbated contemporary imperialism, racism, and sexism. H. Rider Haggard's novels, for example, have been criticized in these terms, although some critics have also noted the ways in which his novels contest certain popular stereotypes.[30] However, what is less often noted about such popular works of the fin de siècle and after are their self-subverting ironies and their association of reason with romance.[31] By linking the rational with marvels and adventure, New Romance and the works it inspired may have inculcated among the public a sense that modern rationality can be a source of animism rather than anomie, that analysis can be numinous rather than numbing; it may have encouraged them to think logically in emulation of such romantic yet rational heroes as Sherlock Holmes. (One individual who was so affected was the psychoanalyst Robert Lindner, who confessed to being a lifelong science fiction "addict," writing: "I owe to science fiction much more than gratitude for entertainment. Re-enforcing a native curiosity and an inclina-

tion toward science, such reading has led me toward the serious study of subjects like Semantics and Cybernetics, to say nothing of laying a foundation for intellectual hobbies like philosophy, higher mathematics and physics.")[32]

The use of the rational vernacular at the mass-cultural level to redress disenchantment suggests that contemporary cultural pessimists mistakenly identified a narrow, "means-ends" instrumental rationality as the hallmark of modernity and were too quick to dismiss more playful forms of rationality as deceptive froth pandered to by the culture industry. Indeed, the romance of reason and the ironic distance fostered by New Romance and later literary forms may tend to shore up one definition of enchantment— "to delight"—over its more pernicious meaning of "to beguile."[33] Ernst Bloch has argued that turning to the imagination can be a mere soporific for the ills of the present, but it can also be a resource for the ways in which those ills might be surmounted. And, as Bloch stressed, this is especially the case when the imagination is grounded in a rational vernacular: "Everybody's life is pervaded by daydreams: one part of this is just stale, even enervating escapism, even booty for swindlers, but another part is provocative, is not content just to accept the bad which exists, does not accept renunciation. This other part has hoping at its core, and is teachable. It can be extricated from the unregulated daydream and from its sly misuse, can be activated undimmed. . . . Then let the daydreams grow really fuller, that is, clearer, less random, more familiar, more clearly understood and more mediated with the course of things."[34]

Indeed, Bloch suggested that the genre of science fiction was specifically suited for this function. As he argued in his essay on the utopian resources embedded in traditional fairy tales,

> if one turns from . . . the old story which remains eternally new, to the really new and newest history, to the fantastic changes of technology, then it is not surprising to see even here a place for forming fairy tales, i.e. for technological-magical utopias. Jules Verne's [works] and other creative narrations of a technological capacity or not-yet-capacity are still pure formations of fairy tales. What is significant about such kinds of "modern fairy tales" is that it is reason itself which leads to the wish projections of the old fairy tale and serves them. Again what proves itself is a harmony with courage and cunning, as that earliest kind of enlightenment which already characterizes *Hansel and Gretel*: consider yourself as born free and entitled to be totally happy, dare to make use of your power of reasoning, look upon the outcome of things as friendly. These are the genuine maxims of fairy tales, and fortunately for us they appear not only in the past but also in the now.[35]

In what follows, I discuss how New Romance emerged to reconcile modernity and enchantment through the use of the rational vernacular and the ironic imagination. I then examine several "spectacular texts" of this genre to illustrate how they created virtual "geographies of the imagination" that adults could inhabit for protracted periods of time. Finally, I discuss how this habitation of imaginary worlds constructed through the rational vernacular was both legitimated and enabled through the emergence of communities of readers at the turn of the century. Such shared participation in fantastic worlds amounted to the creation of public spheres of the imagination, reenchanting modernity without repudiating its central tenets.

The "New Romance" of the Fin de Siècle

The genre of "New Romance" appeared in Britain in the 1880s, combining realism and romance. To contemporaries, the new works by Robert Louis Stevenson, H. Rider Haggard, Rudyard Kipling, Arthur Conan Doyle, Bram Stoker, and others appeared to redress the sense of pessimism expressed by the dominant genre of literary realism and the general cultural climate of scientific naturalism during the last third of the century. "The world is disenchanted," wrote the critic Andrew Lang in an 1887 sonnet about Haggard's *She* (1886). But, he continued, it can become reenchanted through imaginative leaps, exemplified by Haggard's epic.[36] Writing about Haggard's *King Solomon's Mines* (1885) and *She*, the critic W. E. Henley observed "just as it was thoroughly accepted that there were no more stories to be told, that romance was utterly dried up, and that analysis of character . . . was the only thing in fiction attractive to the public, down there came upon us a whole horde of Zulu divinities and the semipiternal queens of beauty in the caves of Kor."[37] If it weren't for the enormous success of Haggard's two novels, which immediately followed it, Stevenson's popular "boy's book" *Treasure Island* (1883) might have appeared to be an anomaly, a work of romantic adventure written to please the sensibilities of adults as well as children. Taking them together, however, critics felt that a new genre had emerged, and their opinions were confirmed by the subsequent publication of many other works in the same mode: writing in 1892, the critic George Saintsbury noted, "we have revived the romance . . . on a scale which a whole generation had not seen. We have wound ourselves up to something like the pitch of Romantics of sixty or seventy years ago."[38]

But this pitch was a distinctively new note in literature, not just a refrain from the implausible extravagances of the Gothic fiction or romances of the

early nineteenth century.[39] What distinguished New Romance was not just that these books were exuberant fantasies, bursting like fireworks against the somber background of literary realism, but that they appropriated the techniques of literary realism and thus could command the attention of adults schooled in naturalism yet yearning for the marvelous. A contemporary reviewer of Haggard's novels, for example, cited his "hybrid species of invention—jolting you at every step from the naturalistic to the fantastic and back again."[40] Another reviewer called *She* "a marvelously realistic tale of fantastic adventures," and *Blackwood's Edinburgh Magazine* praised its author as "the avatar of the old story-teller, with a flavour of the nineteenth century and scientific explanation."[41] Haggard, explained the *Scots Observer*, "describes his fabulous action with a realistic minuteness and full relative truth."[42] It was these qualities that characterized New Romance as a whole, according to another critic: "The methods of the new *raconteur* are not refined. . . . His object is to work in as many marvels as possible, with so many realities as to make the whole look as if it might have been."[43] The merger of these two modes inspired heated debates in the late 1880s about the relative merits of realism and romance, which gave New Romance wide publicity. According to Andrew Lang, "a new Battle of the Books is being fought."[44]

Regardless of the positions writers took in the debate, their essays drew attention to the pervasive climate of intellectual disenchantment that seemed to preclude the existence of marvels and wonders in everyday life. One critic wondered if, in a world governed by scientific rationality, "we shall ever find anything really marvelous, anything which will deflect the whole current of human thought, or even make us question the accuracy of what we know. We doubt it greatly. One can dream of such things."[45] The imagination became widely recognized as the locus for modern enchantment, just as it had been for the early romantics, although now the imagination had to be disciplined and rational. In a culture that valorized positivism and materialism, even imaginary enchantments required grounding in realism, objectivity, and fact—the rational vernacular of modernity. *King Solomon's Mines*, according to a critic, was so popular because it met these criteria, addressing modern readers' demands "that the lust of wonder should be fully and, so to speak, honestly satiated." Previous generations had been satisfied with ghost stories or chivalric romances, but "their descendants, unable to believe in magic . . . seek a similar gratification in discovery,—scientific, antiquarian, or geographical."[46] The New Romance writer was thus required to steer a narrow course between the Scylla of fan-

tasy and the Charybdis of realism, or risk alienating his audience. As Haggard himself reflected, "adventure in this narrow world of ours is a limited quality, and imagination, after all, is hemmed in by deductions from experience. When we try to travel beyond these the results become so unfamiliar that they are apt to lack interest to the ordinary mind. . . . The lines which close in the kingdom of romance are very narrow."[47]

By delimiting the "kingdom of romance" to an autonomous sphere of the imagination permeated by the rational vernacular, adults were able to actively engage in the pretense that the enchantments were real, while simultaneously acknowledging this mental sleight of hand. The novels created a ludic space in which mature readers were authorized and enabled to play. They could immerse themselves in these fantastic worlds because the authors of New Romance intended to create an atmosphere of verisimilitude instead of the estranging effects found in earlier metafictions like *Don Quixote* or *Tristram Shandy*. Romances, Stevenson argued, were distinguished from other forms of fiction by their emphasis on plot, which was the most powerful narrative element in captivating readers: "It is not character but incident that woos us out of our reserve. Then we forget characters and plunge into the story without reserve—then we are reading romance."[48]

New Romance's emphasis on linear narratives full of engaging incidents more than offset the texts' sly ironies, at least in terms of capturing and maintaining the reader's attention. Nevertheless, experienced readers knew they were reading an extravagant fiction even as they gave themselves over to it wholeheartedly. New Romance novels were akin to the "artful deceptions" of American popular culture perpetrated by P. T. Barnum and others in the early nineteenth century, which have been insightfully analyzed by James Cook. Cook demonstrates that many suspected or knew that popular exhibitions of marvels were deceptions, but because these exhibitions were so artful in their presentation, so "incredible" yet so "real," the audiences allowed themselves to be enchanted but not deceived by the illusions presented to them: "It seems clear that artful deception in the Age of Barnum routinely involved a calculating intermixing of the genuine and the fake, enchantment and disenchantment, energetic public exposé and momentary suspension of disbelief. . . . In the nineteenth-century arts of deception, then, illusionism and realism were always interconnected. . . . There was no need to *choose* between illusionism and realism. The public was amused even when it was conscious of being deceived."[49] Similar examples of artful deception, as Cook and others have shown, are to be found in

the literary hoaxes of Edgar Allan Poe, in which fantastic events are narrated with such naturalistic detail that they were thought by many to be true.[50] Poe's tales were among the inspirations for Jules Verne's own "scientific romances" combining realism and romance, which began to appear in the 1860s, and Stevenson, Haggard, Doyle and other New Romance writers cited one or both of these authors as important influences on their own work. Indeed, some of the texts by these latter authors did function as inadvertent hoaxes for naïve or less experienced readers: Haggard reported receiving a fair amount of correspondence from those who believed that *King Solomon's Mines* was true,[51] just as Doyle received similar letters about Sherlock Holmes. (After the second Holmes story was published in 1890, Doyle wrote to his editor expressing surprise that "a . . . tobacconist actually wrote to me under cover to you, to ask me where he could get a copy of the monograph in which Sherlock Holmes described the difference in the ashes of 140 different types of tobacco.")[52]

New Romance's emphasis on science, rationality, technology, and bourgeois adventure would seem to set the genre at the opposite pole from aestheticism, and Andrew Lang's definition of romance as "stories told for stories' sake" was no doubt intended to tweak the aestheticist credo of "art for art's sake."[53] Certainly, aestheticism could appear to be a reaction against prominent aspects of modernity, reveling in irrationalism, mysticism, and elitism, whereas New Romance accepted the modern vernacular. Yet the two had much in common. Both aestheticism and New Romance represented attempts to reenchant the world by creating autonomous secondary worlds of wonder, divorced from the banal commonplaces of the everyday. And both New Romance and aestheticism were self-conscious genres that drew attention to their works as being artifacts of the imagination. In the new age of the "spectacle," the public was becoming more aware of the polyvalent uses of representations, given the increased deployments of images in everyday life fostered by the new mass media and advertising.

Many New Romance novels were themselves spectacular, using the latest advances in printing technologies to complement the literary creation of secondary worlds with images, usually in the forms of photographs, drawings, diagrams, and maps.[54] There was a clear discrepancy between the "reality effect" produced by this combination of text and images—a *Gesamtkunstwerk* between two covers—and the fantastic events being retailed; the reader was encouraged to be of two minds, accepting the reality of the fantasy on the one hand and noting its carefully contrived status on the other. Forewords, dedications, footnotes, and picture captions also might be writ-

ten in a slightly arch style, further underlining the ironies inherent in the work, drawing attention to its status as an aesthetic artifact.

But while New Romance, like aestheticism, cultivated and addressed an ironic imagination, its irony was not so heavy-handed as to inhibit imaginative immersion. It provided just enough distance to ensure that the form of enchantment one experienced was one of playful delight instead of unwitting deception. If a secondary world was especially rich (as in Tolkien's narratives of "Middle-earth") or its characters sufficiently fascinating (as in Doyle's stories of Sherlock Holmes), readers might continue to inhabit these worlds long after the narrative itself was finished. Unlike the eponymous protagonist of Flaubert's *Madame Bovary* (1857), many readers of the fin de siècle and after approached fictional worlds in an ironic spirit, encouraged to do so in many instances by the texts themselves. Emma Bovary came to a bad end because of her inability to distinguish reality from romance, but readers at the turn of the century were being trained to make such distinctions and invited by the richly detailed marvels of secondary worlds to inhabit them for protracted periods.

In what follows we shall see how New Romance writers created literal geographies of the imagination, combining the rational vernacular and new printing technologies to produce spectacular texts for the new spectacular culture that burgeoned at the turn of the century.

Geographies of the Imagination: "Spectacular Texts"

Many contemporaries cited Stevenson's *Treasure Island* (1883) as the beginning of New Romance; Haggard recalled that it had inspired him to write *King Solomon's Mines*, and both novels were published with elaborately detailed foldout maps. Publishers' artifices such as these were critical to the New Romance project. Metonymically, the maps signaled that the text itself was to be taken as a "geography of the imagination," subject to imaginative habitation; more prosaically, they underlined the author's commitment to literary realism, no matter how fantastic the narrative. Stevenson's map began as a sketch he made in the course of improvising his story for a young friend, and he admitted that the more "realistic" map that was eventually published lacked the spontaneity and naïveté he associated with the narrative's genesis:

> It is one thing to draw a map at random, set a scale in one corner of it at a venture, and write up a story to the measurements. It is quite another to have to examine a whole book, make an inventory of all the allusions contained in it, and

with a pair of compasses, painfully design a map to suit the data. I did it, and the map was drawn again in my father's office, with embellishments of blowing whales and sailing ships, and my father himself brought into service a knack he had of various writing, and elaborately forged the signature of Captain Flint, and the sailing directions of Billy Bones. But somehow it was never "Treasure Island" to me.[55]

Nevertheless, Stevenson commended to aspiring writers the importance of mapping out their secondary worlds in detail, admitting that he himself even used an atlas: "The author must know his countryside, whether real or imaginary, like his hand; the distances, the points of the compass, the place of the sun's rising, the behavior of the moon, should all be beyond cavil."[56] The built environment of Stevenson's island was laden with pirates' treasure, but also with the rational vernacular, the latter facilitating belief in the former in a positivistic age.

Other writers of New Romance would follow Stevenson (and important predecessors like Poe and Verne) in creating enchanting worlds of the imagination distinguished by the rational vernacular. Their efforts were assisted by new developments of printing in the 1880s, such as halftone lithography, which enabled the reproduction of photographs and detailed drawings containing fine gradations of shadow and tone. Neil Harris has noted that this innovation rendered illustrations more "objective" and real-seeming than earlier forms of lithography and woodcuts, which drew attention to the hand of the individual artist: with the halftone improvement, "the illusion of seeing an actual scene, or receiving an objective record of such a scene, was immeasurably enhanced."[57] The illusion of objectivity was also evoked through paratextual elements associated with scholarship, such as footnotes, glossaries, and appendices. New Romance novels that combined these diverse elements deserve to be called "spectacular texts," presenting empirically detailed secondary worlds able to appeal to rational adults.

H. Rider Haggard's *She* is a prime example of a spectacular text. Haggard had taken great pains with the map for his earlier book *King Solomon's Mines*, commissioning the artist Agnes Barber to create a weathered map that looked as if it had been etched in blood on linen.[58] Many were fooled into thinking the map real,[59] which encouraged Haggard to create an even more elaborate set of visual and verbal deceptions for *She*. The frontispiece of *She* is a photograph—a contemporary mark of truth[60]—of a "Facsimile of the Sherd of Amenartas," Haggard's invented potsherd that provides the protagonists with key information for their fantastic quest in search of She-Who-Must-Be-Obeyed. Haggard had Barber create an actual sherd and to

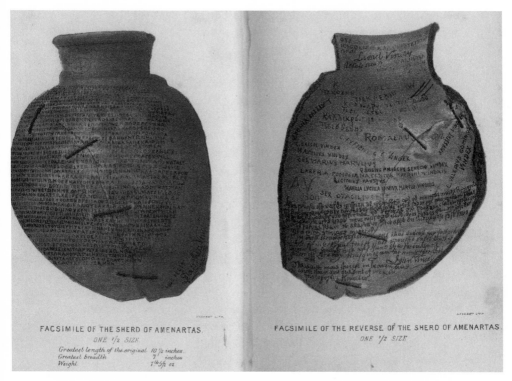

FACSIMILE OF THE SHERD OF AMENARTAS.
ONE ½ SIZE.

Greatest length of the original 10 ½ inches
Greatest breadth   7   inches
Weight   1 ℔ 5½ oz

FACSIMILE OF THE REVERSE OF THE SHERD OF AMENARTAS.
ONE ½ SIZE

FIG. 2.1. "Fascimile of the Sherd of Amenartas." Frontispiece photographs (originals in color) in H. Rider Haggard, *She* (London, 1887).

ensure their accuracy had two scholars compose the classical Greek, Latin, and Old English inscriptions on it. In addition to being visible in the frontispiece image of the sherd (fig. 2.1), these inscriptions are also presented in the three languages in the text itself. When Haggard showed the finished sherd to the antiquarian Sir John Evans, the latter remarked, "All I can say is that it might possibly have been forged."[61]

Haggard also used footnotes throughout the work, attributed to two distinct authors. The book begins with the framing device of an introduction by an "Editor" (presumably Haggard, as it is claimed that the Editor has written an earlier "Central African adventure"). The Editor receives a manuscript from "L. Horace Holly," who insists that his text is "a real African adventure."[62] The rest of the novel consists of this manuscript, with footnotes by either the "Editor" or "L.H.H." The footnotes elaborate on the events of the novel, or provide factual support or emendations to state-

ments in the text. (Thus one early footnote, attributed to "L.H.H.," begins "The Kallikrates here referred to by my friend was a Spartan, spoken of by Herodotus [Herod. Ix.72] as being remarkable for his beauty. He fell at the glorious battle of Plataea [September 22, B.C. 479].")[63]

There are several remarkable aspects about these footnotes. First, footnotes were not common in works of fiction, let alone works of fantastic fiction. Haggard uses them prominently, to drive home the point intended by his frontispiece: that *She* is an objective account of a genuine adventure. However, the very prominence of sober footnotes in such a fanciful narrative, like the incredible elaboration of the sherd, has, of course, the opposite (and intended) bathetic effect: to remind the reader again and again that the text is a fiction. But this estranging technique is also undercut by having two authors write the footnotes. The reader assumes that Holly is fictitious, but is not sure about the "Editor," who is implied to be Haggard; and the Editor's notes indicate that he accepts the reality of Holly's manuscript. Haggard has been rightly criticized for being a poor stylist, but his techniques for evoking a double-minded consciousness in his reader are brilliant. Other novelists used framing devices, or illustrations, or occasional footnotes, but Haggard combines them all, facilitating imaginative immersion while encouraging ironic detachment.

There is little doubt that Haggard's use of irony in *She* was intentional, although this is an aspect that many critics of his works tend to underplay or ignore. Contemporary readers were aware of it, however. After reading a draft of *She,* Haggard's friend Andrew Lang suggested that he diminish some of the more evidently facetious remarks in the citations: "I'm sure the note about a monograph on Ayesha's Greek pronounciation for the use of public schools, will show the Public you are laughing—a thing I can never help doing, and the B[ritish] P[ublic] hate it."[64] Haggard's own ironic self-parody encouraged others to write parodies and pastiches of his works, which would also happen with Arthur Conan Doyle when he created Sherlock Holmes. In such ways the secondary world takes on a life of its own, encouraging readers to continue to inhabit an imaginative space that has become more ubiquitous through multiple publications, and also to contribute to its ongoing creation by offering their own versions.

Lang himself wrote an anonymous parody of *She* published in 1887, entitled *He*—said to be "by the author of *It*"—and his text directed attention to the ironic, realist, and spectacular aspects of Haggard's work. For example, paralleling the footnotes by two authors in *She*, there is throughout *He* a running dialogue in footnotes between the "PUBLISHER" and the "ED-

ITOR" about the realist aspects of such a fantastic narrative, such as the lengthy translations from ancient Greek and Latin. ("Don't you think this is a little dull? The public don't care about dead languages.—PUBLISHER. Story can't possibly go on without it, as you'll see. You *must* have something like this in a romance. Look at Poe's cipher in the *Gold Beetle*, and the chart in *Treasure Island*, and the Portuguese scroll in *King Solomon's Mines*.—ED.")[65] And, highlighting the spectacular nature of the new mass consumer society and its role in fostering an ironic imagination among the public, the two discuss ways to sell advertising within the story. Here is an example of one such footnote exchange, instigated by the following line of the story:

> The wine was procured, as I would advise every African traveler to do, from Messrs.——[1]
>
> 1. Messrs. Who? Printers in a hurry.—PUBLISHER
> Suppressed the name. Messrs.——gave an impolite response to our suggestions as to mutual arrangements.—ED.[66]

He has many other references to advertising, and the plot itself is revealed to be an elaborate confidence trick, in which a man claiming to be an ancient wizard (the "He" of the title) bilks the female versions of Holly and Leo, Polly and Leonora, out of their money. Once again drawing attention to the spectacular nature of that text and situating it within the context of the modern culture of the spectacle, Lang's satire also mocks the typographical tricks Haggard employed in *She* (fig. 2.2).

While there are many other spectacular texts one could cite, I'd like to focus briefly on four others in order to make my earlier generalizations about the ironic, aesthetic, and rational elements of these texts more concrete. The American John Uri Lloyd's *Etidorpha* (1895), initially issued by the author in a limited edition, proved so popular it went through many commercial editions in the next two decades, all lavishly illustrated. Lloyd was a practicing scientist who was dismayed by the narrow materialism and reductivism of his peers. *Etidorpha* was intended to reenchant the speculative inquiry of science by illustrating the important findings of earlier alchemists and non-Western approaches to nature as a rebuke to the instrumental rationalism of the modern scientific worldview.

The complex frame narrative has Lloyd publishing a manuscript left with him by a "Mr. Drury," who himself had been entrusted with it many years earlier by the narrator of a fantastic journey into the earth who calls himself "I-Am-The-Man." (In the course of this latter narrative, the reader learns

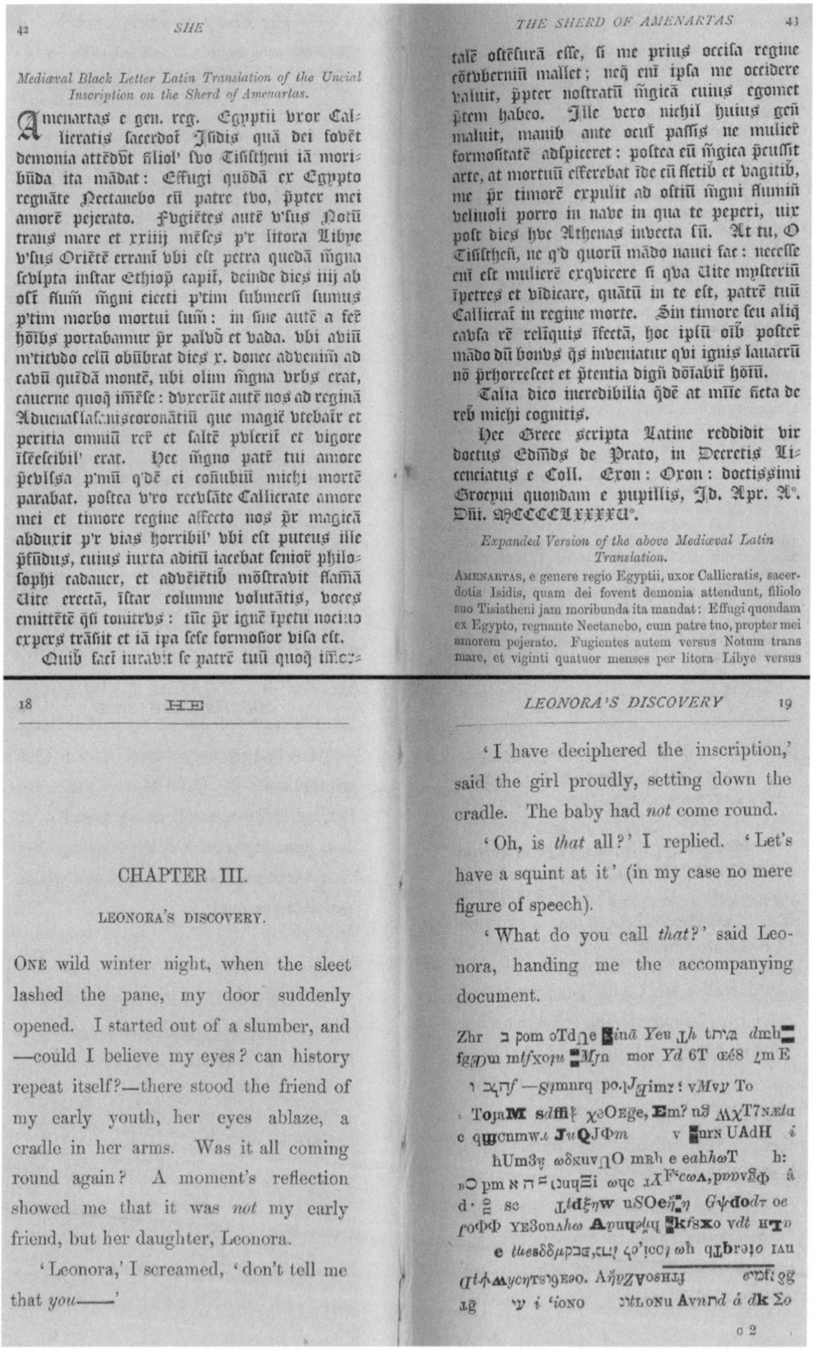

Mediæval Black Letter Latin Translation of the Uncial Inscription on the Sherd of Amenartas.

Amenartas e gen. reg. Egyptii vror Callicratis sacerdos Isidis qua dei fovet demonia attedut filiol' suo Tisistheni ia moribuda ita madat: Effugi quoddam er Egypto regnate Nectanebo eu patre tuo, ppter mei amore pejerato. Fugietes aute v'sus Notu trans mare et rriiij meses p'r litora Libye v'sus Oriete errans vbi est petra queda magna sculpta instar Ethiop capit, deinde dies iiij ab ost fluii magni eiecti p'tim submersi sumus p'tim morbo mortui sum: in fine aute a fez hoibs portabamur pr palvo et vada. vbi aviu m'tirvbo celu obubrat dies r. donec abveniu ad cabu quida monte, ubi olim magna vrbs erat, caverne quoq imese: dvreriit aute nos ad regina Advenaslascuiscoronatiu que magie vtebaiz et peritia omniu res et salte pvlerii et vigore isesctibil' erat. Hec magno patri tui amore pevilssa p'mu q'de ei conubiu michi morte parabat. postea v'ro recvlate Callicrate amore mei et timore regine affecto nos pr magica abdurit p'r vias horribil' vbi est puteus ille psudus, cuius iurta aditu iacebat senior philosophi cadaver, et abveietib mostravit flama Uite erecta, istar columne volutatis, voces emittete qu tonitrvs: iue pr igne ipstu nocuo expers trasut et ia ipa sese formosior visa est.

Quib faci iurabit se patre tuu quoq imez—

tale ostesura esse, si me prius occisa regine corvberniu mallet; neq eni ipsa me occidere valuit, ppter nostratu magica cuius egomet ptem habeo. Ille vero nichil huius gen maluit, manub ante ocul passis ne mulier formositate adspiceret: postea eu magica peussit arte, at mortuu efferebat ibe eu sletib et vagitib, me pr timore erpulit ab ostriu magni slumiu velinuoli porro in nave in qua te peperi, uix post dies hoc Athenas invecta su. At tu, O Tisistheu, ne q'd quoru mado nauci sac: necesse eni est muliere erqvicere si qva Uite mysteriu ipetres et vibicare, quatu in te est, patre tuu Callicrat in regine morte. Sin timore seu aliq cavsa re reliquis isceta, hoc ipsu oib poster mado bu bonvs qs inveniatur qvi ignis lauacru no prhorrescet et ptentia dign dolabit hoiu.

Talia dico incredibilia qbe at mile sicta be reb nichil cognitis.

Hec Grece scripta Latine reddidit vir doctus Edmubs be Prato, in Decretis Licenciatus e Coll. Exon: Oron: doctissimi Grocpui quondam e pupillis, Jo. Apr. A°. Dni. MCCCCLIIIIU°.

Expanded Version of the above Mediæval Latin Translation.

Amenartas, e genere regio Egyptii, uxor Callicratis, sacerdotis Isidis, quam dei fovent demonia attendunt, filiolo suo Tisistheni jam moribunda ita mandat: Effugi quondam ex Egypto, regnante Nectanebo, cum patre tuo, propter amorem pejerato. Fugientes autem versus Notum trans mare, et viginti quatuor menses per litora Libye versus

---

CHAPTER III.

LEONORA'S DISCOVERY.

ONE wild winter night, when the sleet lashed the pane, my door suddenly opened. I started out of a slumber, and —could I believe my eyes? can history repeat itself?—there stood the friend of my early youth, her eyes ablaze, a cradle in her arms. Was it all coming round again? A moment's reflection showed me that it was *not* my early friend, but her daughter, Leonora.

'Leonora,' I screamed, 'don't tell me that *you*——'

'I have deciphered the inscription,' said the girl proudly, setting down the cradle. The baby had *not* come round.

'Oh, is *that* all?' I replied. 'Let's have a squint at it' (in my case no mere figure of speech).

'What do you call *that*?' said Leonora, handing me the accompanying document.

Zhr פ pom oTdᴎe 𝐆ina Yeʊ ⅃h trⱱa dmb
fgᴎᴖua mtʃxoɼu 𝐌ʃᴎ mor Yd 6T œ68 ⏌m E

1 ⤞ᴎ̄ʃ—𝑔ᴝmnrq po.ᴉⱼᵍimɪ꞉ vMvy To
Toɉa𝐌 sdffi⳨ χᴏOʙɡɛ, 𝐄m? n𝕵 ᴍχT7ɴæla
c qᴝcnmⱳ꞊ Jʋ𝐐Jꟼm v 𝐆ɴrꓤ UAdH ⅰ
hUm3ᵽ ꞷꝺxuvᴎO mɐh e eɑhhoT h:
ᴎOᴏ pm ꝁᴨᴲⸯᴎuq𝚵ꟾ ꙍqc ⱴⅬᶠᶜ꙯ꙍᴀ,pʋᴐⱴꝘp ã
d꞉⅝ so ⅃ᵼ𝟒ᶍᴎw uꟚOᴇᵑ̣ ᴎ G𝗏dodꞇ oe
ɼoꟼ𝚽 YɛꝪonᴧhꙍ 𝐀puᴖ⳧ꞕᴗ 𝔊kꞙꜱxo vdꞇ ʜᴛɳ
e ⱦᴜesᵟᵟμᵽᴐᴄ,ᴄⱢʃ꞉ ꞁꙍꞌꞁcꞁ ꙍh qꞀbꞅəꞁo ᴵᴀu
ꞁꞇ𝟒ⱳʏcꞎꞇs̵ꞀᵍʙꝪo. AꜱʏꙀꝩᴏꜱʜ꞊ꞁꞁ ꙍᴏꝏꝼꞛ ꝺꝪ
ꞁꝪ ꞓⱬ ⅰ 𝓲ꙍɴꙮ ꙲ꞇⱢoɴu Avnꞃd ã dk Ꙅo

o 2

FIG. 2.3. Above, one of several foldout maps of an alternate world in Joseph M. Brown's *Astyanax* (New York: Broadway Publishing Co., 1907); below, realistic yet ironic photograph of the "author" and a skeleton in John Uri Lloyd, *Etidorpha* (Cincinnati, 1895), vi.

that the earth is actually a hollow sphere harboring a multitude of wonders.) In Lloyd's Preface, which is accompanied by photographs that are apparently of his study, he states "whether I stood face to face with Mr. Drury in the shadows of this room, or have but a fanciful conception of his figure,—whether the artist drew upon his imagination for the vivid likeness of the several personages figured in the book that follows, or from reliable data has given us facsimiles authentic,—is immaterial." Immediately we are situated in the double-minded consciousness of the ironic imagination. That we are encouraged to doubt that anything in the narrative is true seems to be evident from the Prologue that follows the Preface, supposedly written by the man who left Lloyd the manuscript, "Johannes Llewellyn Llongollyn Drury." Drury relates his background, including the fact that, because his name is so cumbersome, he decided "to select from and rearrange the letters of my several names, and construct therefrom three short, terse words" to use for casual acquaintances—obviously John Uri Lloyd. But "Drury" also insists on the factual nature of the narrative, and the reader's sympathy for this point of view is elicited by the numerous and detailed diagrams, maps, and illustrations in the text; there are also footnotes by the real "J.U.L." that corroborate statements in the text left to him by Drury. In the spectacular and ironic pages of *Etidorpha* a rigorously logical yet patently fantastic world is created, designed to challenge modern disenchantment without relinquishing modern rationality (fig. 2.3).

Similarly, Joseph M. Brown's *Astyanax: An Epic Romance of Ilion, Atlantis, and Amaraca* (1907) undergirds its premise that Northern and Central American civilizations were founded by survivors of the Trojan war and Atlantis with four foldout maps ("prepared by the hand of the author, of the greatest interest and importance to the reader"), an appendix, a calendar, many illustrations, footnotes, and "about 40 tailpieces, almost as fascinating as the illustrations themselves."[67] The spectacular nature of the text as both "real" and "artifice" is highlighted by the inclusion of a photograph of a woman in costume, captioned "Columbia." On a tissue overleaf, the author has written: "Miss Maxine Elliott, fitting the author's ideal of Princess Columbia. Miss Elliott's personality has, with her gracious consent, been embodied in the various drawings of Princess Columbia in this work. The author thus considers it fitting that one of the most charming of Miss Elliott's photographs should preface the work." The succeeding illustrations of a fictitious character modeled on a photograph of a real woman dressed as a fictitious character nicely encapsulate the ongoing juxtaposition of the "real" and the fantastic, the objective and the artificial, that charac-

terizes these spectacular texts. They are explicitly theatrical and yet aspire to render the fantastic plausible by using the rational vernacular to legitimate that which modernity disavows.

We see this as well in Arthur Conan Doyle's *The Lost World* (1912). Doyle took care that the photographs and illustrations for the book appeared realistic, going so far as to don makeup, wig, and beard to appear as his character Professor Challenger for the frontispiece photograph, which is captioned "Professor Challenger in his Study. From a photograph by William Ramford, Hampstead" (fig. 2.4). Ramford was the actual photographer. Doyle scrupulously supervised the creation and placement of other photographs, sketches, and illustrations of the Lost World itself and its prehistoric inhabitants; the legends to the illustrations represent them as being from the sketchbook of one of the characters in the novel. In a letter to the actual illustrator, Doyle wrote, "I feel that we shall make a great joke out of this. . . . I look forward with great interest to see your first studies of fakes."[68] Doyle, too, invoked the double-minded consciousness of the ironic imagination to evoke a peculiarly modern form of enchantment.

Finally, the hardcover edition of Rudyard Kipling's tale about mail delivery by dirigibles in the twenty-first century, *With the Night Mail* (1911), was published as if it were a nonfiction account from a magazine of the future, accompanied by other departments of the spurious magazine: Letters to the Editor; Reviews; an "Aerial Board of Control Report" on weather conditions, accidents, and pilot infractions; an advertising section offering dirigible parts and custom-designed dirigibles; a "help wanted" section, and so on (fig. 2.4). The story was a straightforward futuristic adventure charting a voyage of a mail-ship between London and Quebec, which in the course of its evening run encounters damaged dirigibles, inconsiderate pilots, an aerial hospital ship, and an electrical storm. Kipling manages to present a detailed secondary world in this short narrative, which he continued to explore in a story set in the same world, "As Easy as A.B.C." (written in 1912; published in 1917). The reader of *With the Night Mail* who scrutinizes the "magazine back matter" as well as the story itself will learn in passing how dirigibles supplanted airplanes as major modes of conveyance; how all air transport (and thus virtually all commerce) is governed by a worldwide organization known as the Aerial Control Board (A.B.C.), whose motto is "Transportation is Civilization"; how the average human lifespan has been extended thirty years due to the beneficial consequences of traveling in the thinner air of high altitudes, and other internally consistent facts of this secondary world. Thus, in one of the "Answers to Correspondents," the reader

FIG. 2.4. Above, photograph of "The Members of the Exploring Party" (with Arthur Conan Doyle disguised as Professor Challenger seated at center) in Doyle, *The Lost World* (London, n.d.), 80; below, one of the numerous "advertisements" from the alternate world depicted in Kipling's *With the Night Mail: A Story of 2000 A.D.* (New York, 1909), n.p.

learns that the A.B.C. was formed in 1949, and that as a result "war, as a paying concern, ceased in 1967" (although "The convention of London expressly reserve to every nation the right of waging war so long as it does not interfere with the world's traffic").[69]

Kipling resorts to the rational vernacular of science and engineering to impart verisimilitude to this world, as well as to the advertising vernacular of the new spectacular society. The narrative makes several references to the replacement of religion by commerce as the unifying faith of modernity. In the course of describing an electrical storm buffeting the dirigible, the narrator makes this clear in his choice of metaphors: "If one intrudes on the Heavens when they are balancing their volt-accounts; if one disturbs the High Gods' market-rates by hurling steel hulls at ninety knots across tremblingly adjusted electronic tensions, one must not complain of any rudeness in the reception."[70] The numerous advertisements reproduced within this spectacular text reinforce this point, but the ads themselves are often gently ironic, helping the reader maintain the balancing act between immersion and distance that characterizes the ironic imagination. Kipling nicely captures the tone and layout of contemporary newspaper advertisements in his copy for the year 2000, as in this listing under the "Wants" column: "FAMILY DIRIGIBLE. A COMPETENT, steady man wanted for slow speed, low-level Tangye dirigible. No night work, no sea trips. Must be a member of the Church of England, and make himself useful in the garden. M.R., The Rectory, Gray's Barton, Wilts."[71]

The rational vernacular of the New Romance novels of the late nineteenth century became a common attribute of the succeeding genre of "science fiction," which was christened in American pulp magazines during the 1920s. These early genre magazines also used footnotes, charts, maps, and other indices of scientific respectability for what were often outlandish tales with little inherent scientific plausibility. But comments in the editorial and letters pages of magazines like *Amazing* or *Wonder* or *Astounding* indicate that many of the editors and readers took science and its methods seriously.[72] They also extol the imaginative enchantment, or "sense of wonder," elicited by the fictional secondary worlds of the stories themselves. Indeed, science fiction "fans" of the 1930s were among the earliest groups of readers to form organized communities devoted to their favorite fiction; these communities in turn deepened their members' immersion in fictional worlds, while maintaining interpersonal interactions in the real world. It is to this process of communal engagement with secondary worlds of the imagination that we now turn.

Communal Imaginations and Imagined Communities

As we have seen, the rational vernacular of New Romance was used to legitimate fictional marvels and to foster imaginative engagement in secondary worlds. This immersive process was facilitated and encouraged by changing attitudes to the playful use of the imagination by adults during the fin de siècle. But there was a third factor that made these secondary worlds sites of virtual habitation: the active participation of readers, which in certain important respects had become more intensive by the turn of the century.

This assertion contests an influential paradigm of the history of reading, which suggests that reading in the West had been "intensive" prior to the mid-eighteenth century but became more "extensive" with the rapid profusion of reading material afterwards. But critics of this model argue that extensive reading does not necessarily preclude intensive reading,[73] an observation that is sustained by the near-devout interest inspired by certain fictions of the late nineteenth century, such as Arthur Conan Doyle's Sherlock Holmes stories. The Holmes stories were undoubtedly made popular by their intrinsic qualities (characterization, plot, style, etc.), but extrinsic factors, having to do with the dynamics of mass publishing at the end of the nineteenth century, were also important. Increased competition for readers led periodical writers and publishers to forge innovative strategies aimed at securing reader loyalty; as an unexpected by-product, several of these strategies resulted in sustained reader involvement in the fiction itself. For example, Doyle's Holmes stories in *The Strand* were self-contained, permitting new readers to become involved with the characters in any given issue. Yet they also had elements of a serial narrative, each successive story reinforcing the depth and familiarity of this particular secondary world, heightening readers' anticipation of the next installment of Holmes's wonderful adventures. Doyle claimed he pioneered this technique of combining the addictive elements of serial narration with the "immediate access" of self-contained narratives to make it easier for readers to take up the series at any point; while it did this, the technique also increased his readers' immersive experience by situating the individual stories within an overarching secondary world as their referent. Certainly George Newnes, the publisher of *The Strand* (for upper- and middle-class audiences) and *Tit-Bits* (for lower-middle-class and working-class audiences), capitalized on the series' popularity by publishing the Holmes stories in both magazines, sponsoring con-

tests around them, and encouraging and publishing enquiries regarding them.

This creation of an ongoing public dialogue in the pages of a magazine about that magazine's fiction, in which readers were rewarded for paying careful attention to the details of the stories, was another innovation of the fin de siècle: earlier, individual readers might have written directly to an author or editor, but magazines did not actively solicit or publish readers' opinions concerning the fiction. Newnes's publicity innovations were followed by similar attempts by other publishers to secure the opinions and loyalty of their readers. After the turn of the century, for example, American "pulpwood" periodicals devoted to fiction, such as *Munsey's Magazine*, *The Argosy*, and *Adventure*, established letters pages in which readers were encouraged to discuss the fiction with one another, the editor, and the writers.[74] Editors initially did this as a marketing device, to discover what their readers preferred, but the letters pages became very popular among readers, who actively engaged in topics devoted to the fiction's veracity, style, and other attributes. Some letters pages were more intellectually engaging than others: whereas fiction magazines that targeted children and adolescents, such as the "hero pulps" (*The Shadow*, *Doc Savage*, and the like) tended to receive formulaic letters, other fiction magazines with a more adult audience (such as the science fiction pulps) often had energetic exchanges among their readers about the fiction published and the editorial policies of the periodical itself.

These letters pages reflected and supported the development of the ironic imagination and the growing tendency to inhabit fictional secondary worlds buttressed by the rational vernacular, in at least three ways. First, the readers themselves treated the stories as, on a certain level, "real"—worthy of intelligent debate about the plausibility of the narrative, its facts, and the author's point of view. Thus, in several issues of *Adventure* magazine during 1925, readers debated the merits of Talbot Mundy's serialized *Tros of Samothrace*, a fantastic adventure involving Julius Caesar's invasion of Britain. Mundy's fictional depiction of Caesar was controversial at the time: he presented Caesar as a neofascist, which enraged as many readers as it inspired others. The controversy surrounding Mundy's interpretation elicited cogent letters replete with historical data from a wide spectrum of the magazine's audience, ranging from professionals to the working classes. Readers of *Adventure* were as enthralled by the debate as they were by the fiction. "The Caesar-Mundy . . . shindy . . . has given me more enjoyment than any-

thing I've seen for a long time," one reader remarked. "It is extremely interesting, and probably the truth—as in most cases of the kind—lies somewhere in between. However, I think I can voice the real feelings of several thousands of invigorated readers when I say: Attaboy Caesar! Attaboy Mundy! Sic' em! It is a lovely row and brings out points I never learned before."[75] Interactions among readers and writers such as this could only increase immersion in the fictional worlds. Readers were encouraged not to be merely passive consumers of a tale but to contribute their own imaginative and cognitive perceptions of the secondary world. Similarly, science fiction readers often wrote to magazines when they spotted errors in scientific accuracy in the stories, or to suggest possible plots, authors, and sequels the magazine should publish. By writing about the fiction, readers became more active participants in it.

But if the first effect of letters pages was to augment the reality effect of the fiction, thereby enhancing imaginative immersion, the second effect was to reinforce in readers' minds the artificiality of such secondary worlds: that they were aesthetic constructs that could be imaginatively inhabited for a time but were nevertheless unreal, the creation of an author whom the letters pages had made into a recognizable personality. Letters pages probably helped acclimate readers with minimal education to an understanding of how fiction was constructed in terms of plot, style, and point of view; and all readers were reminded that, though worlds of fiction and reality might occasionally overlap, they were also quite distinct, bracketed between the covers of a book or magazine. In other words, fiction did not function simply through the "willing suspension of disbelief": Flaubert's Madame Bovary had attained that when she read romances, but lacking the ironic consciousness of her author, she still elided fiction and life to her detriment. The willing suspension of disbelief was necessary for fiction to be immersive, but the post-Bovary world of bourgeois reading (which Flaubert himself helped to create) was also suffused with ironic distance. Letters pages in fiction magazines were thus a manifestation, as well as facilitator, of the double-minded consciousness of the ironic imagination that came to the fore during and after the fin de siècle.

The third important effect of letters pages in mass-circulation fiction magazines is that they established communities of readers, in effect becoming "public spheres" of the imagination. Adults were encouraged to indulge their imaginations with other adults, and one consequence of this was that readers with a shared taste for an author, character, or genre began to communicate with one another outside the pages of the magazine. Organized

science fiction fandom, for example, originated in the 1930s through the mediating influence of the letters pages of the science fiction pulp magazines; the addresses of writers were printed with their letters, and soon individuals were contacting one another by mail and meeting in person, forming clubs, writing fanzines, and staging conventions. Similarly, the American "Baker Street Irregulars," a group devoted to Sherlock Holmes (devoted to such an extent that they insisted Holmes was real and that Doyle was at best Watson's literary agent) was also formed in the 1930s under the auspices of the *Saturday Review* and its editor, Christopher Morley. Such reading communities helped legitimate each member's habitation of fictional worlds. Edmund Wilson expressed a residual Victorian revulsion against this practice when he called the Sherlock Holmes society "infantile,"[76] but the society itself provided its members with a sanction to continue their extended immersion in a detailed secondary world, just as science fiction fandom helped its members withstand the scorn of others in the 1930s for "that crazy Buck Rogers stuff."

Reading communities, like the letters pages of magazines, enabled their members to become creative partners with the writers of the fictions they shared. The Baker Street Irregulars published articles seeking to reconcile the apparent contradictions and lacunae in the Holmes "canon" (Was Watson shot in the shoulder or the leg? Which college did Holmes attend? etc.). Since the eighteenth century, readers had been writing to authors to discuss the plots and characters of novels, but with the establishment of letters pages and reading communities in the early twentieth century, readers received substantially more feedback for their investment in secondary worlds—not only from authors, but also from editors and fellow readers. Communities of readers thereby enhanced each individual's sense of imaginative immersion in these worlds by providing a synergistic effect, while also reinforcing the general awareness of all members that each was participating in a game of the ironic imagination.

The letters sections of popular-fiction magazines, and the accompanying communities that developed around certain characters or genres, were thus sharply defined instances of new public spheres of the imagination, in which rational adults came together to play in secondary worlds of the imagination. At the same time, the new mass media of this period contributed to culture itself becoming a more diffused public sphere of the imagination. Popular characters in fiction, film, radio, and advertising were part of a shared common currency that brought people from diverse backgrounds together.[77] These new media, like the letters pages of magazines,

also acclimated individuals into inhabiting secondary worlds: for example, radio, the "theater of the imagination," became a common companion to most people's lives in Britain and America in the interwar period. In America, many children's radio shows had clubs that enhanced the imaginative participation of their listeners by issuing premiums, such as decoders; these modern reliquaries enabled their young listeners to interact with the program and with one another, and also provided each child with a token redolent of the magical charisma of such enchanted figures as Captain Midnight, Superman, The Lone Ranger, and Little Orphan Annie. Just as children's literature carved out a separate imaginative space for its readers in the 1860s, the radio clubs of the interwar and immediate postwar period prepared a new generation to inhabit imaginary secondary worlds in a communal fashion, which many of them continued to do as adult fans of *The Lord of the Rings* or *Star Trek* in the 1960s. Television, videos, and other information technologies have only made this process more ubiquitous, accessible, and acceptable. But our present ease with secondary worlds of enchantment built out of the rational vernacular and inhabited through the ironic imagination is still a relatively recent constituent of modernity, and would have been incomprehensible to many for much of the Victorian period.

There are dangers to this form of habitation. The psychoanalyst Robert Lindner recounts a case history of one of his patients who had created a secondary world, a detailed futuristic universe indebted to the patient's extensive (and intensive) reading of science fiction. The patient not only documented this world in great detail but also believed it to be real; without any irony, he spent many waking hours "visiting" it to the detriment of his work and personal life. Lindner's initial therapeutic strategy was to enter into his patient's fantasy in order to wean him from it. Yet the therapist unexpectedly found himself nearly as captivated by the documented fantasy realm as its creator: "My condition throughout was . . . that of enchantment developing toward obsession."[78] The wish fulfillments provided by this secondary world proved too alluring for Lindner, especially as they were couched in the rational vernacular that he had been acculturated to value. This secondary world tempted him to be "geologist, explorer, astronomer, historian, physicist, adventurer" instead of the sedentary analyst he had become. Despite his better judgment, Lindner found himself engaged in an "intense pursuit of error and inconsistency in the 'records' . . . with the obsessive aim of 'setting them straight,' of 'getting the facts.'"[79] This negative, "beguiling" form of enchantment overtook Lindner at an especially vulnerable period in his life, when he was most susceptible to its blan-

dishments; fortunately, he was able to extricate himself from the growing delusion through self-analysis before he succumbed completely to its spell. But his account of "The Jet-Propelled Couch" is a classic example of how the ironic imagination can lose its prophylactic distance from the immersion it also enacts.

Nevertheless, Lindner's own experience, while valuable as a cautionary reminder, does not seem to be a common one. The abuse of secondary worlds may be no more prevalent than other forms of obsessive behavior among the general population; many people today are able to successfully combine their imaginative immersion in worlds of wonder with their everyday responsibilities and goals. Ideally, the continued practice of an ironic imagination should inoculate one against the predilection to conflate secondary and primary worlds. And the corresponding advantages of this modern form of enchantment may well outweigh not only its own dangers but also those of other, less rational and more emotive forms of enchantment. Secondary worlds of the imagination can provide a vantage point from which to criticize prevailing ways of thinking and acting; communities of readers devoted to these worlds can engage in socially mediated thought experiments that may yield concrete results in the real world. (The origins of aeronautics, for example, have been traced to early enthusiasts of science fiction.)[80] Finding a home in the imagination that does not repudiate the rational vernacular, while still permitting the satisfaction of the deep desire for enchantment, means finding a secure domicile in modernity as well: to be neither alienated from nor complacent about it.

Spaces of the Vernacular: Ernst Bloch's Philosophy of Hope and the German Hometown

BERND HÜPPAUF

I

Theories of modernity tend to operate on a macro level, offering explanations of the processes of modernization through highly general concepts. One such concept is abstraction. Its principal elements are rationalization of space, acceleration of time, and urbanization. It constructs the world in terms of a process that over the course of time inevitably creates uniformity and makes space and spaces immaterial. Models of modernization make the category of space appear insignificant in relation to time. Observers have suggested that from the beginning of the traffic revolution, the acceleration of time conquered space and destroyed place. The abstractness of modern existence is interpreted as a consequence of the rule of standardized international time independent of place, the seasons, the movements of the sun and moon, or individuals' inner physiological sense of time. Rationalized and abstract urban life in big cities is considered the universal objective of modernization, rendering all other forms of life anachronistic.[1]

A second constitutive concept in theories of modernity is that of a bourgeois, or *bürgerliche*, society. It is broad and ill-defined. Many of its theorists, such as Hegel, Marx, and Adorno, defined it in terms of its intrinsic contradictions. Bourgeois/*bürgerlich* for them was identical with a system of antagonisms, of dividing and splitting and a resulting "anomic," to use Durkheim's term, condition of society and the individual.[2] Constructed in a framework of Hegelian dialectics, these contradictions contribute to the process of creating a homogeneous order, eradicating opposition by marginalizing or absorbing it. The powers of internationalism, now called globalization, appear to be successful in completely marginalizing or ab-

sorbing the resistance of space and the particular. The new Guggenheim Museum at Bilbao has been called a prime example of this tendency. In the view of many critics, the $100 million building represents the ongoing "McDonaldization" of Spanish art. The franchise ideology is supported, Dina Smith argues, "by the fact that the museum is almost completely managed by its New York branch. Most of the recent acquisitions have been works by famous American artists, with very little indigenous Spanish or Basque art represented."[3]

Will continued homogenization leave room for the indigenous and for local identification, given that, as Niklas Luhmann puts it, "spatial boundaries make no sense for functional systems aiming at universalism"?[4] Are we experiencing a time when the specific character of places is disappearing as a result of the modernizing of Europe and the world?

These questions are associated with varying value judgments. They give rise either to expressions of the triumph of modernity or to an animosity toward the culture of the bourgeoisie that defines the anonymous market, economic rationality and the accumulation of capital as universal objectives and has no place for the particular and individual. Problems emerge as soon as we leave the macro level and focus on the particular rather than the general. There are differences that resist inclusion in the paradigm, details that will not fit, and countermovements and retardations at the margins of the European-American model. Theories favoring semantic structures construct the world in terms of a process that over the course of time inevitably creates uniformity and leaves no room for space. It is surprising then to note that globalization has led to the return of space by transforming the temporal category of modernity into a spatial framework.[5] To be sure, global space is being emptied of its qualities and subjected to the requirements of the time of rationalization. Yet a new awareness of the importance of space and the tension between internationalism and places of distinct local cultures is emerging.

Modernity, its furor of change and innovation notwithstanding, may have lived off values and images inherited from previous times for which it demonstrated little but contempt. Antinomies hardly noticed now appear to have been more constitutive than had been imagined until recently. Among the contradictions of modernization, the one between the tendency toward economic, financial, or architectural internationalism and an insistence on cultures of local identification was never seriously addressed. A tacit dependence on the local and concrete appears to have been much deeper than the dominant self-image in the name of progress toward ab-

straction would suggest. A theory of modernity capable of accommodating this dependence might lead to a very different image of modernity, its genesis, and its current condition. Critical theory has demonstrated a lack of sensitivity to the local and regional, and to spaces of the vernacular. The binary opposition of place and internationalism could well be an oversimplification resulting from theoretical blindness and a more complex theoretical framework needs to be developed. From a different perspective, it seems that the small and local, although hopelessly overshadowed by the gigantic creations of modernity, has been a potent concealed counterforce in the construction of the modern world. Rather than disappearing under the mounting pressures of globalization, space, it can be argued, has never lost its constitutive power and is at present being rediscovered.

Recent debate has made it obvious that the construction of the modern as a linear process of accelerated centralization and abstraction creates a distorted image. The relationship between modernity and space and place is no longer easily identified with that between emancipation and a naïve longing for a lost place free from alienation. There is a rising awareness that a sense of place and the desire for the experience of identity in a small and familiar environment was as much a part of modernity as the spectacular changes in the world through progress and internationalism.[6] It could be characterized by the perspicuity of its repudiation and simultaneous but subconscious fostering of the vernacular.

The term "vernacular" conveys a tension between closed domestic space and the open public arena. It does not exist in German and is usually translated by the noun *Heimat*.[7] This equation is problematic, because during the nineteenth century, the term *Heimat* acquired immense emotional weight. In contrast to "vernacular," it emphasizes emotional ties to the place of birth and childhood, set in opposition to a sense of "otherness" and being alien, *fremd*.[8] Like "vernacular," *Heimat* refers to a space defined in terms of a physical, cultural, or mental place of belonging. The word designates a sphere set aside from the public, protected from exposure and designed for the creation of identity. The ambiguity of *Heimat* easily turns into aggressive opposition. Identity requires boundaries and exclusion, whereas the imperative of modernity is unrestricted openness through a destruction of borders. The challenge of this contradiction remains one of the unresolved philosophical problems of the present. It has profound political implications.

In opposition to the internationalism of modernity, the vernacular is de-

fined as the category of the particular, based on an unequivocal sense of place, and it was therefore trivialized and written out of history until recently. Theories of modernity failed to take into consideration the vernacular and excluded it as insignificant or identified it with the obsolete. Its disappearance seemed imminent. But, humble and contemptible though it was, the vernacular demonstrated the strength to survive the ideologies of internationalism and power of scale, changed but not obliterated. The assumption that the triumph of the modern inevitably spells the death of the vernacular, although widespread, is difficult to sustain.[9] Rediscovered and raised to the level of theoretical reflection, it is gaining a surprising significance and the potential to contribute to the ongoing reconstitution of images of modernity and modernism.

The question can be raised of whether the vernacular was not only a suppressed detail but modernity was tacitly shaped by it much more than its self-proclaimed program seemed to permit. If the acceleration of time is significant for modernity, the vernacular is a retarding element. The question arises as to whether this retardation is a vanishing relic of the past or rather an integral element of modernity that calls for a reconsideration of the role of time. This essay contends that closer examination of the vernacular will lead to a revision of received theories of the relationship between modernity and time.

II. A Philosophy of the Vernacular

Discourse on space and the vernacular is burdened by a past when theories of space were closely connected with reactionary anti-modern ideologies. An unstable amalgam of a veneration of the vernacular, propagated as the base for identity, and an aggressive advocacy of modernism characterized European fascism. This polarity was expressed not only in practical politics but in the architectural policies and literature associated with the fascist movement. The fate of the Bauhaus and, after its closure, of biographies and works of its former members who stayed in Germany were symptomatic.[10]

National Socialism was sly in appropriating the appeal of the vernacular for its political purposes. In the "struggle for the soul," National Socialism was extremely successful in appropriating literary, artistic, and architectural versions of the vernacular. However, the weakness of this *Heimat* movement was apparent. The emphasis placed on identity as an essential state of being and authenticity was unconcerned with freedom and required a de-

valuation of history and historical time. This political definition of *Heimat* as a concrete place leapt back into an oversimplifying idea of an anti-modern romanticism. It defined both the self and its place in terms of an early moment in the history of metaphysics. History had to be conceived of as a movement that made an end of history. For this ideology, there was no transition from one phase to the next but only an abrupt emergence, a jump, an inexplicable discontinuity. *Heimat* was presented as presence by turning it into vulgar metaphysical fundamentalism. The simultaneous fascination with speed, aviation, communication technology, and other innovations of an aggressive modernization remained an unrelated juxtaposition.

By comparison, the philosophical and political position of the Left was unambiguous. Committed to a teleological vision of historical progress, critical theory constructed an opposition between the modern and the vernacular. Hegel's concept of a universal history and Marx's theory of international capitalism made space immaterial. The intellectual horizon of the dialectical philosophy of history was delineated by an abstract concept of time that privileged the future. Consequently, this philosophy of history was wary of any association with the tangible, the present, the local and provincial. The vernacular was identified with a problematic politics of identity. Adorno spoke for many when he associated *Heimat* with identity politics, which, in turn, he identified with "untruth" and, in concrete political terms, with fascism.

Ernst Bloch's Philosophy of the Vernacular

Ernst Bloch's philosophy was an exception. He shared Adorno's indictment of identity politics, yet by the same token, he made an attempt to free space from its ideological identification with immobility and reactionary nostalgia. Bloch (1885–1977) was the philosopher of the vernacular, one of the first to consider it worthy of theorizing.[11] In opposition to academic philosophy since Plato, his thought elevates the simple, the narrow, and the concrete to the level of philosophical reflection. His "vernacular" does not just refer to a place but signifies an emotional state and resonates with a spatial definition of being. He turns place and the tangible banalities of existence, mere obstructions for transcendental and analytical philosophy alike, into prime objects of philosophical enquiry. Endemic specificities of places, such as local customs and regional proverbs, become moving forces in a thinking that fuses philosophy and an ethnology of space. Bloch's philosophy is engaged in a search for spaces of revelation. At the same time, he

continues the Marxian tradition of theory engaged in changing rather than interpreting the world and he elaborates upon the small and the concrete, upon a focus on the vernacular as a model of the envisaged new world.

Bloch's philosophy grapples with the time-space relationship. His point of departure is a spatial turn in philosophical reflection on past and future. His philosophy avoids the identification of space with the immobile and of the vernacular with insignificant detail, with ornament or arbitrary motif, and treats it instead in the same way as the romantics philosophized about the fragment. In the tradition of Georg Simmel, and not unlike his contemporaries Siegfried Kracauer and Walter Benjamin, Bloch develops a phenomenological gaze that discovers the vernacular as the matrix of a different way of perceiving the world.[12] In contrast to most interpretations, Bloch's philosophy of space shows him to be less indebted to Hegel's teleological theory of history than to Hegel's critics Schelling, Schlegel, and the romantics.[13] Not abstract concepts and conceptual models but images of the vernacular constitute the hinge connecting the individual and society, the natural and built environments. Bloch's vernacular is concrete and tangible and preserves traditions derived from a world familiar to us as an imagined past, although it may never in fact have existed. The vernacular is at the center of his attempt to connect philosophical theory with a world outside of thinking, a world of concrete things and of action for which the social practice of building, represented by architecture, provides the model. Spaces need neither logical connections nor continuities. Like Kracauer, Bloch describes them as discrete miniatures,[14] in a world that Adorno called "micro-Marxism" with an "aesthetic radiance" bestowed on it by a Hegelian language.[15] To the degree to which history is predicated upon the construction of discontinuous and discrete spaces, but not the flow of time, it is freed from the constraints of teleology.

Time, Teleology, and Freedom

In contradistinction to mainstream philosophy, Bloch is not concerned with a philosophical legitimation of being but with the potentialities of becoming. He developed no theory of history, yet his way of thinking aims at combining potentiality with a theory of concreteness. It is an attempt to fuse fact-bound history with philosophical abstraction and pursues two aims, namely, liberating the empirical world from its status as an object in a system of data and transforming philosophy by directing the gaze to the small and the concrete. This is not a philosophy of history but a philosophical history that rescues history from the tyranny of factuality and philoso-

phy from hollow abstraction. If we take his philosophy of space and the vernacular as the point of departure, the question arises of how imagined space can be linked to observed space and time. Is a philosophical ethnology of space and things possible?

In contrast to the Hegelian concept of history, space is pivotal for Bloch's way of thinking.[16] He is critical of a construction of history that subjects the individual to the necessity of an abstract law. For him, the conflict between freedom and necessity results from a transcendental concept of history that needs to be dissolved. From his perspective, freedom is inextricably linked to liberation from the domination of time as the defining category of being. He makes an attempt to rid philosophy of this disquieting contradiction through a spatial turn. He develops a complex dialectic of temporality that attaches a special significance to space and refuses to absorb it into time. The early Bloch refers to the specifics of geographical regions, southwestern Germany and its democratic traditions, for example, or the "motherland" instead of the nation-state. He emphatically speaks of the need of a site (*ein Fleck*) for the individual to stand on. Space in terms of specific sites and concrete locality is crucial to his attempt to overcome the contradiction between freedom and necessity. The imaginary process of making reality emerge is the driving force of his thought. He envisions a new world hidden in the folds of the old world, which can be unfolded by focusing on hidden spaces. They can be made visible through imagination and daydreaming. In opposition to necessity created by teleology, his philosophy of space fragments unity and continuity and creates spaces for self-determination.[17] His preoccupation with space charges the vernacular with specific significance for a philosophy in search of freedom.

Varying Nietzsche's term "untimely" (*unzeitgemäß*), Bloch coined the term *Ungleichzeitigkeit* for an analysis of his present.[18] It refers to a life distanced from the fashionable, the adapted life of the man who is always up to date, streamlined, and simultaneous with his epoch. Bloch's definition of the basic idea of nonsimultaneity (*Ungleichzeitigkeit*) creates a semantic field that emancipates the events of the present and the past from a temporal continuum and makes it possible to link them to space. History is not a succession of phases determined by necessity that results from purpose. Bloch relieves history of the predicament of a causa finalis and replaces the historical telos with the eschaton, the jump rather than the continuous flow toward an end. By deconstructing the function of time for history, Bloch rehabilitates a concept of space that has always been fundamental for eschatological metaphysics. It is true, however, that this spatial and anti-histori-

cist turn contains a danger: the danger of involuntarily rescuing a philosophy of essence, which he was eager to reveal as fake, precisely by the introduction of nonsimultaneous contradictions.

In an eschatological view of the future, a space for the emergence of freedom needs to be determined. *Heimat* is his term for this space. His turn toward space transforms the theoretically insignificant word *Heimat* into a notion of philosophical reflection. In his interpretation, it is not a word designating an ethnographic place. *Heimat* is absent from modern life and needs to be made present as an imagined space of promise, a land to come. It is a sophisticated construction, and its simplicity is artificial. *Heimat* becomes a topos of the individual's right to a self as soon as it can be rehabilitated against the domination of the temporalized and homogenized space of modernization without falling prey to an ideology of stable identity. In open contrast to Heidegger's rejection of anthropology and ethnology, Bloch's philosophy opens theoretical thought to ethnological observation. He turns the ethnographic term *Heimat* into the philosophical term for an imagined space of emergence. His eschatological thinking takes utopian speculation into service for a rebellion against philosophies of necessity and of pessimism. It is a historical potential that his "Prinzip Hoffnung," or "hope as a principle,"[19] associates with future reality. *Heimat* is identical with images and imaginations that point into a space of the "not yet." It is rooted in the anticipatory function of thinking. The invention of *Heimat* is a continuous task and the passage to it requires imagination and philosophical reflection.

Heimat as an Imagined Place

Reconstituted as an imagined space, *Heimat* can be rescued from the fetters of the parochialism of identity politics and its stigma of an anti-modern idyll. Bloch's philosophy creates *Heimat* as an alternative place determined, first and foremost, by negativity. Bloch makes it very clear what *Heimat* must not be. It is a negation of capitalist productivity as well as of nostalgic anti-capitalist escapism. It is *unzeitgemäß* in every respect. He calls hope a "principle," disassociating it from romantic words such as "longing" or "melancholia," and is prepared to accept the linguistic impurity for the sake of rescuing it from the nostalgic longing for an ideal past. Any memory of *Heimat* is deceptive. Bloch knows that searching for a free society in the past is akin to the untruth of the idyll. He cannot share the romantics' idealization of the Middle Ages or the rural life of the past as a golden era before modern alienation.

In Bloch's definition, *Heimat* is not a place that can be visited or reconstructed in individual memories, because it never existed in any known past. He insists that *Heimat* is neither the space of a bygone age nor the final destination of the individual's unhappy journey through the hostile modern world. *Heimat* cannot provide a space for reconciliation, because it needs its opposite and would be inconceivable outside of a structure of differences and struggle. *Heimat* is not, Bloch maintains, a place for stable identity isolated from the contingencies of modernity. It is not to be understood as a naïve belief in the pure character of the unspoiled soil of the virgin countryside. It cannot be defined in terms of its essence, because "community" is a symbolic construction and not based on soil or blood.[20] *Heimat* therefore never connects to a first beginning but is always already the product of imagination and dreaming. Being at home is not to be identified with a final arrival, because *Heimat* is an imagined space within the parameters of modernity and a creation through language.[21] Bloch shares this anti-essentialist definition of place with other critical thinkers of his time, notably Simmel, Kracauer, and Benjamin. In a related way, Francesco Passanti reads Le Corbusier's diary from his Balkan trip as an example of the experience of the vernacular without an anti-modern escapism that idealizes the premodern world. Maiken Umbach's interpretation points to a similar problem perceived by Hermann Muthesius, who, in sharp contrast to Bloch's antibourgeois way of thinking about space, opted precisely for a timid *bürgerliche* (civic) architecture. It can be interpreted as a sign of the time that these architects and theoreticians of architecture shared the conviction that the aesthetics of building should serve an ethical (and political) purpose.

A critical view will reveal how uncanny anti-modern idylls are. *Heimat* can be conceived of only in close connection with a sense of contrast nurtured by the open space of the world. It is a state of mind in which happiness is associated with a sense of belonging and, at the same time, a sense of the freedom to leave. *Heimat* is a relational term, not one that defines a static, solipsistic life. *Heimweh* (homesickness) is inconceivable without its contrary, *Fernweh*, the pull of the unknown and desire for faraway places.[22]

Heimat needs to be invented and remains a mental sketch, an *Entwurf*. The German word *Entwurf* contains the verb *werfen*, to throw. A throwing of the imagination into the space in front and into the future is required by the sketch, the *Entwurf*. The house of a sketch is different, less and at the same time more than the house that finally materializes, less inasmuch as it is not present and cannot be touched or entered, and more inasmuch as its absence opens possibilities, a potential that is lost in the final material product. Bloch's image of *Heimat* is not a modern myth. In contrast to Celia Ap-

plegate's definition of *Heimat* as a "myth about the possibility of a community in the face of fragmentation and alienation,"[23] Bloch's attempt to reconstruct philosophy in terms of a theory of the concrete is not concerned with myth creation. It is also a misconstruction to interpret his association of *Heimat* with the principle of hope as a precursor of later theories of the virtual. To be sure, Bloch's philosophy of hope must be seen against the background of a life that equals suffering, sorrow, and pain. Bloch perceives a tacit coalition between a temporal philosophy of necessity and the capitalist order, with its quest for timeliness, productivity and efficiency. He shares Marx's characterization of bourgeois capitalism as a system of misery (*Elend*). However, an unacknowledged proximity to Heidegger's *Sorge* is beyond doubt and even stronger. For Bloch, *Heimat* is neither a modern myth born of the traumatic experiences of industrialization nor a quest for the authentic life. The world's incessant coming into being through fantasy and imagination is a refutation of Hegelian teleology and a politically committed appropriation of Heidegger's central concept of *Sorge*.

Empty Spaces and a Philosophy of Revelation

In an attempt to defend Bloch's image of *Heimat* from the anticipated criticism of naïve romanticism, Adorno once referred to it as a space "des begriffslos Erscheinenden,"[24] that is, of revelation beyond conceptual models. Bloch speaks of hollow spaces in the world. This negative space came into existence through the end of metaphysical systems, spaces vacated by God and theology. Negative space creates a desire that demands to be filled with new images, images of a humane world that has to be imagined without recourse to transcendental philosophy and with no connection to transcendence. What these spaces call for is not abstract theory but a theory of praxis. They suggest a decomposition of the grand picture of teleological history into little stories which, in turn, can be used as ethnographical material for the construction of concrete spaces, of small worlds liberated from the terror of abstract time and uniformity. Human existence is not predetermined, not final and never fully present or complete. It is not tightly woven but loose, and leaves room for the unexpected and the unknown. Philosophy needs to reclaim the attitude of surprise by confronting unknown territories, like the child who is surprised to discover cracks in a seemingly continuous reality. Through these cracks, the light comes in from no-where. It is neither the light of Plato's metaphysics nor the Christian metaphor of God as light. This is philosophy's contribution to a new way of thinking and living in which the world becomes a home. This world, Bloch once

wrote, is the only example of the possibility of a creatio ex nihilo, it can be invented out of nothing but dreaming.[25] Its elements derive from existing reality, which needs to be subjected to a decontextualizing gaze that discovers traces of the new in fluid constellations of the most banal spheres of life, traces conspicuously overlooked by philosophy.

Bloch's Kleinstadt

Philosophical and architectural discourse rarely interact. Yet it is architecture, Bloch contends, that needs to redefine its mission and prepare for the inclusion of the imaginary. At the same time, philosophy needs to embrace practical questions of building and living as a precondition of humane life. A philosophical ethnology of space would provide a common ground and meeting place of the two distinct disciplines. Bloch carries his idea through into a model of architecture. His idea of architecture is characterized by concreteness and smallness, and the architectural space of the small town, the *Kleinstadt*, plays a significant role. In Bloch's philosophy, the small town is not a space of nostalgic longing for the premodern. It is, rather, an architectural space where loss can be addressed and where modernity meets its own contradictions and offers compensation for its destructions. Regardless of negative or positive connotations, *Heimat* is for Bloch the central term for the place of emotional attachment, love, or hate, and, in its own way, it contributes to paving the path into modernity. It needed a postmodern mentality to acknowledge this contribution.

Heimat and the *Kleinstadt*, resist the destruction of space. In opposition to a life congruent with modernity, the *Kleinstadt* provided a space "far away from the stream of the time, in a remote region." The opposition to a life continuously adapting to modern trends needed a space removed from the domination of time in order to create an attitude of independence "that has been achieved by many hometown citizens. They are provincial in a way that adds a much older life to retardation."[26] This reevaluation of the "provincial" and of slowness in terms of an alternative to the destructive process of acceleration links the space of the town to the future for which we crave. In Bloch's view, it is the recourse to an older life—a life before the emergence of the modern, the bourgeois society and the rule of the clock—that invests the *Kleinstadt* with negativity, which, in turn, he interprets as a genuine power of resistance within modernity. This resistance creates the vernacular's character as a dream into the future. He constructs the vernacular of the *Kleinstadt* as an urban space that, in spite of the capitalist perversion of ideals of urban civilization, keeps the utopia of the good life alive.[27]

III. Heimat as Space—Epistemological Problems

I shall now attempt to describe and recreate the experience of the *Kleinstadt* as a specific space in the framework of a broader attempt to understand its effects for the process of modernization. This will be done in an ethnographical framework combining philosophical reflection with historical observations.[28]

Kleinstadt is a fuzzy term referring to both real and imagined space, a place for living and a frame of mind, characterized by sets of values and norms. As a result of this ambiguity, the term can be used as a descriptive category only with a great deal of caution and easily conflates distinct dimensions. As a critical term that sensitizes one to contrasting theories of modernity, it is, however, worth elaborating on. It subjects universalizing theories to testing scrutiny and points to their deficiencies as well as to damages and casualties resulting from the process of modernity. The *Kleinstadt* was simultaneously the swan song of a doomed community and a product of the new period of industrialization and urbanization. The ambivalence intrinsic to both the *Kleinstadt* and its image defined its position, including its specific productivity, in public discourse during the 150 years of its existence.

I shall start with the *Kleinstadt,* or German hometown, as it can be historically reconstructed, followed by a discussion of the imagined *Kleinstadt* as a place of resistance, of communication, of creativity, and, finally, of nightmares and self-destruction. These are linked to three fundamental traditions of urban life: political institutions that attempt to achieve the impossible by securing both social coherence and individual freedom; the classical importance of a shared language; and the restless mind called the creativity and innovation of modern man. At a time of social and cultural upheaval, when the fragile combination of these conflicting traditions was endangered, the culture of the *Kleinstadt* made a significant contribution to maintaining them and passing them on to a new period.

From Small Towns to Hometown

The only substantial study of the German small town defines the *Kleinstadt* as a specific political and social space that emerged in the form of residential towns after the end of the Thirty Years' War and persisted until the foundation of the Reich in 1871. Mack Walker uses the term "home town" in an attempt to capture the specifics of the German *Kleinstadt* of this period.[29] "Small town" is the more literal translation. However, by using the

FIG. 3.1. Ludwig Bartning, *Weimar: Abendseite* (view of Weimar), 1785, from *Damals in Weimar*, ed. Wilhelm Bode (1912; facs. reprint, Weimar, 1991).

comparison of scale, the mental characteristics of the German word are neutralized. But they are vital to the concept, setting the *Kleinstadt* in opposition to both the country idyll and the urbanism of the emerging modern city. For Walker, a basic feature of German hometowns was their isolation, because "there was almost no penetration into their internal affairs from the outside."[30] Visual representations often emphasized the town wall, inherited from a time before the invention of modern artillery, indicating that progress, growth, and expansion were not seriously affecting the *Kleinstadt* (fig. 3.1).[31] Its sociological basis was a middle-class milieu of moderate wealth made up of professionals, teachers and professors, retired officers, civil servants, merchants, and minor aristocrats. Above all, it was a place that maintained its own political structures, spatial arrangements, and its own time in contradistinction to the homogenized space and time of the modern city, slower than the time of individual lives and the time of modern political and social institutions. A deescalation of pace can be observed at its center.

Rationalization of Space

In spatial terms, the modern city's objective was the eradication of the crooked anatomy of old towns and its replacement with clear and geometrical arrangements. The ideal was symmetry and perfect geometrical forms, which although ultimately unattainable were pursued with rigor. The pervasive ideal of geometrical order ruled the modern period from Newton on; in political terms, it was a reflection of the order of absolutist rationality. This spatial organization left deep traces in the construction and reconstruction of the modern city. The order of the medieval town was now perceived as disorder, and as such, it had to be banished.[32] Traces that the premodern and pregeometric thinking of individuals, guilds, and the church had left in the arrangements of streets, squares, big and small houses, and factories became intolerable to an aesthetic mind that was dominated by the ideal of reason and identified reason with geometrical order. These apparently anarchic relics of the past had to be destroyed. Untidy quarters where lanes wriggled like worms, where no façade was regular and everything seemed warped, had to be erased. Room for a space of rational planning needed to be created by the destruction of the crooked. This was often done against strong resistance by the inhabitants of these quarters.[33] In the course of the nineteenth century, Paris with its systems of boulevards and squares where they cross, dividing the space of the city into elements of a geometrical figure, became the model. This fundamental change was two-sided. It created the pleasure of ruling over space by subjugating it to the aesthetics of geometry and symmetry and at the same time, it subjugated those living in the city to the new rigid spatial order. The metropolis was a space where the nation-state, modern socioeconomic forces of centralization, rationalization, and political domination, and a state of mind expressed in literature and the arts were intricately interwoven.

The Hometown between Country and City

The big city was the center of gravity during the era of the nation-state and national literatures in Europe. From the eighteenth century on, history, and specifically literary history, was made in the metropolis, which not only shaped forms of life, genres of writing, and styles of performing but controlled their dissemination. The history of western European literatures was centered on the capitals of the nation-states, where pervasive norms were defined according to which the world had to live and write. In opposition to this centralization and domination, images of the countryside were

closely tied to romanticism and reactionary politics. In the course of the nineteenth century, the idealization of the countryside came to be increasingly associated with anti-modernism and lost its attraction. The nineteenth-century novel became "the most centralized of all literary genres."[34] From Balzac to Dickens and Joyce, the big city, places like London, Dublin, Moscow, and Paris, provided the cognitive and emotional anatomy of the modern novel. It created an ideal space for a narrative that lost its paradigmatic position only in the late twentieth century.

Life in the big city, as portrayed in French and English literature throughout the nineteenth century, and later also in German texts, was not ideal but "hard, artificial, complicated."[35] In nineteenth-century English fiction with an urban setting, city life is seen as inauthentic, and few people actually wish to live there. In Franco Moretti's words, the characters in these novels live in the big city out of "mere narrative inertia . . . London . . . is stupid, arrogant, grotesque, aggressive—but can easily be avoided: it exists 'around', or better still outside the characters, not in them."[36] In Germany, Bettina von Arnim's book on the poverty of life in the city, dedicated to the king of Prussia (1843),[37] is an example of this critique. A split between individuals and their spatial environment was the product of the modern city. This split gave rise to counterworlds, such as the suburbs (Dickens) or country mansions (Fontane), that provided shelter for moral values. The harder the life in the city, the greater the need for relief and compensation. Urban culture—the opera, music halls, salons, gambling, and all forms of entertainment, soon including the cinema—was a compensatory product of the pressures of urban life and therefore inevitably not genuine.

The absence of a unitary state, and of a metropolis, with its power of centralization and concentration, set Germany apart, not only from Britain and France, the nations conventionally regarded as the European model, but also from eastern Europe, where Moscow's significance as an ideological powerhouse and place of identification seems to have been even more pronounced than that of Paris and London for western Europe. A metropolis that both served as a centralizing magnet and radiated its influence into the remotest corners of the nation (and its colonies) was lacking in Germany. Yet the metropolis was imagined as a threat to German political, intellectual, and literary life. Although far less important than London, Paris, or Moscow, Berlin was increasingly identified with this threat. The big city's artificiality and fragmentation of time were considered hostile to human nature. German novels of the time narrate stories of an aggressive anti-urbanism in the countryside and villages. They developed a genre suitable for the

nostalgic reconstruction in memory of life in the good old days, of a sense of authenticity, located in the country, in opposition to the destructive forces of the metropolis. Forests, meadows, fields, mountains, and village lanes were substituted for the streets, theaters, display windows, salons, and squares of the city novel.

It is, however, an oversimplification to juxtapose the urban novel as the medium of the modern with the novel of the country and village as its opposite. The spatial constellations are far less clearly defined. Provincial towns in French novels could be modern without, however, replicating the living conditions of Paris. Kenneth Clark suggests that provincialism could be interpreted as "merely a matter of distance from a center, where standards of skill are higher and patrons more exacting . . . and the provincial artist is launched on his struggle with the dominating style."[38] Such a view presupposes a unified field and linear forces operating between center and periphery. It is predicated on the perception of a national culture constituted by a linear center-periphery distance. As a result of the increasing distance from the metropolis, the centripetal force of the center is gradually decreasing, but it nonetheless remains the defining power in the entire field. However, the space of cultural production is far from being unified and homogeneous. Systems theory also speaks of the center-periphery relationship but defines it as "a form of difference."[39] This difference is never characterized by a linearity of distance. The powers of cohesion, repulsion, and gravity of a uniform Newtonian space do not operate in the space of cultural production. It is polycentric. It is a field with a plurality of forces and conflicting movements, localized gravitational pulls and epicenters. This uneven space was a precondition of the survival of the vernacular in a world of rapid centralization.

In Germany, it was not only the idealized countryside and its hamlets that gained significance but also a geographical and sociopolitical structure that differed from the city-province divide of England and France; the cultural historian Wilhelm Riehl, an astute observer, called this "individualized country."[40] It created a space that liberated itself from the pervasive pull of the center and the dominance of its geometry and ideological and political power. It was less unifying and compelling than the big city and opened up opportunities for local democracy, for joining in or staying away, from circles of friendship, and for celebrating creativity. It was an architectural and political space that protected one from the pull toward uniformity. Its foremost representation was the unique *Kleinstadt*.

In contrast to the metropolis, the *Kleinstadt* retained its curved streets

and lanes, and its lack of geometrical order. It did not follow the imperative of rationalized order and could still be experienced as a place of one's own. It was familiar and offered a sense of security and protection from the violations inflicted on the subject by modernity. It not only created a time independent of the time of social modernization but also saved the time of individual biographies from the ossification associated with the countryside. The hometown was urban, yet it was also a site where the conflict of modern history between freedom and compulsion, strongly experienced in the big city, appeared to be resolved in favor of the individual's autonomy. These were the preconditions of a life in which the individual was not lost but able to maintain a sense of self. It was conceived of as a space fit for the attempt to maintain a sense of place and concreteness in a world that dissolved all that had once been concrete and tangible into abstraction.

The *Kleinstadt* created an imagined space for cultivating subjectivity, including its irrationality—in contrast to the rationalization of industrializing societies—and for the local and particular—in contrast to the universalism of Enlightenment values. But at the same time, it was also the space of the eminently modern struggle of the self to determine its place in a society of growing abstraction and in the anonymity of a world increasingly defined by instrumental rationality. Under the conditions of modernity, the *Kleinstadt* provided a space for a life of untimeliness. It did not fit into patterns of efficiency and time management and maintained a degree of authenticity otherwise absent from modern life. Its space remained crooked, the way Kant thought human nature was crooked. It created not only an irregularly striated space for physical and social movement, but a space to which its inhabitants were attached, not wishing to be anywhere else.

The *Kleinstadt* thus served as an obscuring force that rendered the clear image of the center-periphery power struggle obsolete. It obfuscated the unilinear power relations by creating many small centers and shifting peripheries, and it provided a space for the unfolding of cultural distinctions between tangible and invisible groupings.

Provincialism is not a function of the distance from the center; rather, it is defined by a state of mind and a sense of inferiority.[41] The literature of the *Kleinstadt* was not defensive, but conscious of its innovative qualities and independent standards. Its vernacular actively obscured the relationship of dominance and dependence. It did not cringe culturally.

From the perspective of a nationalist like Heinrich von Treitschke, the strong position of the *Kleinstadt* in Germany's literary and cultural life was a deplorable hindrance on the way to a strong nation-state dominated by a powerful capital.[42]

The Imagined Hometown as a Space of Subtle Resistance

In contrast to its historical definition, the German *Kleinstadt* as a frame of mind was an invention of the late eighteenth century. It was invented as an imagined space loosely related to the small towns located on maps and described in travel guides. Its emergence was predicated on the tension with the simultaneously emerging *Grosstadt*, or big city, as the center of the changing physical and mental geography of the industrializing century. It gave a name to a space characterized by a specific lifestyle. It seems justifiable to interpret the hometown's spatial decentralization and retarding of momentum as a complementary attempt at creating a modern world, less consistent, less glamorous, and ultimately less dominant in terms of political power and philosophical persuasiveness, yet with a queer obstinacy. In the arts and literature, the hometown developed into an imagined space that differed equally from the built environment of city dwellers and that of peasant farmers.[43] Paradigmatic for this *Kleinstadt* are not only Goethe's Weimar (fig. 3.2), but Kant's Königsberg, Schelling's Jena, Hölderlin's Tübingen, Mörike's Cleversulzbach, and the romantics' Heidelberg. Jena and Heidelberg were not only centers of German romanticism but also imagined spaces of fantasy and thinking, geographical and architectural representations of the ideal type of the *Kleinstadt*. It was an imagined place that merged the small towns of the century with the idea of a vanishing urban culture. It created a place in the history of mentalities that invented a space for modern life at the margin of modernity defined in terms of the politics and polity of the western European nation-state.[44] During an extended period of transition from a society of early manufacturing to high capitalism, the *Kleinstadt* offered a space for a specific form of cognitive and emotional productivity, for reflection, self-searching, and the transformation of tradition into new ways of thinking.

The Kleinstadt as a Way of Life—Subjectivity

The *Kleinstadt* was not a place of simplicity whose inhabitants were unaware of the changes resulting from modern rationalization; rather, it was a place of deep complexity, easily missed by the uneducated eye. It was a place of gentle resistance against the present and its profane reverence for progress, which the *Kleinstadt* was unable to reverse but impacted through its retardation. It was characterized by a life based on the moral cosmos of *Bildung* (education and cultivation). The *Kleinstadt* provided the space of tranquility necessary for the reflection of a *vita contemplativa*. It was the

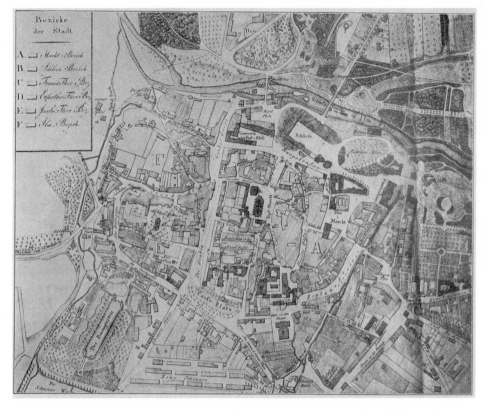

FIG. 3.2. Weimar town plan, 1825, from *Damals in Weimar*, ed. Wilhelm Bode (1912; facs. reprint, Weimar, 1991).

place that in both physical and mental senses gave birth to nineteenth-century German Idealism. At a time when the process of industrialization and urbanization turned into a threat to the individual and symptoms of a deterioration of the self were analyzed in literature and philosophy, the *Kleinstadt* became the place where the individual experienced the possibility of resistance to being absorbed into the condition of modernity. It is the central paradox of the *Kleinstadt* that some of the most pertinent analyses of these destructive elements of modernity emerged precisely under its auspices.

The relative independence of the hometown was a pillar of cultural pluralism and lived democracy. The *Kleinstadt* functioned as a microsphere that was constitutive for specific ways of living and communicating resonating with and at the same time opposing modernization. Alongside membership

in a profession, a religion, a state, and, possibly, a secret society, the small town offered its own membership to its inhabitants, one endowed with distinctive cultural values and virtues that rendered the importance of other memberships relative. It was not lost on *Kleinstadt* dwellers that this membership was a constitutive part of the competition between systematic order and creative disorder, between centralism and particularism.[45] Members of the community of a *Kleinstadt* did not give up or attenuate their other memberships. However, they entered into a specific commitment that set them apart from others as a result of a voluntary decision. This added to the palette of cultural distinctions available to them. By combining visible and institutionalized with informal and invisible memberships, they continued an old tradition of opposing the power of central and local authorities. ("Stadtluft macht frei" was the slogan of bondsmen who succeeded in escaping from their lords and obtained their freedom after living in a town for more than one hundred days.) A cultural history of the *Kleinstadt* could be written in terms of this emancipatory spirit, vital for the self-perception of individuals and literary groups like the Göttinger Hain until the age when the democratic spirit of this culture crumbled under the growing weight of the big city, its masses, and its popular culture.

The literature of the big city offered images of an "unlimited" freedom, but at the expense of a defenseless exposure and vulnerability of the subject. In opposition to these places of isolation and loneliness where personal bonds were severed, the *Kleinstadt* provided a space for the cultivation of intimate relationships. Shielded from the acceleration and commercialization of life in the city, but also distanced from the anachronisms of the quest for identity and authenticity in the back-to-the-origin discourse, the *Kleinstadt* became the site where memory could evade the erasure of the past characteristic of big cities. Emotion and the nonrational could thrive without being caught in a binary opposition between a false memory of the premodern and the vanishing of memory in the continuous flux of the modern.

The state of mind associated with the *Kleinstadt* inevitably clashed with the ways of thinking and being in the world emanating from the metropolis. It created an autonomous space for writing and living, neither isolated nor subjected to a center's domination. Identification with the local as a place of difference was the response to the modern world's insistence on a unified central standard. This image, it needs to be emphasized, was not "innocent" or idyllic. It interfered with the power play between center and periphery that was at the core of the creation of modern Europe. It would

be naïve to portray the struggle for domination as a painless redirection of influence and pure rearrangement of the distribution of knowledge. The relationship between center and hometown was characterized neither by harmonious exchanges nor by diffusion, but rather by conflict.[46] In the increasingly international Europe, the focal points of orientation and power over the mind were Paris and London, and, from the end of the nineteenth century, also Vienna and Berlin. The position of the *Kleinstadt* within this field of shifting power relations was one of resistance to a totality of space organized according to geometric-political imperatives.

As a result of radical political and cultural changes at the outset of industrialization, a unified moral code vanished, and the ancient philosophical question about the right way of life was asked anew. The *Kleinstadt* imagined was one response. It resisted the abandoning of an ethics that, Bloch argued, transcends the world as we know it, and functioned as a counterbalance to growing insecurities and a loss of orientation.

It maintained disintegrating principles of social stability and morality and at the same time was creative in transforming them. When Goethe, in his epos *Hermann und Dorothea*, transformed the religious refugees from the Salzburg of 1731 into a group of displaced persons fleeing from the upheavals of the French Revolution, he created the dichotomy that designates modern life. It creates upheaval and at the same time attempts to construct a humane space free from uncontrollable threats of nature and political terror. The refugees arrive at a place of tranquility and stability characteristic of the *Kleinstadt*, a "happy corner" (*glücklicher Winkel*) populated by unselfish and caring people, who respond to the misery of the refugees with emotional generosity. In this epos, it is the pride of the hometown ("small as it may be") to be as orderly and moral as demanded by the Enlightenment ideal of humanity. What sets the *Kleinstadt* apart in this epos is its stability, which in turn links it to an idealized image of Greek antiquity. The modern period is represented by revolution, but at the same time its *Kleinstadt* also provides the power to put an end to destruction and create a space of morality and belonging. It is a time of political chaos and destruction, but at the same time, the arts and literature are holding human life in high esteem comparable only to the idealized Greek polis.

This *Kleinstadt* is characterized by an absence of the tragic. In contrast to the *Elective Affinities* and other texts by Goethe concerned with love, the *Kleinstadt* of this epos is a space of love without drama and deep conflict between the sexes, a type of love that is close to an ideal friendship and the realization of the neoclassical ideal of humanity. It was the ideal space for, and

created a specific form of, friendship as an attitude that shunned politics, detested the increasing subjugation of private life to centralized authorities and the pervasive, rationalized unifying power of the metropolis. In terms of social culture, the *Kleinstadt* was the space for the ambiguities and dialogical forms of communication that we associate with modern culture. During this period, friendship was a central playing field of moral culture. It created emotional bonds that liberated personal relationships from the dominant powers of politics by putting the emphasis on personal preferences rather than egalitarian ideals and on emotional motifs rather than rational decision-making. Friendship can be associated with an anti-political mood endemic in the space of the *Kleinstadt*.[47] It was primarily this space of the *Kleinstadt* and its corresponding mentality that gave *Hermann und Dorothea* its astounding popularity among the German *Kleinstadt*-intelligentsia of the nineteenth century. In his enthusiastic comments on *Hermann und Dorothea*, Wilhelm von Humboldt expressed the hope that this image of the *Kleinstadt* had created a model for the future and would give rise to a whole new epic literature dealing with the life of the *Bürger*. This did not happen.

Communication

The cultural construction of the *Kleinstadt* provided space for the vernacular as a state of mind. It did not offer itself as a place of escape. The *Kleinstadt* remained equally distant from the city as a place that made subjectivity vanish and the idealized countryside as the ideological opposite of the city. It occupied a unique position in the uneasy relationship between the countryside and a metropolis characterized by both participation and negativity. Its resistance to rationalization was based on a political tradition of individual freedom and, in the middle of the nineteenth century, also a tradition of Christian heresy and an opposition to Rome and the Vatican. Its forms of communication were an attempt to reconstitute a dialogical culture of persuasion and an immediate contact alien to modern political institutions of mediation.

The city offered new and "unlimited" forms of political freedom and independence for intellectual productivity. It also created its own casualties. An increasing realization of the egalitarian ideal was accompanied by the breakdown of traditional social and communicative structures, which were gradually replaced by open markets. Unlimited freedom to publish was merely the flip side of the silencing of the individual by market forces that have no ears to listen and no mouth to speak. Networks of communication

and social intercourse were destroyed, and the subject was exposed to a threatening anonymous and unbridled market. Under the conditions of the *Kleinstadt*, other forms of communication developed, maintaining a certain degree of orality and emphasizing the authenticity of face-to-face communication rather than equity of the exchange of symbolic values in anonymous markets. An important aspect of *Kleinstadt* culture was that it retained polycentric functions of public discourse dismantled in the modern city, which had no physical or mental space for the agora. The imagined *Kleinstadt* was conceived of as a polis. It was based upon an idealized view of classical antiquity and created private and public institutions and clubs devoted to intensive communication that requires presence.[48] The physical and narrow place of the agora was being replaced by the space of the town as an imagined sphere of genuine dialogue.[49] In contrast to the anonymity of the big city, it was the *Kleinstadt* where the ideal of unmediated communication continued to be cultivated. This was not communication as a result of a struggle with the deindividualizing powers of the metropolis, but dialogue embedded in lived structures of physical presence and corporeal proximity. The well-known scene when Goethe and Schiller first met after a lecture and began a conversation that was followed by a lifelong flow of letters, exchanged nearly every day, can be read as the archetypical scene of *Kleinstadt* communication.

The relaxed communication of these small urban communities was the positive side of a culture oscillating between recreating ideals of the classical past and bourgeois presence. It stands in equal distance to the medieval town built around centers of worship and the collapse of central authority in the industrialized modern city. It maintained a certain degree of direct and polycentric communication through orality. Friendliness or comitas (comity) of social interaction imbued life in the *Kleinstadt* with an aspect of a civil society threatened by the rough conditions of the big city. This civility of communication operated on two different levels. It was characteristic of communication in everyday practices, which Wieland, Goethe, Schiller, and Herder attempted to frame in theoretical and literary terms, and it was also operative in distinct discourses of philosophy, philology, history, and aesthetics, all of which thrived in eighteenth- and nineteenth-century Germany, not least due to the conditions provided by the *Kleinstadt*.

Creativity

The literature of the *Kleinstadt* was not a derivative of the metropolis. Referring to Kotzebue's drama *Die Kleinstädter* in her report on Germany

based on her visit in 1803 and 1804, Madame de Staël compared France, where the focus of literary life was only on Paris, with Germany, where small towns created "an empire . . . for the imagination, serious study, or simply benevolence."[50] She experienced the *Kleinstadt* Weimar as a place whose citizens inhabited "the universe and, through reading and a width of reflection escaped the narrow boundaries of the predominant circumstances."[51] The latest European developments in arts, literature, and fashion were discussed within the spatial constraints of this humble place. In contrast to her expectations, the narrow conditions of individual lives did not lead to claustrophobia but, instead, were channeled into intellectual productivity. Her idealized assessment contributed to the emergence of an image that created its own momentum and its own reality of the mind. It provided the context for the surprising cultural productivity that made a substantial contribution to the concept of the modern.[52] It borders on the grotesque that the term "world literature" was born in an obscure town in provincial Germany. Goethe's term *Weltliteratur* was indicative of ways of thinking that came from within but transcended the narrow boundaries of provincial places, extending Rousseau's *citoyen* and Kant's vision of a citizen of the world in an emerging world society.

There are numerous examples in nineteenth-century literature where the tension between the *Kleinstadt* and the open space of the world is transformed into aesthetic creativity. Jean Paul's novels oscillate between the narrowness of the *Kleinstadt* and the unlimited world of imagination, of an idealized, borderless love of humanity. Turgenev paints a favorable picture of the German *Kleinstadt*. The opening pages of Gottfried Keller's novel *Der Grüne Heinrich* sing the praises of the open-minded small towns, pulsating with traffic and commerce, on the river Rhine and Lake Constance.[53] At a time when the capital's artistic preferences were conventional and nationalistic, it was at provincial Weimar where the modern French art of Manet, Cézanne, Gauguin, and Rodin was celebrated.[54] Rodin devoted fourteen modern watercolors to this provincial place, where they were exhibited. The Bauhaus was founded at Weimar by Henry van de Velde, Walter Gropius, and others. It certainly was not the brainchild of the *Kleinstadt* spirit. Yet it was conceived under the conditions and in the specific environment of this provincial place where, as Madame de Staël had observed a hundred years earlier, the narrow streets bred a universalism of the spirit that resonated with the innovative centers of the world. When, in 1922, representatives of the Dada and constructivist movements gathered in Weimar, it was a signal to the world that the German hometown still had the poten-

tial to create a space open for imagination and creativity. However, the *Kleinstadt* and its image soon deteriorated. Instead of providing images of an ideal of life, it became an isolated exception and in a way a mere figment.

Nightmare and Decline

The *Kleinstadt*'s construction as a homogeneous sphere is a purposeful deception. The preservation of its architecture and spaces of memory had its price. In the literature of the *Kleinstadt*, this price was not glossed over but, on the contrary, contributed to its fascination. As a peculiar space, it was paradigmatic of ambivalence. While it offered a breeding ground for creativity, shielding the subject from the fragmentations of the city, it was also built upon a curtailing of freedom and a domestication of subjectivity. It was a space of nightmares (fig. 3.3), where the "black wings of metaphysics," to use Hölderlin's phrase, encircled the mind.

While the *Kleinstadt* reduced the threats of modernization by separating life into inside and outside, it provided protection only from outside threats and not against violation from within. This was part of the paradoxical situation created by the imaginary *Kleinstadt*, which, in a sense, was more "real" than the real *Kleinstadt*. Its ideal typical existence was opposed to the surrounding reality, and it posited the individual in an ambiguous relation to the modern mind. Its assertion of autonomy created lonely souls subject to nightmares of isolation and helplessness. For the autonomous soul, another autonomous soul becomes the prime object of desire. After the disintegration of metaphysical systems, the lone individual created a new space designed for relating to other equally isolated individuals, giving rise to a secular cult of friendship.

This desire created a space protected both from nature and the process of modernization, where the individual was free fully to explore its deepest abyss. Under a surface of harmony, the *Kleinstadt* was a crucible of conflicts and unresolved struggles of the soul. Here, the dramas of nature were not replaced by the artificiality of a synthetic reality typical of the modern city. Karl Philipp Moritz's miserable protagonist Anton Reiser and the pietist origins of the masochist search for the self required the *Kleinstadt* as their physical site and mental setting. The theatrical space of Goethe's *Faust*, Hölderlin's *Heidelberg*, E. T. A. Hoffmann's deranged places (which only faintly resemble the Berlin known from other stories of his time), and the town of night watchmen and nightmares in the anonymous *Nachtwachen von Bonaventura* are all examples of the psychological abyss hidden under a friendly appear-

FIG. 3.3. Egon Schiele, *Tote Stadt III*, oil on wood, 1911, Leopold Museum, Vienna. Reproduced by kind permission.

ance and of the return of repressed nature. At night, the *Kleinstadt* turned into a sphere of the imagination run wild. It attempted to protect itself by paying for a nightwatchman, who, with his horn and pike, fought in vain against the specters that haunted those who longed for the quiet life.

The history of the modern "I" is stretched out between the poles of freedom associated with open spaces and the longing for a place of security and belonging. These two poles have their reverse sides, anxiety produced by openness and hatred resulting from the oppressiveness of the closed space of villages and small towns.[55] Belonging to a home can turn the experience of security into its opposite, giving rise to feelings of claustrophobia. The

oppression of space and a repressive domination over space and over the self are disquieting topoi of nineteenth-century literature and art. Detached from the outside world, the hometown revolves around its own center, which is unchanging and denies individuals the right to distance and a space of their own. The closed chamber, the narrow street, the village enclosed by a medieval wall typify the vernacular's capacity to produce suffocation and terror. As Freud observed, the *heimlich* (homely or secret) glides easily into its opposite, the *unheimlich* (uncanny)—the home becomes sinister and scary.[56]

The crisis of modern civilization at the end of the nineteenth century wrote finis to the story of the German hometown. Modernist poets rebelled against the fake ideal of this remote, closed space. They imagined extreme sites in nature, such as the high mountains (*Hochgebirge*) and the sea, as counterworlds to the narrow world of the *Kleinstadt*, now derided as a fossil paralyzed with sterile idealism. Nietzsche's Zarathustra experiences the town as being inhabited by philistines and leaves it for the mountains and deep woods. Brecht's "Baal" and early poetry contributed to the reevaluation of nature in opposition to the philistine life in the small towns. Equally, the big city is now perceived in a different light. Gottfried Benn, Alfred Döblin, and Bertolt Brecht created images of the big city that, with joy or cynicism, destroy every positive aspect of the vernacular. The *Kleinstadt* had become hollow, the country a faded past, and only the big city (or wild nature) appeared to offer the space for brutal competition, antagonism, and enmity now identified with the modern. The enemies of modernity held the *Kleinstadt* in equally low regard. When the project of a modernist architectural and artistic future was abandoned in Weimar in 1925, a sinister ideology took its place. When it was forced to engage in a political struggle with the center, the hometown had no power of resistance.[57] From 1929 on, the National Socialists formed the state government in Thuringia (of which Weimar was the capital), and Hitler's minister of the interior, Wilhelm Frick, subsequently began savaging "Nigger culture" and calling for a national and *völkisch* revival of pure German art. The vernacular of the hometown offered no resistance but was appropriated in support of this racism and provincial sterility.

Viewing the *Kleinstadt* through the eyes of its modern despisers, informed by their disdain for its narrowness and hypocrisy, will inevitably bar our understanding of it as a productive site, which it was in the real and symbolic worlds for more than a century. It was never a place only of creativity, or only of provincial sterility, but a fragile mix, an ambivalent combination of contradictory forces.

IV

In his assessment of the victory of reactionary politics in the 1930s, Bloch contended that the vernacular had been abandoned by intellectuals and architects engaged in shaping the condition of modern life. It needed to be recaptured. While Bloch shunned identity politics, he was equally aware that human life is impossible without boundaries and exclusions. His philosophy of hope is characterized by an idealized space made present through the imagination, which, as he was well aware, is deceptive, but which he was unwilling to abandon. Bloch mourned a loss, and his oeuvre is undeniably motivated by nostalgia for a place that never existed. Despite his lifelong dialogue with Nietzsche, Bloch's philosophy of hope was based on an (intentional) misreading of Nietzsche. Nietzsche's attack on the modern world and his critique of morality was not, as Bloch's reading suggests, the springboard for a project to change the world.[58] Nietzsche's analysis of deception included the "gay" and gleeful invitation to embrace the world as a never-ending play of ambiguities and delusions. It abandoned all the dreams associated with *Heimat*. In opposition to Nietzsche, Bloch regarded this kind of play as indicative of an inauthentic life. His hope was identical with the expectation that the play of presence and absence will come to a happy conclusion. In a short but significant passage, Bloch refers to a memory of children building a play house in the branches of a tree that could not be seen from below. "Sitting in it high above the ground, and having pulled up the ladder, interrupting the connection to the ground below, we felt absolute happiness."[59] The combination of concrete childhood memories and the lofty dream of an imagined place of happiness referred to a fragile and transient, primitive structure that, despite its imaginary constitution, contained within it the promise of a humane future. Could a dream of the future be farther away from Nietzsche's myth of a new man in a newly mythologized world?

Bloch has been criticized for his mysticism.[60] He was well aware of the pitfalls of his project to reconstitute the popular term *Heimat* by deconstructing its ontology. But he insisted that the hollow spaces created by the retreat of the gods must not be left to the contemptuous opponents of modernity.[61] Bloch's philosophy is that of a visionary architect of imagined spaces designed to replace the world of capitalism with something radically different, a space and time for which he had no better word than *Heimat*. It was reminiscent of the security, trust, and good experiences of a time experienced in life, a time that in memory combines events, dreams and imagi-

nation, the time of childhood. Read as a guide for action, Bloch's paradoxical combination of utopia and place calls for the dismantling of the modern city and the substitution of transient, weightless structures that would make it possible to experience *Heimweh* and *Fernweh* in the same space. This vision was clearly informed by romantic fantasies. Bruno Taut's "Dissolution of the City"—an architect's fantasy of realizing a speculative imagery of building—is far from Bloch's ideal of building, dwelling, thinking for a free subjectivity. Bloch shared the architectural utopian dream of a decentralized city, built for small, self-sufficient communities organized around a childlike ideal of altruistic mutual support. But he conceived of it in strong contrast to the international style of Bruno Taut or Le Corbusier's idea of the city and the house as machines for living and working. Bloch occasionally polemicized against modernist architecture, notably against the work of Gropius and Le Corbusier, whom he considered practitioners of the soulless craft of engineers. If Le Corbusier's motto "Architecture or revolution" was symptomatic of the attempt to maintain modern civilization through reform in the face of threatening revolution, Bloch's ideal of a vernacular architecture turned the relationship around. His architecture of revolution used building and dwelling for the *Entwurf* of a new world that has the potential of becoming a space for the experience of *Heimat*. Yet Bloch failed to take the historical experience of the twentieth century into consideration. In the wake of the catastrophes of his century, we need to ask whether it is still legitimate to maintain images of *Heimat* as an ideal for modern architecture, or whether it may have turned into a crime of the mind.

Bloch knew that modern architecture is not guided by ethics but by aesthetics. But he rebelled against this preference and dreamt of maintaining an ethics of place. His hope was that a philosophy of space would lead to liberation from teleology, and he never thought of exposing the liberated space to a philosophy of language games. *Heimat* was in need of being protected from both reactionary politics and theories of the arbitrariness of signs. In Bloch's concept of history, the absence of *Heimat* is transitory. The subdued but continuing presence of the vernacular in modernity can be interpreted as a sign indicating the temporary absence of *Heimat* but not its obliteration. Its hidden existence speaks of the possibility of putting an end to the inauthentic play of signs. Modern architecture, he wrote, faces the impossible task of building where "there is no cleared building site and . . . appropriate tools for building the human house have not yet come into existence."[62] This resonates with Heidegger's lament that we do not know

how to build and shall have to learn how to dwell. This impossibility did not lead Bloch down the slope to a postmodern notion of existence as a play of metaphors in the absence of a "transcendental signifier." His dreams do not belong in the adult world of frivolous games, but in the serious playing of children, who associate dreams with promises that burst reality open. Bloch shared children's belief in dreams' power of becoming real. They represent the promise inherent in eschatological thinking. An architecture that corresponds to the needs of the subject in a postindustrial world would need to develop responses to the challenge of fusing modern aesthetics and the ethics hidden in the inconspicuous vernacular. There is no need to reemphasize that the vernacular must not be reduced to a matter of building materials, ornament, or local motif but needs to be incorporated into the constitution of architecture and the creation of the image of a new world. In spite of globalization's pressure for uniformity, there are signs that modern architecture may be responding to this challenge.

CHAPTER FOUR

The Deutscher Werkbund, Globalization, and the Invention of Modern Vernaculars

MAIKEN UMBACH

Globalization is a buzzword of our times. Yet it is not a new phenomenon. As recent research has revealed, a "very big globalization bang" occurred in the mid to late nineteenth century.[1] This means that in Europe, the emergence of an integrated global market coincided with the arrival of most classic features of modernization, such as industrialization, urbanization, and nation-state formation: it was an integral part of the experience of modernity.[2] Much like today, around 1900, contemporaries regarded these developments both as an opportunity and a cause for anxiety about the erosion of identities. This chapter argues that globalization, thus perceived, sparked off a fundamental rethinking of the significance of place in the modern world. The vernacular, as the element in culture connected with place, came to be seen as a hallmark of distinctiveness that needed to be carefully guarded. At the same time, however, the vernacular also informed what became known as "national types," which were in turn mobilized in a project of economic imperialism at the expense of "less distinctive" cultures. The following pages examine this linkage in late nineteenth-century Germany. Imperial Germany was not only a major player in the competition to conquer the global market. It also became a "laboratory of modernity" in the cultural sphere—decades before the more spectacular modernist experiments of the Weimar Republic decisively shaped the image of modernism worldwide.[3] Thus, if we are to understand the role of the vernacular as a constitutive feature of modernist culture, we have to revisit the nexus between *Heimat* and globalization in late nineteenth-century Germany. Yet the reasons for revisiting the formative years of German modernism are not just historical. A long-term perspective onto the genesis of modernism has

important implications for our thinking about globalization today. If globalization was integral to the evolution of modernism, then the present-day search for a vision of modernity that respects and preserves vernacular peculiarities does not have to reinvent the wheel. Instead, the genesis of German modernism offers numerous insights into how the vernacular, understood as that which is particular to place, and the universal idiom of modernity can be reconciled.

Like any highly politicized term, "globalization" is more often invoked than defined. Broadly speaking, we can identify three important characteristics, which feature with varying degrees of prominence in most accounts.[4] Firstly, globalization denotes a strategy used by the most highly industrialized nations of our world to maximize exports of their products to less developed nations. This, as critics point out, often has problematic consequences for domestic economic development in the importing countries.[5] Secondly, globalization implies that this process is not purely economic in nature: typically, political pressure and military threats are used to prop up the relationship of economic dependence or exploitation. And thirdly, to speak of globalization is to draw attention to the wider cultural implications of this economic imperialism. Through its goods, "the West," consciously or unconsciously, superimposes its own identity upon other cultures, thus undermining the pluralism of local, regional, tribal and national identities worldwide, and reshaping the globe in its own image.[6] None of the above were specific to the late twentieth century. There are many similarities between nineteenth-century imperial expansion and present-day "globalization." Elites within the nineteenth-century British Empire were, if anything, more mobile than they are today—Oxbridge graduates joined the civil service in India, and children of Indian elite families studied at Oxbridge. Similarly, unskilled workers emigrated from Europe to the New World in vast numbers during the nineteenth century.[7] Conversely, twentieth-century attempts to promote the free flow of labor, for example, within the European Union, have been surprisingly unsuccessful: Europe's labor force today is significantly more stationary than in previous centuries. In fact, as Alan James persuasively argued, the twentieth century is perhaps better regarded as the "end of globalization" than as its beginning.[8] Like international labor mobility, the international flow of goods, too, is not specific to the twentieth century: the nineteenth century witnessed a dramatic intensification of trade, both within and outside the framework of formal colonialism, which only ground to a halt with the arrival of protectionism and world war.[9] What is more, economic globalization was not only a fact of life in nine-

teenth-century Europe: contemporaries were also acutely aware of these changes. As the century progressed, global competition radically transformed people's perception of the world they inhabited, and their sense of identity within it. The history of the great world fairs is a case in point.[10] Historians have toyed with different metaphors to capture the profound sense of novelty and uncertainty that characterized the globalization experience of these generations. As we come to appreciate this period as the birthplace of global modernity, older paradigms that characterized the later nineteenth century as an "end," a historical moment when an older era drew to a close, have lost their hegemonic status. Where labels such as "fin de siècle" or "the age of decadence" saw the urge to retreat from real life into a realm of fantasy and subjectivity as emblematic of the era, terms like "the age of nervousness" better capture the mentality of excited helplessness with which people observed, chronicled, promoted, or attempted to prevent these seismic changes.[11]

Yet we cannot properly understand contemporaries' reactions to globalization without also revising the other side of modernization theory's supposition, namely, the notion that the local had been rendered obsolete by the national in the same way that the global then rendered the national obsolete. As the relationship between nationalism and globalization is being redefined from one of succession to one of simultaneity, the idea of a linear progression from localism to nationalism also requires revision. Only then can we begin to appreciate how both the local and the national were invoked to make sense of the new global world. In 1990, Celia Applegate published her influential *A Nation of Provincials: The German Idea of Heimat*.[12] The book sparked off a new trend in nationalism studies, which sees localist or *Heimat* sentiments as a constitutive and necessary feature of the nation-building process. Far from standing in the way of national integration, the concrete, familiar imagery of *Heimat* helped ordinary men and women imagine the abstract category of the nation. The local sphere of experience came to be seen as a "metaphor" or vehicle for the invention of the nation.[13] It is therefore neither surprising nor paradoxical that we find vernacular revivalism and the proliferation of *Heimat* images peaking precisely when popular nationalism was at its height: just before and during World War I. Not only did idealized representations of the (rural) homeland play a crucial role in war propaganda. In Germany especially, the *Heimat* cause (the preservation and revival of local and regional traditions) attracted an unprecedented mass following from the 1900s on.[14] Yet the bulk of historical studies examining the iconography and choreography of *Heimat* still

classify it as backward-looking, nostalgic, and essentially anti-modern. If *Heimat*-style localism was compatible with nationalism, they suggest, this was because the two phenomena shared conservative characteristics. Like nationalists, the defenders of *Heimat* may have mobilized localist sentiment to boost their popular support—but they also mobilized imperialism and xenophobia, themselves hardly progressive ideas. Most existing studies maintain that those elements of nationalism that were indeed progressive, that is, democratic and socially inclusive (in a different terminology: "modern"), had little in common with the resurgence of localism in this period.[15] This is a point that the German literature on this subject emphasizes particularly prominently. Much that was associated with the idea of *Heimat* in the Wilhelmine period seemed to resurface in the *völkisch* "Blut und Boden" ideology of the Nazis.[16] Even if not all *Heimat* advocates before World War I were outspoken racists, at the very least, institutions like the Bund Heimatschutz were ideologically wedded to a romanticized rural past that had no place for progress, urbanism, and democratic pluralism—let alone multiculturalism. This was something that the Nazis could draw upon in their own propaganda—and they did. The career of the Wilhelmine *Heimatschutz* proponent Paul Schultze-Naumburg, who became a major figure in Nazi cultural politics after 1933, is often cited to illustrate the connection.[17] Insofar as there were differences, they were caused by the fact that the Bund Heimatschutz was so reactionary that even the Nazis found it difficult to assimilate this ideology wholeheartedly into their partially modern Reich. The problem with the *Heimat* ideology from the point of view of the Nazis was that it opposed even those aspects of modernity that National Socialism thought to assimilate: technological process, urbanization, and life in a modern "mass society."

This chapter does not seek to downplay or whitewash the reactionary features of the idea of *Heimat*. It does, however, advocate a reassessment of the role the vernacular played in the genesis of modernism—not only in Germany, but throughout Europe, and even in America. To this end, we need to distinguish between different types of *Heimat* sentiments. The invention of *Heimat* was no less ambiguous than the invention of the nation. Just as there was no "one" nationalism, there was no one localism or regionalism. Not to take the scope of variation into account will inevitably lead to distorted findings. Some idioms of *Heimat* had nostalgic overtones—these tended to allude to a rural, preindustrial past, and, relying on standardized iconographies of the local idyll, ironed out the specificity of particular regions that they claimed to celebrate. Politically, these images

FIG. 4.1. Wilhelm Schulz, *Den Feinden zum Trutz, der Heimat zum Schutz* (To Defy the Enemy, to Protect the *Heimat*). Poster advertising German war bonds, 1914–18. From *Das Plakat* 10 (January 1919), figure 23.

proved particularly useful in war propaganda during World War I (see, e.g., fig. 4.1).[18] We encounter them frequently in British and French as well as in German posters, picture postcards, pamphlets, and even soldiers' own letters.

Yet alongside these *Heimat* tropes, we also find others that were less unequivocally anti-modern and that placed greater emphasis on difference and regional specificity (even if this specificity, too, was partly a cultural construction). As we shall see, these images consciously and visibly incorpo-

rated distinctly urban as well as technical features. And although this second type of *Heimat* image actually predated World War I, it was by no means superseded by the more standardized and "idyllic" imagery of war propaganda. The fact that boundaries between these ideal types of *Heimat* are fuzzy, and that many tropes in the verbal and visual discourse of the early twentieth century drew on both types, does not invalidate the analytical distinction. Indeed, it makes it all the more necessary if we are to make sense of *Heimat's* deeply ambiguous role in the history of modernity.

To do so, we need to ask what contemporaries understood modernity to be. In economic terms, the answer is clear. At the end of the nineteenth century, England was widely regarded as the modern nation par excellence. Not only was England at the heart of a vast empire. It had also pioneered the Industrial Revolution and exported products all over the world. From the point of view of many German reformers, the way forward lay in imitating this success story. Yet some voices warned that mere "copying" was not enough: they suggested that English products were successful because they expressed a distinctive national character, which by definition defied direct imitation.

> Decisive for a leading role is only the ideal value that is inherent in a national performance, in other words, its cultural value. The fact that England in the late eighteenth century, when she experienced stunning successes in shaping middle-class taste . . . could participate in the world market was her independent national achievement. Also more recently, the influence of English Arts and Crafts on the world market is instructive enough. Only because England gave something that was specifically her own could her products . . . represent a distinctive feature of the world market. Commercial success marched behind dominant internal values.[19]

The author of these lines was Hermann Muthesius (1861–1927), a perceptive and influential political commentator on this era.[20] Muthesius also played an important role in promoting German economic modernization on the ground. His views thus provide a useful starting point for an investigation into the way in which continental Europeans, responding to the challenge of British global success, turned to the vernacular in search for the roots of national authenticity. Muthesius, who was trained both in the arts and the applied sciences, began working for the Prussian civil service in 1893.[21] In 1896, he was sent to England, where his official role was that of "technical attaché" at the German embassy in London, for a seven-year period. His brief was to compile reports on British industrial success and suggest ways in which the German empire might emulate it. Back in Germany, in the Royal Prussian Ministry of Trade and Industry, Muthesius himself helped

promote and implement the English-inspired agenda of reform that he had devised during his years abroad. He remained in that office until 1926.

If in 1907, Muthesius had depicted national distinctiveness as the secret to British success in the global market, by 1915, he confidently announced that Germany was now ready to step into England's shoes: "This German form will be more than just a term used in patriotic speeches: it will become the world form. Today the ascendancy of German peoples on this earth is a certainty. . . . It is not just a question of ruling the world, financing the world, educating it, or providing it with goods and products. It is a question of shaping its appearance. Only when a nation accomplishes this act can it truly be said to stand at the top of the world: Germany must be that nation."[22] This statement, although blatantly jingoistic, was not totally unfounded. Between 1870 and 1913, Germany's share of world industrial production rose from 13 to 16 percent. In the same period, England's share dropped from 32 to 14 percent.[23] There were other symptoms of this trend, more visible to contemporaries than abstract statistics. The history of the label "Made in Germany" is one of them.[24] In 1887, the British Merchandise Act forced German manufacturers to label all products destined for export to Britain or any of her colonies "Made in Germany." The assumption was that British consumers, once warned that particular goods were German-made, would shy away from buying them: they were regarded as cheap, inferior imitations of English products. This impression was shared by many Germans, especially after the debacle of the 1876 Philadelphia world exhibition.[25] By the late 1890s, however, the picture had changed dramatically. "Made in Germany" was no longer a pejorative term. It was now identified with goods of a high technical and aesthetic standard. English manufacturers even began to forge the label, printing it on their English-made products.[26] At this point, the conjunction between economic modernization and cultural modernism becomes very apparent. In 1896, the English journalist E. E. Williams published a book entitled *"Made in Germany,"* which analyzed the decline of British manufacturing and technology, and described the German takeover of the world through the proliferation of objects "Made in Germany," penetrating even into the privacy of ordinary English homes. The protagonist of his account is horrified to discover the creeping "Germanization" of his world. Despairing of the extent to which German consumer goods have come to dominate even the intimacy of his personal sphere, he falls asleep and in a nightmare, discovers that even the gates of Heaven are now guarded by a German St. Peter, and can be unlocked only with keys "Made in Germany."[27] Williams's observations were indicative of widely held perceptions at the time.[28] During the 1890s, substantial parts of

German production successfully shifted to "quality work," thus overcoming the Philadelphia syndrome. This was not just a question of export statistics. The German-made goods became vehicles for a spiritual conquest of the world. Most contemporaries agreed with Muthesius that being "on top of the world" was a question of "shaping its appearance."

Such were the power-political realities behind the rediscovery of the vernacular as an asset that could be marketed globally. On the surface at least, the motivation was economic.[29] Organizationally, the supposedly conservative Prussian government played a decisive role, linking the project to political imperialism.[30] Yet these practical concerns coincided and benefited from a much more far-reaching and broadly conceived reevaluation of the role of "place" in modernity. This is very apparent in the history of the Deutscher Werkbund.[31] While German industrialists and politicians alike looked to this organization to achieve their immediate goals, in doing so, they tapped into and—perhaps inadvertently—aided a reform program that aimed at a much more fundamental reform of "culture." This becomes apparent if we examine the core membership of the Werkbund. Ostensibly, the Werkbund, founded in 1907, was supposed to unite industrial designers and producers, who would collaborate in producing quality work of a distinct and internationally recognizable "German" character. Various manufacturing organizations joined immediately, such as the Deutschen Werkstätten für Handwerkskunst (with around 600 employees) and the Thonet Stuhlfabriken (with 6,000 employees at seven sites). In the period up to 1914, large industrial enterprises also became Werkbund members, including AEG, Siemens, Bosch, BASF, and Mercedes Benz. Yet amongst the creative minds in the Werkbund, the vast majority were not, or at least not primarily, industrial designers. Rather, they tended to be men like Hermann Muthesius, Bruno Paul (1874–1968), and Peter Behrens (1868–1940). Often trained as artists (with the exception of Muthesius), they were practicing architects first, theorists of vernacular modernism second, political reformers third—and object designers only on the side.[32] It is true that the Werkbund amassed a sizable collection of model objects that were to inspire and guide industrial designers.[33] Yet it is unsurprising, given the protagonists in the process, that the Werkbund's efforts to inject industrial culture with a "sense of place" quickly transcended questions of design, image, and marketing. In fact, much Werkbund activism was based on the premise that "mere design," in the sense of the "style" that decorated an object or a building, was to be rejected. The cultivation of a sense of place in manufacturing was to be grounded in a far-reaching project of cultural reform, in which the vernacular was to serve as a launchpad for the transformation of every

aspect of daily life. In this, the Werkbund's activities differed dramatically from the proliferation of nationalist "icons" that had characterized the later nineteenth century.[34] The latter had taken the form of national monuments, such as the statue of Arminius in the Teutoburg Forest, and grand public buildings, such as the Paris Opera House or the Vienna Ringstrasse.[35] Such projects had drawn on an allegorical vocabulary that, for all its ostentatious nationalism, had little room for "place." The official architecture of nation-alism was dominated by a stylistic eclecticism known as historicism or beaux-arts (named after the part of the French Academy where it was taught). It drew on a range of preestablished stylistic idioms that were eith-er universal to all European cultures or freely mixed different national tra-ditions. The Flemish Renaissance, Italian Renaissance, German Renais-sance, and French Renaissance (or so-called château style), for example, enjoyed equal popularity in later nineteenth-century European architecture. The agenda of the Werkbund rejected this legacy, which it associated with stylistic and ideological falsity. Instead, it looked to the English Arts and Crafts movement as a model for vernacular modernism. In England and abroad, John Ruskin (1819–1900) was heralded as the forefather of the new place-based culture required in an age of globalization. "He [Ruskin] suc-ceeded in opening the hearts of the English people to art," Muthesius wrote. "That is, to art in that special, Germanic sense: for the craftsman-ship, the character, the rootedness in the soil [*bodenwüchsig*], the authentic-ity in art, the art of daily life and the human environment in its entirety. His principles were the quest for honesty and depth in art, the turn against false splendor and mere elegance, his conviction that art had to be a necessary part of the life of the human soul."[36] Although the designs of Ruskin and William Morris (1834–1896) drew on neogothic motifs, the underlying ide-ology was anti-historicist.[37] They saw vernacular idioms as the only legiti-mate source of culture. From traditions of indigenous craftsmanship and a visual language that had emerged in response to the practical requirements of the English people, functional yet "homey" forms were derived.[38] Ulti-mately, the aim was a moral rejuvenation of British society.[39] Ruskin, Mor-ris, and their followers thought that the problem of "alienation" was first and foremost a cultural one. Not the ownership of the means of production but the process of production had to be changed. The task was to abolish "labor"—a state of alienation that prevailed in industrialized societies—and return to quality work, offering a sense of identity and pride to the human producer.[40] It soon became apparent, however, that returning to preindus-trial methods of manufacturing created practical dilemmas. The techniques

employed in Morris's workshops were ill suited to an industrial age; moreover, the products were so costly that they missed Morris's main target group, the alienated masses.[41]

As early as the 1860s, German practitioners sought to reconcile the ideological aims of Arts and Crafts with the modern techniques of production that Ruskin had rejected. Rather than abolishing factory-production, machines were to be used in a more worker-friendly way: they were to perform those tasks that were purely mechanical and thus help restore creativity and craftsmanship to the work of the human producer. In Hermann Schwabe's words, "turn machines into the forth estate and get as many workers as possible back to the third estate."[42] The Werkbund took up this agenda. And as Adolf Vetter pointed out in a keynote speech on the annual Werkbund conference of 1910, the organization's aim to promote German *Wertarbeit* represented a direct translation of Ruskin's categories.[43] In England, too, "medieval modernism" produced a progressive faction advocating a pro-industrial stance. Yet its impact remained more limited than in Germany. As Noel Rooke observed: "We changed not only the face but the direction of German industry. [Yet] in all those pre-war years, those of us who were interested could make very much less impression on British industry."[44]

The reasons for this difference were manifold but had little to do with a uniquely German idealism about "joy of work," as is frequently claimed.[45] Instead, the tendency to invest work with immense meaning, which defined the quality of any social and cultural system, was part of an international movement, with reformers throughout Europe and America looking to the vernacular in their quest to recover place for modernity. The reasons for the Werkbund's relatively greater success were quite concrete. First, there was the geographical isolation of the major London-based design schools from the provinces, where British industrial production was concentrated. There was no single British organization like the Werkbund to unite the designers and those who might use the designs on an industrial scale. Another reason was political. In Germany, state administrations, even the allegedly conservative and Junker-dominated Prussian state, played a major and direct role in promoting modern industrial design. In Britain, by contrast, the Board of Education provided little more than symbolic encouragement of reform in this sector.[46] This difference in attitude persisted at least till World War II. In Germany, the quest to achieve a global industrial economy was seen as a project in the pursuit of which the state and a number of voluntary agencies such as the Werkbund systematically collaborated. In Britain, by contrast, few perceived the need for such a concerted effort—after all, Britannia al-

ready ruled the waves. Where reform initiatives emerged, these usually remained isolated, tackling individual symptoms of the modernization. Some aimed at overcoming workers' alienation, others strove to improve public taste, foster national pride, or, as the inventors of the British Merchandise Act, to tackle German commercial competition. These individual initiatives were not conceived or synthesized into a single strategy. It would be wrong to assume, however, that this meant that Ruskin's and Morris's ideas were by definition unsuited to being applied to industry and the global market. The German case proves the opposite. The political and economic framework was simply better suited to this synthesis.

On a conceptual level, the notion of the "vernacular" bound together the two decisive components of this reform project: the tradition of craftsmanship and a sense of geographical "rootedness" that countered the threatening alienation between people and the material culture of modernity. While often ardent nationalists, most members of the Werkbund did not feel that the nation could bring about the recovery of this sense of place. Even while Muthesius outlined the creation of national "types" as the ultimate aim of the organization,[47] in actual fact, national idioms proved of little consequence in the development of the new language of forms. The space of the nation, after all, was itself an abstraction. Instead, the concrete imagery of *Heimat* was invoked as the key with which to unlock the door to recovering a sense of place in modernity. *Heimat* denoted a set of material conventions that were specific to a locality or region; they found their purest expression in the privacy of the domestic house. Again, there was nothing peculiarly German about this move. In fact, it was not even the German home that first kicked off the debate. In 1904, Muthesius published a multivolume work entitled *Das Englische Haus* (The English House), in which he argued that domestic vernacular architecture embodied the spirit of English national identity.[48] "The simple house that is developed from rural motifs and constructed according to logical objective [*fachlich*] principles" was to replace the "polished villa that is overloaded with all manners of historical ornamentation."[49] Other preferred adjectives were "simple," "rational," "comfortable," "practical," "homey," and, of course, *heimatlich*. These were the values to which the Werkbund was to aspire. And they were to be realized first and foremost through the built environment—and only by extension in object design. Yet this was an architecture that, although designed by the Werkbund's most prominent figures, features rarely in the historiography of modernism. Today, we rarely question the assumption that modernism in architecture was defined by the very rejection of domes-

ticity.[50] Yet this is no more viable than the claim that all modernism defies "place." The Werkbund, for its part, pursued a modernism that was vernacular in the original sense of the word: its spirit emanated from things pertaining to the home.[51] Hence, it cannot surprise that Muthesius's own architectural production, while including some industrial buildings, was overwhelmingly concerned with private houses. It is only through a close analysis of this material evidence that we can properly understand his use of buzzwords like "function," which are so easily misunderstood.[52]

Muthesius' domestic building projects had an emphatically rustic feel to them: key motifs, such as the use of timber framing, the high pitched roof, and unadorned, brick walls were reminiscent of German farmhouse architecture. Other features were clearly borrowed from English vernacular revival buildings. These included the extensive use of bay windows and the fact that some of the timber framing featured neo-Celtic ornamental painting. In particular, the unusual, inward-curving front of Muthesius's Haus Freundenberg (fig. 4.2), recalled Edward Prior's The Barn in Exmouth, Devonshire, designed 1896 (fig. 4.3).

FIG. 4.2. Hermann Muthesius, Haus Freundenberg, An der Rehwiese, Berlin-Dahlem (completed 1920). Photograph by Maiken Umbach.

FIG. 4.3. Edward Prior's The Barn in Exmouth, Devonshire, designed 1896.
Reproduced by kind permission of English Heritage.

As the vernacular motifs are relatively easy to spot, given their "narrative" character, it is easy to read these buildings as a straightforward vernacular revival. Yet on closer inspection, it becomes clear that both houses also translate the traditional vernacular prototype into a modern context. Comparatively speaking, Prior's building, which served Muthesius as a model, is relatively more archaic. Yet even here, what appears authentic at first glance turns out to have the character of a deliberate quotation. Prior's building, constructed in 1896, hides a modern concrete structure: when the thatched roof caught fire in 1905, the house itself did not burn down, and the roof was subsequently replaced by a slate roof. Here Prior used a device often employed by Arts and Crafts architects. Another example would be William Richard Lethaby's All Saints Church in Brockhampton, Herfordshire, built in 1901–2. It, too, had a thatched roof—but the traditionalism of the construction was an illusion, the thatch was immediately attached to concrete.

In Muthesius's *Das Englische Haus,* both these buildings are depicted as exemplary pieces of reform architecture. We have already seen that they also inspired his own architectural work. It is not surprising, therefore, that Muthesius's use of the vernacular had a similar, quotation-like quality, per-

haps most apparent in the timber-framing in the gable of Haus Freudenberg: a memory trope, but not a structural feature. What is interesting,
however, is not the use of such "fakes" per se, but, rather, the rational thinking behind them. Vernacular architects all shared a suspicion of façades: an
imposing, symmetrical, and highly ornamental façade, was, after all, the
hallmark of the historicist villa. But while some *Heimat*-architects simply
went for an "Olde Worlde" crooked appearance, the inward curve of The
Barn and Haus Freundenberg had a particular function. As the spectator
approaches these houses, he or she is visually drawn into a semi-enclosed
space. The boundaries between exterior and interior dissolve—an impression reinforced by the symmetrical garden surrounding Muthesius's house,
which is divided by low-cut hedges, white fences, and pergolas into little
subunits resembling rooms. In this way, vernacular modernists sought to
achieve a closer integration of the building with its environment, without,
however, embracing nature as anti-civilization: it, itself, was civilized, urbanized by the process, transformed into a highly rational, habitable garden.

The same sort of rational thinking is apparent when it comes to the ir-
regular positioning and sizing of the windows. In Haus Freudenberg, the
windows are apparently just another "quaint" feature, disturbing the symmetry of the façade, to give it a seemingly more organic quality. In fact,
however, as Muthesius explained, the size and position of the windows in
houses like Freudenberg were dictated by the interior space behind them. A
sitting room would require a large and relatively low window to let in
plenty of natural light and permit a pleasant view of the gardens. Views
were not a consideration for the adjacent kitchen, which did, however, need
good natural light for work, while a bathroom window was to shield the
user from the outside gaze and bedroom windows needed to be positioned
so as to catch direct sunlight only at carefully selected times of the day. This
architecture, then, was eminently functional. Its functionality encompassed
technical features, but also, importantly, the pragmatic and emotional requirements of its inhabitants. Sensitivity to function united the vernacular
and the modern—and set both in opposition to traditional representational
and aristocratic architecture.

Functionalism thus understood implied a sensitivity to difference: difference of climate, difference of lifestyle, and difference of cultural context.
English models could not simply be imported to Germany. As Muthesius
said: "I did not want to recommend imitating the English house or its details but to explain to the German reader the ideology [*Gesinnung*] that lies

at its heart."⁵³ Muthesius's own houses, designed to set the new trend for modern German *Heimat* architecture, were not only emphatically German. They also engaged with issues specific to Berlin, where he lived and worked. In other words, the quest for national types not only started with vernacular motifs: it also resulted in forms that took regional specificity into account when defining what was functional. The beginning of the twentieth century saw Berlin at the heyday of industrialization and population growth. Vast new suburbs were created, facilitated by the construction of a local train line. These not only housed the workers. Some, like Dahlem, Zehlendorf, Wannsee, and Nikolassee were prestigious locations where the new industrial and banking elites settled. They were Muthesius's primary clientele. He saw it as his main task to provide homes that would serve the cultural and political assertion of the new industrial elites vis-à-vis the Prussian landed aristocracy, the Junkers, who had dominated the region's life up to this point. To overcome the Prussian obsession with representing social status, Muthesius wanted to promote an authentically "bourgeois architecture." Politically, he worked in close collaboration with Friedrich Naumann, a leading left liberal thinker of the time, and MP for the Progressive People's Party. Naumann's influential 1909 essay "Der Industriestaat" (The Industrial State) argued that while the German economy had become industrial, politically and culturally, the country was still ruled by largely aristocratic agrarian elites and shaped by their reactionary value system.⁵⁴ The task for the future was to create an "industrial state," that is, a political order that would truly reflect the interests and values of those who defined Germany economically and socially.

What Naumann called the industrial state, Muthesius called a *bürgerlich* society. "An alarming mania prevails for glossing over real conditions, to overrefine until something is considered 'distinguished,' to force one's self into a pseudo-aristocracy," he declared. "We seem to be ashamed of the very thing that should make us proud, our *Bürgertum*. We want to be aristocrats at the very moment when the *Bürgertum* has become the basis of our economic, social and political life, when it has reached such a height that it is able to determine the culture of our time."⁵⁵ This was written in 1904. By 1911, Muthesius already saw the situation in less pessimistic terms, declaring: "Many people, especially the rich and the aristocracy, reject our movement, because they dislike its purifying character and because the *bürgerlich* confession [*Bekenntnis*] of our new understanding of art appears frightening to them."⁵⁶

The use of the term "confession" to describe a movement for the im-

provement of architecture and design is indicative: what was at stake was a quasi-religious quest for spiritual renewal. Remnants of aristocratic culture were to be eradicated from this architecture, which would emerge purified and cleansed. This rhetoric was reminiscent of "New Liberalism" in contemporary England, whence so much visual inspiration was derived.[57] In keeping with the social dynamics of this movement, traditional signifiers of hierarchy were eliminated within the house. In Muthesius's houses, functional spheres, whilst separated, were all accorded equal importance. The same rules about space, air circulation and light applied to the sitting room, the kitchen, and the servants' rooms. Radically, the servants' quarters were to be located on the same floor as and have the same height as the rooms of the house's owners. The second task was to facilitate new patterns of sociability. The aim was a reform of urban life, not a retreat into a rustic premodern idyll. This was all the more important because the enemies of the modernizers launched their attacks from a "countryside" platform: the Prussian landed aristocracy were Naumann's main opponents. There was little question, then, that the site of "vernacular modernism" was to be the city, moreover, the big, industrial city. But life in this city required reform. For this purpose, various strategies emerged.

To Muthesius and his associates, the modern city that they strove to create was one that would be purged of false ostentation and representation as embodied by traditional cultural institutions such as the opera. A reformed sense of urban identity was to arise out of bourgeois values of domesticity as the prime sphere for social intercourse. Music played a crucial role in this. Where opera represented a false, alienated way of enjoying music, the private "music chamber" became the spiritual centerpiece of many of Muthesius's houses. Here, in quiet contemplation and serious conversation, the new middle classes would enjoy the true spirit of culture in musical soirées and poetry readings. One is reminded of Daniel Nikolaus Chodowiecky's (1726–1801) famous polemical cartoons, in which he opposed false, ostentatious, and outward-directed social mannerisms with the authentic, inward-gazing, and contemplative poses of enlightened sentimentality. This notion became so crucial to Muthesius's thinking that in many of his designs, the music chamber replaced the grander hall in the English houses that had inspired him.[58]

This did not mean that German vernacular houses were generally smaller or more modest than their English counterparts. Indeed, when we compare Muthesius's work with that of the British Arts and Crafts architect-designers Sir Edwin Lutyens (1869–1944) or M. H. Baillie Scott (1865–1945), we

notice that German neovernacular houses had a more public character. While Muthesius's houses employed plenty of *Heimat* motifs, these were used in a "narrative," not a literal, manner. While rejecting ostentation, these houses could (and should) be "read." Like the essentially affirmative view of (reformed) urbanism that underpinned much of the vernacular movement in Germany, the desire to depict a catalogue of bourgeois virtues distinguished these houses from purely rural, conservative *Heimat* architecture. Though suffused with a sense of locality and nature (many of Muthesius's houses engaged with the open landscape on the garden side),[59] they could also be viewed with great ease from the street, many even from several sides. Hedges were kept very low indeed—no more than a foot or two—and Muthesius's characteristic white fences, which he used as geometrical ornaments in the style of the Scottish architect and designer Charles Rennie Mackintosh (1868–1928), offered little more than a symbolic suggestion of private space. These houses "spoke," they projected private values onto the public sphere. For all their dislike of representation, they were proud flagships of the ideology of a new age. By contrast, Baillie Scott's houses were typically crouched behind large trees, totally hidden from public view, with their grounds protected by that archetypal English signpost "No trespassing." Muthesius himself described the experience of "not seeing the English house" during his travels in Britain. It is easily replicated today, further enhanced by the presence of high-tech burglar alarms and guard dogs that threaten the life of the researcher.

This was not just a difference of taste. In the English Arts and Crafts movement, "privacy" signaled a retreat from society and public culture, not a resource to be mobilized for the regeneration of an "alienated" public culture.[60] In a sense, the difference in physical accessibility is but a mirror image of the process on which Muthesius embarked by writing his book *Das Englische Haus*. In explaining its ideological agenda, in trying to capture its visual language in analytical categories, Muthesius achieved a curious paradox. His work was hailed in the English press as the first attempt by a foreigner to come to a real appreciation of the English spirit—and simultaneously regarded with bewilderment for having turned an "implied" practice into an issue of philosophical investigation. Under the heading "A German View of Modern English Architecture," the *Architect and Contract Reporter* reviewed Muthesius's first publication on the topic, and described the peculiarity of his approach in the following terms: "The text reveals in almost every line the pains which the author must have taken to arrive at the truth, and we have only to compare it with essays in which French architects have

endeavored to describe our modern architecture in order to perceive the difference not only between individuals but between two races. The German, being more of a philosopher, endeavors to get at the root of things and to explain why they assume one form rather than many others."[61] As the vernacular object moved between cultures, not only its visual features, but also its ideological significance changed. *Heimat* became "peripatetic" and, as a consequence, more conceptual.

A second major vehicle for creating an urban environment that reconciled the vernacular and the modern was the idea of the garden city. Again, this was an idea that was first developed in England and that spread to the Continent in the first decades of the twentieth century, reaching particular prominence in Germany.[62] Muthesius played a vital role in transmitting the concept from Britain: *Das Englische Haus* contains detailed descriptions of several examples. Yet he later became extremely suspicious of the whole concept—and with good reason. Early twentieth-century garden cities developed from a nineteenth-century English prototype. Paternalistic employers had built model villages to house mainly the workers employed in their own factories, often on green-field sites. The most famous examples were Titus Salt's Saltaire of 1853, Cadbury's Bournville of 1878, and the Lever Brothers' Port Sunlight of 1887. The latter two had been built in an Arts and Crafts–inspired neovernacular, and both cities were discussed and, to varying degrees, praised in Muthesius's works. Developing this model one step further, in 1903, Ebenezer Howard and the "Garden City Pioneer Company" created the first "modern" garden city in Letchworth.[63] Their achievement marked the transition from philanthropic project to modern town planning, and they were partly inspired by the urban planner F. L. Olmsted, creator of New York's Central Park, whose work Howard had seen in the United States. Letchworth had not one factory but several. It was to function as a self-sustaining settlement, complete with living quarters, its own manufacturing sector, and collectively owned agricultural land. At the same time, its location close to London was deliberate; Howard soon built a second garden city in the proximity, Welwyn, and envisaged a ring of garden cities growing up around the overcrowded and "unhealthy" capital. This was, in a sense, the birth of the modern suburb; indeed, Norman Shaw's development at Bedford Park, already started in 1875, and later Hampstead Garden, made no claims to being self-sustaining, but served very much as suburbs in the modern sense.

All these garden cities had one common denominator. They were to provide a more varied, "greener" living environment for industrial workers that

was not only physically "healthier" because of better air quality and less overcrowding, but also allowed for the development of a "sense of place" to counteract the anonymity of the modern metropolis. Unsurprisingly, then, vernacular modernists in Germany emulated the concept. From 1907, a number of leading reform architects, including Muthesius and Richard Riemerschmid (1868–1957), joined forces to create the first German garden city, Hellerau.[64] Though relatively close to the industrializing city of Dresden, Hellerau was to be largely self-sustaining. At its heart was a large manufacturing enterprise, the Deutsche Werkstätten, which produced reform furniture according to Arts and Crafts principles. The history of Hellerau can serve as an archetypal case illustrating the ideological problems inherent in vernacular modernism. Hellerau's Deutsche Werkstätten were part of the Werkbund, and hence, as we have seen, an emphatically modernizing project. Yet they failed to overcome the conservative impulse of the Arts and Crafts ideal in much the same way as Morris's workshops had. Riemerschmid's factory building at Hellerau of 1909 illustrates the problem (fig. 4.4). In his analysis of the building, Matthew Jefferies argues that it provides a perfect illustration of the "architectural characteristics most loudly championed by the *Heimatschützer*—honesty, simplicity, solidity—[which] were ethical qualities above all else."[65] Riemerschmid would have been delighted by this summary. Yet these buildings illustrate, in a sense, the precise opposite: an appropriation of the vernacular that was not functional, and in which, as a result, the conspicuous display of "honesty, simplicity, solidity" degenerated into a hollow propaganda device. Riemerschmid's dilettantism was self-referential. His "early modern" porter's lodge, crouched under a gigantic Dürer-style roof, the low archway, the fairy-tale-style window shutters, the disparate connection with the adjoining buildings, creating a mock-medieval curving effect of the front—all these suggested a rural idyll, an archetypal German village untouched by modern civilization, rather than a modern factory. What is more, the factory building itself was divided into three wings according to the baroque formula: a type of "historicism" that Muthesius would have avoided at all cost. Gropius was not entirely off the mark when he proclaimed that Hellerau's factory was a "dishonest piece of rustic romanticism."[66]

Judged in this light, Hellerau's economic failure was not entirely coincidental. As the modernists amongst its supporters, including Muthesius himself, became gradually more disillusioned with the whole project, it was taken over by more other-worldly "life-reform" groups, who were more concerned with expressionist dancing than with homes for industrial work-

FIG. 4.4. Richard Riemerschmid's factory building at Hellerau (1909). Reproduced by kind permission of the Fotoarchiv Marburg.

ers. Yet it would be wrong to dismiss all aspects of Hellerau's original conception outright. Alongside Riemerschmid, more progressive architects like Muthesius had taken part, and the innovative town plan they achieved—simultaneously historical and functional—had enduring attractions, which were imitated elsewhere in Germany. As part of this movement, a new his-

torical sensitivity entered the modernist movement. In 1908, Paul Mebes published his book *Um 1800: Architektur und Handwerk im letzten Jahrhundert ihrer traditionellen Entwicklung*, which became an instant success. Reform architects saw this as an acceptable form of historical reference.[67] This did little to diminish the reformers' rejection of historicism. We are dealing, instead, with two different forms of memory. Historicism invoked concrete and distinct precedents: its purpose was representational, and its models were derived from an architecture of power. By contrast, when modernists of the early twentieth century evoked the period "around 1800," they referred not to a specific moment in political history but rather to the *longue durée* of a culture they wished to celebrate and promote, which they called *bürgerlich*. The term *bürgerlich* was used not in the Marxist sense but in the way in which German literature had employed it since the Enlightenment: to denote a certain mind-set, the virtues of an unassuming lifestyle, economic self-reliance, and an emotional individualism shaped by the movement of sentimentality.[68] In the Biedermeier era, vernacular modernists believed, a synthesis between the high culture of the eighteenth century—classicism—and a vernacular simplicity characteristic of *Bürger* had been achieved. Culture had successfully emancipated itself from the dictates of courtly representation and assumed a modest, simple form appropriate for the average middle-class home. Goethe's garden house in the Ilm Park at Weimar became the prototype of this ideal. On the one hand, it was modest and unassuming; its very location in the park, signaling Goethe's withdrawal from the courtly life of Weimar to a more contemplative existence, was idiomatic.[69] On the other hand, it was not a primitive farmhouse, but bore witness to the increasing self-confidence and cultural achievements of the *Bürgertum*. To the reformers, the Biedermeier house became the house *an sich*, the archetype of a house.[70] Heinrich Tessenow (1876–1950), one of the participating architects at Hellerau, proclaimed the Biedermeier house his model. Hermann Bahr wrote in 1900:

> We shall no longer be fooled, we know that the façade has become meaningless. This has to be our first demand when we think about modern architecture: that a house has to be built from the inside out, and that the façade should be nothing but the pure expression of the living quarters inside. The house of the [Viennese] Ringstrasse is a sham, it is unnatural, it negates the purpose of building. The house of the Biedermeier era is genuine, it has a form appropriate to its content, it is the house *an sich* of *bürgerlich* requirements.[71]

After World War I, the situation changed. A new version of modernism emerged that rejected the pragmatic, historical, and individualist features of

vernacular modernism. In Germany, this new modernism came to be embodied in the Bauhaus, though it was far from confined to the exclusive school. The existing literature has dealt with this shift in two ways. One school has seen the increasing abstraction of the Bauhaus as a logical culmination of the half-hearted and incomplete modernizing impulse of the prewar years.[72] Others, such as Mark Jarzombek, see prewar vernacular modernism as hopelessly conservative: only Bauhaus-style modernism represented a democratic future.[73] The Bauhaus thus rendered all alternative visions obsolete as an object of serious study—the sheer mass of publications on the Bauhaus, compared to a few largely biographical studies on "other" modernists in the interwar years, testify to this tendency. Yet perhaps vernacular and "classic" modernism (or, to use Charles Jencks's problematic term, "Heroic Modernism")[74] are better regarded as two varieties of the same phenomenon, which continued to coexist and inspire one another. The original Bauhaus manifesto of 1919 certainly continued many crucial Werkbund ideas, and membership of the two institutions often overlapped. Both placed much emphasis on the notion of craftsmanship as a link between vernacular sentiment and industrial production. Even the manifesto's language, harking back, as it did, to the days of medieval cathedral builders and master craftsmen, was "medieval" in Ruskin's sense.[75] And much later, Gropius, one of the Bauhaus's founding fathers and most influential exponents, rejected the MOMA label "International Style" under which many Bauhaus architects reached prominence in the United States after 1933.

This said, it is undeniably true that in the later 1920s, an ideological confrontation between the two brands of modernism emerged that left an important—and almost wholly detrimental—mark on both. The projects of the later 1920s, such as the famous Weißenhof model housing project in Stuttgart, marked the shift toward a more radical idiom of modernism purged of any literal allusions to *Heimat*. The aesthetics of Gropius, Le Corbusier, and, most of all, the mature Mies van de Rohe, director of the Bauhaus from 1930 on,[76] were more concerned with Platonic questions about ideal-typical forms than with preserving a pluralism of local and regional idioms and traditions.[77]

Muthesius and other vernacular modernists in the Werkbund denounced the Weißenhofsiedlung (fig. 4.5). They regarded the philosophical abstraction of this kind of modernism as yet another "style," prioritizing form over function and thus structurally related to the old historicism.[78] They also objected to the increasing internationalization of this formal vocabulary. While the prewar Werkbund had embraced competition in the global mar-

FIG. 4.5. The Weißenhofsiedlung, Stuttgart, 1927. Reproduced by kind permission of the Landesmedienzentrum Stuttgart.

ketplace, it rejected the idea that regional and national distinctiveness should be shed as a result. In the interwar period, the Werkbund split into two factions. Members of the "Ring" such as Mies van der Rohe, Gropius, Bruno Taut, and Hugo Häring moved toward a more universal international aesthetics; in 1928, many of them also became members of CIAM, the Congrès internationaux d'architecture moderne. In response to these developments, more conservative *Werkbündler* formed a rival to the "Ring," the "Block."[79] Two of its leading figures, Paul Bonatz and Paul Schmitthenner, representatives of the "Swabian School," initiated a counterproject to the Weißenhof: the Am Kochenhof housing project, immediately adjacent to it, which rejected internationalism and employed regional and national idioms (fig. 4.6). Indeed, it was to resemble the archetypal German hometown, as discussed in Chapter 3 of this volume. The *Bauzeitung* described Am Kochenhof thus:

> In the Am Kochenhof housing project, a true children's paradise has been created in the spirit of the poetics of the village and the countryside: small gardens, small courtyards, small passageways, and small squares, in which children rejoice in harmless games, where the leisure of the old is to enjoy the happiness of the

young. Romanticism was long deemed outmoded. Yet it is the inevitable outcome as long as one allows all those small coincidences, which disrupt every regularity here and there, to be seen rather than covered up, as long as we embrace them as a welcome ingredient that enriches and enlivens the whole, and that deserves our very special care and attention.[80]

The chief architect of the Kochenhof was Paul Schmitthenner. The direct comparison with the Weißenhof makes his architecture look "conservative." But it was a far cry from the traditional *Heimat* style. Even though the Kochenhof was partly sponsored by an association for the promotion of wood as a building material—the Vereinigung Deutsches Holz für Hausbau und Wohnung—no timber framing was used at all, and all wooden beams were hidden behind smooth surfaces. Schmitthenner himself named his ideal: Goethe's garden house. Indeed, he went as far as to buy some genuine Biedermeier furniture for some of the Kochenhof houses, to make the connection quite clear.

Both the Weißenhof and the Kochenhof were to be funded by the same Society for Research into the Economics of Construction.[81] Yet before the Kochenhof could be completed, it fell victim to the financial pressures of the Great Depression. It was only realized five year later, but now under the direction of Alfred Rosenberg's Kampfbund für deutsche Kultur. Rosen-

FIG. 4.6. The Am Kochenhof Siedlung, Stuttgart, 1933. From *Moderne Bauformen* 32, 11 (November 1933).

berg was a leading Nazi ideologue and editor in chief of the *Völkischer Beobachter*, and the Kampfbund was an organization designed to rally anti-republican, educated German middle-class opinion behind the Nazi movement.[82] It would be unfair to conclude from the changing political patronage of the Kochenhof that its conception was wholly "fascist" in nature, much less that the entire movement of vernacular modernism fueled the rise of the Nazi state. As the analysis of Muthesius's work has shown, the vernacular modernism of the pre-Nazi period was driven by a concern for regional pluralism and *bürgerlich* individualism that was fundamentally alien to the Nazi regime. At the same time, the connections between the vernacular movement and Nazi racial policy were more than mere coincidence. The humanitarian impulse behind vernacular modernism did not prevent several of its key exponents from collaborating with the Nazis: their resentment vis-à-vis international modernism was clearly greater than their resentment of *volkish* ideology. Indeed, some of the vernacular modernists had become so doctrinaire about their rejection of anything that smacked of internationalism in the 1920s that their arguments developed a problematic racial dynamic all of their own. The competition between flat and pitched roofs turned into one such ideological battleground. In 1927, Paul Schultze-Naumburg denounced the flat roof as "oriental."[83] Even though the argument started on a pragmatic note, suggesting that flat roofs were only suitable for warmer and drier climates than those of northern Europe, the racial label suggested a problematic propagandistic turn. For the Kochenhof, Schultze-Naumburg actually prescribed a minimum roof slope of 35°.[84]

This new dogmatism was typical of the political polarization of the later 1920s. Around this time, in Berlin, a dispute developed that came to be known as the "roof war of Zehlendorf." From 1926, the Argentinische Alle, which runs through Zehlendorf, became the site for the construction of the radical modernist Onkel-Toms-Hütte housing project by Bruno Taut. The housing blocks were abstract, almost cubist; and the dominant Bauhaus white was supplemented by a color scheme carefully devised to emphasize connections and distances between the housing blocks.[85] While the project was still under construction, a rival development was initiated on its Southern edge, Am Fischtal. The director was Heinrich Tessenow, famous for his work in Hellerau. Another participating architect was Schmitthenner. Like the Kochenhof, Am Fischtal employed a compulsory angle for sloping roofs (45°), the antithesis of Taut's flat cubist shapes.[86] In these days, the issue became so politicized that ordinary residents of Berlin spontaneously joined

into the "roof war." House No 13, Schlickweg, built in a Muthesius-style vernacular, was decorated with an inscription that announced, in the local dialect, that "under a high-pitched roof, decent people dwell."[87]

It is important to remember that as part of the same process, "classical" modernism, too, developed that doctrinaire outlook during the later 1920s for which it was later rightly attacked. Internationalist modernism could be every bit as authoritarian and prescriptive as its vernacular counterpart. In 1925, Gropius published a volume entitled *Internationale Architektur*, in which several model Bauhaus houses were depicted. One of them was Haus Michaelsen in Hamburg, by Gropius's pupil Karl Schneider.[88] This was a thoroughly avant-garde construction, with an experimental composite structure. But it violated the new internationalist orthodoxy because it had a sloping roof—an altogether sensible feature, given its location on the bank of the windy, rainswept valley of the river Elbe. But, Gropius decreed, a sloping roof could under no circumstances be included in this volume. The photograph that was included therefore shows not the house, but only the little tower located in its outer northwest corner: the only part with a flat top. In 1930, Josef Frank pointed out that a general tendency had developed according to which architecture was no longer judged according to its merits but by certain iconic features only, the most important of these being the flat roof, which demarcated the dividing line between "conservative" and "modern."[89] Both sides were guilty of sacrificing their humanitarian pragmatism for the benefit of architectural orthodoxy. Indeed, not only vernacularists, but also modernists in the Bauhaus did at times collaborate with the Nazis.[90]

Politically speaking, then, modernism contained as many utopian dreams as ideological pitfalls. In their preoccupation with "place," and the implicit denial of mobility and multiculturalism that this implied, vernacular modernists were prone to collaborations with politically conservative, at times even racist forces. This does not, however, render their contribution to the evolution of modernism invalid. While borderlines between a nostalgic vernacular revivalism and vernacular modernism were sometimes hard to draw, they certainly did exist. And nobody was more keen to define these lines than vernacular modernists themselves. *Bauernromantik* became a purely pejorative label, with which nobody would identify. Even *Heimat* gradually went out of fashion. As Muthesius once wrote: "Associations for the preservation of folk costumes will not be able to prevent this development [international industrial competition], as indeed *Heimatschutz* movements will not be able to prevent the internationalization of forms and

shape."[91] Modernity had arrived, and it was here to stay. The vernacular was not an antidote: it was, rather, a vehicle of civilizing modernity itself, reconciling it with the practical need and search for "identity" of individuals and particular communities. Just as the geographical vernacular could help people imagine the abstract nation, the metaphorical vernacular of the Werkbund could help them imagine the abstraction that was modernity. This story was not unique to Germany. Throughout Europe, and even in the United States, the vernacular became a vital means for addressing the practical and psychological challenges of industrialization and globalization. The *Sonderweg* framework, which portrays all German history as the prehistory of Nazi state, obscures the universal significance of *Heimat* in the process of modernization. It is more helpful to think of the German story as an integral part of the emergence of a "vernacular international." Vernacular idioms traveled freely between different regions, and different nations. Though the "peripatetics" of the vernacular necessitated multiple cultural translations, wherever these idioms were employed, they shared one underlying purpose: far from undermining the abstractions of modernity and "nation," they rendered them commensurable.

CHAPTER FIVE

The Vernacular, Modernism, and Le Corbusier

FRANCESCO PASSANTI

In Chapter 4, focused on German architecture before and after World War I, Maiken Umbach proposes a congruence between the local, conceptualized as *Heimat*, or native place, and modern industrial globalization. On the one hand, Umbach shows that *Heimat* references played an important role before the war in shaping the commercial and aesthetic strategies of progressive industrial milieus: the central place in this part of her argument is held by the architect Hermann Muthesius and by the "vernacular modernism" of his houses, in which traditional typologies are adapted for new lifestyles. On the other hand, Umbach considers two parallel currents in architecture after the war, one continuing the prewar vernacularist vocabulary, the other (epitomized by the Bauhaus) proclaiming a new aesthetic devoid of traditional references: these currents, she argues, should be seen, not as reactionary versus progressive, but as varieties of the same effort to give shape to the modern industrial world. Figures 4.5 and 4.6, depicting the Weißenhof and Am Kochenhof, two late 1920s model housing projects in Stuttgart, fix the polemical tension between these two currents.

These two figures provide a good starting point for this chapter, in which I seek to show that the vernacular helped to shape an architecture of modernity, not only when it provided an explicit formal model (Muthesius's houses, Am Kochenhof), but also—as a conceptual model—when the architecture emphatically rejected any traditional formal references (the Weißenhof). The Weißenhof (1927) featured model dwellings by several prominent modernist architects from across Europe, and it was intended to show that there existed internationally, by then, a new kind of architecture using new industrial materials such as steel and concrete, and with a com-

mon architectural vocabulary, for example, flat roofs, that broke with traditional forms.[1] The Weißenhof marked the coming of age of modern architecture as an international movement. The following year saw the founding of the Congrès internationaux d'architecture moderne (CIAM). And by 1932, the Museum of Modern Art in New York held an exhibition of the new architecture, accompanied by a book titled *The International Style*, which is what the new architecture has been called in English ever since.[2]

The Franco-Swiss architect Le Corbusier, the name adopted by Charles-Édouard Jeanneret (1887–1965), played a central role in developing and promoting the new modern architecture; and, in acknowledgment of this role, he was asked to exhibit not one but two model houses at the Weißenhof. His book *Vers une architecture* (1923), translated under the title *Towards a New Architecture* (1927), can be considered the Bible of the new movement.[3] In it, Le Corbusier famously defines architecture as "the masterly, correct and magnificent play of masses under the light," argues that houses are "dwelling machines"; and he cites ships, airplanes, and automobiles as examples of fresh rethinking based on function. During the 1920s, Le Corbusier proposed urban designs dominated by skyscrapers and automobiles, and his houses often evoked transatlantic ships (figs. 5.1–5.3).

The architecture of Le Corbusier and of the other Weißenhof participants, with its proclaimed "machine aesthetic" and its claim to be an "international style," would seem to be the built embodiment of the process of modernization, sweeping away traditions, identities, and roots, all in the name of a triumphant globalization driven by technological development. This is how it was attacked by its enemies, and also how it was promoted by its advocates, eager to invest their movement with the quality of inevitability that modernization seemed to have. But this architecture was neither an automatic result of modernization nor stemmed from enthusiastic acceptance of it: it was a *critical response*—in many ways a reluctant response—to modernization, to the wholesale displacement of the old by the new; and, as such, it entailed a critical attitude to both poles of the transformation, old (including the vernacular) and new. One could also say that the critical response to the new was mediated by concepts borrowed from the old. Either way, then, categories such as vernacular, regional, folk, ethnic, and primitive could play a constituent role in the conceptualization of modern architecture. And, as we shall see, for the initiators of modern architecture, these categories overlapped fluidly: in fact, it was precisely this fluidity that allowed the migration of concepts from the old to the new.

This chapter investigates that migration of concepts in the case of Le

Parthénon, de 450 à 550 av. J.-C.

Le Parthénon est un produit de sélection appliquée à un standart établi. Depuis un siècle déjà, le temple grec était organisé dans tous ses éléments.

Lorsqu'un standart est établi, le jeu de la concurrence immédiate et violente s'exerce. C'est le match ; pour gagner, il faut

Cliché de *La Vie Automobile*.

Humbert, 1907.

Cliché Albert Morancé.

Parthénon, de 447 à 434 av. J.-C.

faire mieux que l'adversaire *dans toutes les parties*, dans la ligne d'ensemble et dans tous les détails. C'est alors l'étude poussée des parties. Progrès.

Le standart est une nécessité d'ordre apporté dans le travail humain.

Le standart s'établit sur des bases certaines, non pas arbi-

Delage, Grand-Sport 1921.

FIG. 5.1. Le Corbusier, pages from the chapter "Les Autos" in id., *Vers une architecture* (Paris, 1923), 106–7.

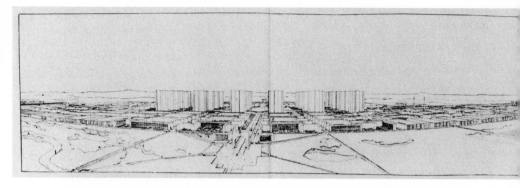

FIG. 5.2. Le Corbusier, Ville contemporaine (1922). From Le Corbusier, *Urbanisme* (Paris, 1925), 182–83, © Artists Rights Society (ARS), New York / ADAGP, Paris / FLC. Reproduced by kind permission.

Corbusier, who provides a particularly interesting case study for this volume because his intellectual formation before the war included broad exposure to the German debate about architecture discussed in Chapter 4.[4] The focus of my essay is intentionally narrow, to allow for sufficient detail; but its implication (that traditionalist concepts played a constitutive role in conceptualizing an emphatically modernist approach) is broader. I shall begin by evoking two paradigmatic moments in Le Corbusier's career: first, a trip through the Balkans in 1911, which was probably his central experience of the vernacular in his youth, and second, his design of that modernist icon the Villa Savoye at Poissy in 1928. After that, the focus shifts to the process by which Le Corbusier constructed a modernist concept of architecture, asking what role the vernacular played in it.

For brevity's sake, I use the term "vernacular" in a very broad sense, as shorthand for the fluid range of categories discussed above. And I use the terms "modern architecture" or "modernist architecture" interchangeably to designate the 1920s architecture of Le Corbusier and other Weißenhof participants and their like.

⌐

The Balkan trip that Le Corbusier undertook when he was twenty-three years old was part of a longer tour from Vienna to Istanbul, Athens, and Rome—a tour that Le Corbusier called his "voyage d'Orient."[5] In the first part of the tour, particularly devoted to vernacular things, Le Corbusier took a boat down the Danube from Vienna to Budapest and Belgrade, then

F I G . 5.3. Le Corbusier, Villa Savoye, Poissy, 1928–31. From Le Corbusier, *Oeuvre Complète*, vol. 2 (Zurich, 1934).

traveled by land through Serbia to Bucharest, and finally crossed the mountains to the ancient Bulgarian capital of Tirnovo, Edirne (formerly Adrianople), and Istanbul.

On the Danube boat in Hungary, Le Corbusier asked the captain to indicate "un village resté dans son état intégral," a village untouched by the Western industrial civilization that he himself came from.[6] In the town of Baja, he found some traditional pottery and commented about "the village potter, whose fingers blindly obey the orders of a centuries old tradition"; "it is the fingers of these potters that work, not their spirit, not their heart."[7]

Of gypsy musicians at a wedding in Serbia, he wrote: "Our beautiful Danube becomes a deity in the song and play of the Gypsies. . . . Standing, the chief, a popular bard, sings the song of his people. He invents some phrases, following the emotion that shakes him, but the elements of his song are ancient . . . the Gypsies let the race speak, the great nation of the dead, through songs from centuries back."[8]

Throughout the trip, he looked at typical local houses. In Hungary, he

noted their layout around a courtyard; in Tirnovo, he noted living rooms with windows wider than they were tall that reached from wall to wall. In Romania and Tirnovo, he was struck by the bright color scheme of the houses, repainted twice a year in brilliant white with accents of sharp blue. "When the blood is young and the spirit healthy, normal sensualism affirms its rights," he commented.[9]

It should be noted that, in these places, Le Corbusier sought not his own vernacular but those of other peoples. In today's parlance, he sought the *other*, a pure and natural man, in contrast to Western man corrupted by the turmoil of the nineteenth century. Le Corbusier's belief in some "original" purity was common for the period.[10] It also reflected the direct influence of Jean-Jacques Rousseau's ideas on his education.[11]

But if Le Corbusier had hoped to find some intact and organic vernacular culture, he was painfully aware of witnessing a disappearing one instead. In Turkey, after the Balkan tour, he noted that pottery had fallen out of use; people preferred ten-liter metal cans (recycled gasoline cans), which did not break; and he commented that "peoples don't stop moving just for the sake of poetic reveries."[12] In Italy, at the end of the trip, he lamented similarly that progress was so ugly, in West and East, and that "there is nothing left of *original* things."[13] But he concluded that the solution to the ravages of modernization should not be sought in the example of premodern cultures, because they are even more vulnerable than our own.[14]

On the basis of this brief sample of observations, we may ask what the significance of the Balkan vernacular was for Le Corbusier. Like all architects, Le Corbusier learned from precedent, and during his travels he noted architectural solutions for later use. Thus, the Tirnovo window can be seen as the source of his *fenêtre en longueur*, the ribbon window that would become one of the defining features of modernist architecture; and the Hungarian courtyards, which he called "summer rooms," can be seen as leading to the enclosed terrace of the Villa Savoye.[15] In learning from precedent, throughout his life, Le Corbusier was particularly interested in solutions of great elementarity and sought these in vernacular or ancient settings like the Balkans or Pompeii, or in examples of functional minimalism like railway sleeping cars, ship cabins, and airplanes.[16] An argument can be made that Le Corbusier owed this interest to Rousseau's ideas on the natural life: the more basic and paradigmatic, ancient or vernacular a solution is, the closer it is to being "natural" and "original."[17] In this sense, one could talk of the vernacular as a reservoir of "original" architectural solutions.

But in fact, during the Hungarian and Balkan part of the trip, Le Cor-

busier was not particularly intent on recording architecture. His notes about Balkan houses are downright skimpy, compared with the attention that he lavished on Pompeian houses later in the trip. The real emotion in his Balkan notes concerns people and their relationship to their artifacts. It was through this relationship, more than the borrowing of specific architectural solutions, that the Balkan experience affected Le Corbusier's modernism.

~

To approach the issue concretely, let us examine the Villa Savoye (fig. 5.3), and in particular its entrance hall (figs. 5.4–5.5). Arriving by car, one gets out under the main boxlike element of the building, which is supported by *pilotis*, or pillars, and finds oneself in the hall. I shall focus on three elements. The first is the industrial glazing, as in factories and greenhouses, that defines the space. The second is the ramp: an ordinary industrial ramp, like those found in factories. The third is the washbasin: an industrially produced object, of the sort found in any bathroom. These are all ordinary elements, "found" elements, not designed expressly for the Villa Savoye. But together, they add up to a ceremonial entry. One is inside, yet not really inside the house; the ramp, like some inclined street, reinforces the sense that one has not yet arrived and evokes ceremonial ramps in the courtyards of medieval or ancient compounds, ramps made to be ascended on horseback or in a litter; the washbasin, in this halfway situation, suggests the ablutions of a ritual entry, for example, in a mosque or a church.[18]

The placement of the columns is careful but not fussy: they are not designed to form a decorative motif, but seem to be there for some commonsense reason. As Le Corbusier wrote to a friend in the early 1920s, with obvious pride: "I have totally lost the taste for the 'motif' and I design like any old chap" (je compose comme un vieux bonhomme).[19] Let us leave aside, for a moment, the larger poetic evocations, and stick to the actual elements from which this place is put together, ordinary "found" elements of everyday life in 1928. They have been found in factories, bathrooms, ships, and so on. They are standard objects of use, intentionally derived from settings that have not been "designed" for aesthetic effect.

Le Corbusier's emphasis on such objects comes from a complex discourse about architecture and the decorative arts, centered on the concept of *Sachlichkeit* (factualness), developed at the turn of the century in German-speaking countries.[20] Two protagonists of this discourse important for Le Corbusier were Adolf Loos in Vienna and Hermann Muthesius in

F I G . 5 . 4 . Le Corbusier, Villa Savoye, entrance hall. From Le Corbusier, *Oeuvre Complète*, vol. 2 (Zurich, 1934), © Artists Rights Society (ARS), New York / ADAGP, Paris / FLC. Reproduced by kind permission.

Berlin. Loos was concerned with the urban bourgeoisie. He found it point-less for decorators and architects to try to invent a new style for this clien-tele: a style appropriate to modern urban life already existed in the shape of the everyday objects that architects had had nothing to do with: men's clothing, shoes, and so forth.[21] For Loos, these were to urban life what the unpretentious farm was to rural life: in short, modern vernacular.[22] Le Cor-busier, who absorbed Loos's ideas in two phases, in 1913 after the "voyage d'Orient" and then again in 1920, extended them to include industrial prod-ucts.[23]

Muthesius requires a longer discussion. While building upon Loos's foundation, he was more concerned with industrial mass society and its commodities.[24] Particularly relevant is his address to a meeting of the Deutsche Werkbund, an association of artists and industrialists, held in Cologne in 1914. At that meeting, which Le Corbusier attended, Muthesius provoked a heated debate by advocating *Typisierung* (literally, "typiza-tion")—a potent prescription because he used the ambiguities of that Ger-

FIG. 5.5. Le Corbusier, Villa Savoye, entrance hall. From Le Corbusier, *Oeuvre Complète*, vol. 2 (Zurich, 1934). © Artists Rights Society (ARS), New York / ADAGP, Paris / FLC. Reproduced by kind permission.

man word to conflate two charged discourses and social visions.[25] The most explicit and recent concerned the evolving structures of industrial society, specifically, the cultural implications of standardization (one of the meanings of *Typisierung*) and marketing by brands (*Typen*), whose uniformity was expected to promote and embody a new cultural unity. This discourse had been developed over the previous fifteen years by such figures as the sociologist Georg Simmel, the politician Friedrich Naumann, and the critic Karl Scheffler. It drew on conceptual structures and reformist concerns derived from the German academic discipline of political economy, out of which sociology emerged as a discipline in 1909, and whose professors sought a third way between laissez-faire capitalism and socialism.[26]

But in visualizing how a unified culture might look, and in the very choice of the root *Typ* to designate standards and brands, those new facts of modern life, Muthesius implicitly relied on an older and more traditionalist discourse as well—implicitly, because the older discourse had already been integrated into the new one ten years before, by two of Muthesius's

mentors, Naumann and Scheffler.[27] This earlier discourse concerned the stable structures of preindustrial society, with its standard vernacular types (*Typen*), for example, the German farmhouse. The best-known spokesman was the writer Paul Schultze-Naumburg, who in turn drew on the German discourse on *Volkskunst* of the late nineteenth century.[28] While conscious of changing conditions, Schultze-Naumburg and his friends insisted on the continued relevance of traditional types, which they held should be adapted, not reinvented anew. They saw these types as solutions perfected anonymously and collectively over many generations and representative of their society precisely because of the anonymity of the process that had embedded the collective identity into the form.[29] During the famous debate at Cologne, a Muthesius supporter also applied this reasoning to Greek temples, perfected anonymously over two centuries before Ictinus designed the Parthenon by slightly inflecting the type.[30]

By conflating the two discourses in the term *Typisierung*, Muthesius bestowed on the products of industry the same ability to embody organic culture that preindustrial vernacular types were deemed to have, thus enlisting in support of expanding industrialization concepts originally advanced by those who would rather contain it.[31] Muthesius dreamt of a modern vernacular—accelerated by intentional *Typisierung*, but a vernacular nevertheless, "found" in the anonymous developments of modern industrial society. Le Corbusier caught the range of Muthesius's argument well and condensed the whole—industry, temples, and all—into two iconic pages of his book *Vers une architecture* (fig. 5.1).[32] *Sachlichkeit* is often confused with *Zweckmässigkeit*, functionality. But the discourse on *Sachlichkeit* was not driven primarily by a concern with function: it was far more complex, and culturalist rather than rationalist. I would argue that a central preoccupation was *representativeness*, that is, a matter of character and identity: things describe the identity of a group when they are "facts" produced unselfconsciously by the group, when people do what they have to do, when they worry about use, rather than image.

⌒

Sachlichkeit had played no role in the early formation of Le Corbusier, and he absorbed this concept starting only in 1913, after the Balkan trip.[33] His education had been that of an artist and had stressed creativity, within a conceptual framework established by John Ruskin and local cultural politics.[34] These cultural politics are particularly relevant to our topic. Le Corbusier had grown up in the Swiss Jura, a French-speaking area close to the

Franco-German linguistic border within Switzerland, and at a time when the issue of Swiss cultural identity was heating up.[35] In the debate on this issue, two positions emerged, one based on geography, in the 1890s, and the other based on race, after 1900. It was the first of these that Le Corbusier absorbed at school from his teacher, the painter Charles l'Eplattenier (1874–1946).[36] The proponents of geographic identity argued that all Swiss, German-speaking and French-speaking alike, have a fundamental thing in common: they are shaped by the mountains.[37] L'Eplattenier's paintings depict mountains, and his didactic ambition was to create a regionalist style and art movement based on the natural characteristics of the Jura mountains. L'Eplattenier's influence is visible in the first house built by his pupil in 1907, the Villa Fallet in La Chaux-de-Fonds, a steep-roofed châlet emphatically covered with decoration based on the motif of rocks and pine trees.

The important point is that L'Eplattenier chose to *invent* a new style, even while drawing inspiration from natural elements. There was indeed a local tradition of splendid farmhouses, built in the same way for 300 years before industrialization, with wide, gently sloping roofs and plain white stucco walls; but L'Eplattenier did not try to reconnect with this tradition.[38] For the purposes of this chapter, the position of L'Eplattenier (inventing a style) and the position of *Sachlichkeit* (finding a style that has already emerged anonymously) represent a point of departure and a point of arrival for Le Corbusier, the first before 1907, the second after 1913. Between those points came two important experiences in Germany during 1910: his encounter in Munich with William Ritter, who inspired the Balkan leg of the "voyage d'Orient," and his exposure in Berlin to the classicism of Peter Behrens, an architect best known for designing the AEG factories and in whose office Le Corbusier spent several months.[39] I shall focus here on Ritter.

William Ritter, a French-speaking Swiss writer, art critic, and painter from Neuchâtel, who lived in Munich, would be a senior friend and mentor to Le Corbusier during the next six years, until well into World War I.[40] Two themes were central to Ritter's thinking. The first was his emphasis on roots: identity cannot be constructed or willed, it comes from the history and place into which one is born. Ritter disliked Americans, urbanized Germans, and Jews, all of them being uprooted in his eyes.[41] Accordingly, his art criticism always started from the givens of an artist's situation (ethnicity, cultural background, etc.), and then proceeded to analyze the manner in which the artist had worked with or against those givens. In the Swiss de-

bate about identity, he favored the position that race determines identity, specifically, that the French-speaking Swiss have a Latin identity.[42] The second theme in Ritter's thinking was his deep attachment to the Slavs, along with an interest in peasant life in the Balkans, where he had spent several years and collected many vernacular objects.[43]

Le Corbusier's Balkan trip was informed by Ritter's attitudes. In line with them, Le Corbusier experienced the trip as an immersion in cultures that had grown over centuries, and that were received and accepted rather than created and chosen, as the passages quoted earlier record: the fingers of the potter "obey the orders of a centuries-old tradition"; the gypsies "let the race speak" through their songs; and so on. Of course, Ritter was not the only source of Le Corbusier's interest in the vernacular; Rousseau has already been mentioned, and Ritter's attitude was echoed by other writers familiar to Le Corbusier.[44] But Ritter provided sustained exposure and broad philosophical grounding for the notion that any real culture is built on previous generations, hence *received*.

Seen in this light, Le Corbusier's experience of the vernacular in the Balkans had two opposite effects. On the one hand (in line with Ritter), it was his first experience of supposedly organic cultures whose forms are not chosen but received. On the other hand (think of the gasoline cans), the Balkan trip was Le Corbusier's first—and decisive—experience of the inevitability of Western industrial modernity, seen not as welcome progress but as a tragically unavoidable reality. Taken as a whole, these two experiences opened Le Corbusier to the notion of a modern vernacular: as integrated and "found" as the ancestral vernacular, yet issuing from the urban cosmopolitan reality of the industrial West, which was winning out in the world. In short, the Balkan experience prepared Le Corbusier to absorb, two years later, the particular way in which that notion was articulated by Loos, Muthesius, and other *sachlich* theorists. Regarding style, Le Corbusier had begun to find the notion of received cultural forms in Peter Behrens's classicism (classicism, by definition, is a received architectural language, to be learned and not invented).[45] Regarding the relationship of style and society, he got that notion of received cultural forms from Ritter, the inspiration behind the Balkan trip, with his insistence that identity is like a destiny.

～

By the 1920s, when he emerged in Paris as a leading modernist, Le Corbusier had arrived at a point of view quite different from the one he had

started from. He had begun within a movement seeking to invent a regionalist style, and he had ended by arguing, with Loos and Muthesius, that modern culture is best described by the work of those anonymous people, notably engineers, who don't try to invent a new aesthetic. This conclusion created a problem for somebody like Le Corbusier, who saw himself as a creative artist: what was his contribution going to be? The question had already preoccupied German artists and had fueled the Werkbund debate Le Corbusier witnessed in Cologne in 1914. In fact, even before Cologne, in a letter of late 1913, written within weeks of reading Loos, he had envisioned what it would be like to design starting from needs instead of aesthetic intent, and had concluded in a sad Ruskinian echo: "That's the huge lamp of sacrifice lighting up. And how hard it is to live each hour sacrificing!"[46] Eventually, he dealt with the problem in two ways, both of them articulated in *Vers une architecture*.

The first was to put the focus on geometric formal relationships, rather than on the particular shape of things. Thus, Le Corbusier defined architecture as the *play* of volumes under the light, emphasized the importance of proportions and regulating lines, and stated that the Parthenon soars above other similar Greek temples because of its refined geometric relationships and precise profiles.[47] He took this approach repeatedly in his designs of the 1920s, for example, when he imparted majestic proportions and rhythmic progression to his skyscrapers (fig. 5.2), and when he justified the proportions of his Villa Stein at Garches through regulating lines.[48] This broad emphasis on geometric relationships had a complex pedigree going back to a modernist emphasis on pure form around 1900, to academic artistic theories of the nineteenth century, and beyond them to classical aesthetics.[49] The second way in which Le Corbusier dealt with the problem has already been suggested in discussing the larger poetic evocations of the entry hall of the Villa Savoye. There, art is achieved by focusing not on relationships of form but on relationships of meaning: in a place that is inside, but not quite, a ramp and a washbasin create a ceremonial entry.

This focus on relationships of meaning had a literary pedigree. It came to Le Corbusier through the French poet Pierre Reverdy, heir to the symbolist poetry of Stéphane Mallarmé and, by the end of World War I, close to cubist painters and Le Corbusier. Reverdy argued in 1917–18 that poetry is constructed from elements found in everyday life and arises when distant realities are brought together.[50] Le Corbusier said the same thing a few years later, in the caption for a photograph of an airplane cockpit that he published in *Vers une architecture* (fig. 5.6). What you see in the photograph

CAPRONI-EXPLORATION.

La poésie n'est pas que dans le verbe. Plus forte est la poésie des faits. Des objets qui signifient quelque chose et qui sont disposés avec tact et talent créent un fait poétique.

FIG. 5.6. Le Corbusier, illustration from the chapter "Les Autos," in id., *Vers une architecture* (Paris, 1923), 113.

is the padded edge of a powerful machine; the dials by which you know its performance; the stick by which you dominate it; the map on which you choose where you want to go; the compass by which you know where you are going. In short, the poetic experience of flying an airplane. Below the picture, Le Corbusier's caption reads: "Poetry is not just in the word. Stronger is the poetry of facts. Objects that mean something, disposed with tact and talent, create a poetic fact."[51] Le Corbusier writes of "la poésie des faits": here he has quite consciously invented *poetic Sachlichkeit*.

To conclude, let us go back to the initial question of this essay: what role did the vernacular play in Le Corbusier's construction of a modernist archi-

tecture? Its principal role, I have suggested, was not as a source of architectural motifs but as a conceptual model for a natural relationship between society and its artifacts, hence between society and architecture; specifically, a conceptual model for the notion of *modern vernacular*—one as naturally issuing from modern industrial society, and as representative of it, as the traditional vernacular of common parlance had been of earlier societies.

Looking forward in time from the 1920s, this vernacular model within modernism suggests a conceptual continuity between Le Corbusier's "machine aesthetic" of that decade and his "brutalist aesthetic" of the following ones, with its reference to rural, primitive, and manual building—two aesthetics whose puzzling contrast has been a central theme of Corbusian literature. The vernacular model was a constant, articulating the persistent hope for a natural and organic modern society, and for a natural relationship of modern society and architecture. As Mary McLeod has shown, what changed was the sense of where to seek the fulfillment of such a hope. During the 1920s, Le Corbusier sought it in the rationalist and abstract organization of industry and in its products; later, disillusioned by them, he sought it in a more direct and holistic connection of people with people, and people and techniques.[52]

Looking backward from the 1920s to Le Corbusier's formation, we have seen that, although intense personal experiences like the Balkan trip played a crucial role in forming his notion of a modern vernacular, he did not come to it by himself but built it upon received discourses. Thus, Le Corbusier's experience of the Balkans was informed by certain ideas of traditional vernacular, of racial and national identity, that he had absorbed through his friend Ritter. And then, upon the personal and ultimately local experience of the trip, Le Corbusier grafted the sophisticated concepts of *Sachlichkeit*, developed over fifteen years in large European urban centers, concepts that themselves incorporated ideas about traditional vernacular and through which Le Corbusier could, in the 1920s, formulate specific architectural strategies meaningful to a larger urban public.

The notion of the vernacular in all of these discourses was focused on collective identity, not the variety and quaintness appreciated by picturesque aesthetics, and it embraced all kinds of artifacts, not just architecture. Around the turn of the century, it took on a central role in architectural thinking, together with classicism, which was about the related theme of order. At a time of rising mass politics, right and left, such evocations of collectivity held increasing appeal for reformers of all persuasions, who felt that the nineteenth century had left a legacy of social and artistic disaggregation.

As a conceptual model, this notion of the vernacular was important, because it could open architecture to a redefinition. Unlike classicism, which was a closed formal system internal to architecture, the vernacular model insisted on connecting architecture to something external to it, the identity of a society; and it further insisted that such a connection be not invented but found. Thus, the vernacular model helped to open architecture to such "facts" as ships and industrial products. On the one hand, this increased openness represented a difficult challenge for architecture, because it weakened its autonomy as a discipline and hence its continuity and accountability: with architecture no longer a closed system, it became more difficult to refine and codify routine design strategies (such as eighteenth-century apartment planning in France) that could provide standards for teaching and judgment. On the other hand, like all disciplines, architecture has always been open to ideas from other disciplines or cultures (think of the Italian influence on France during the sixteenth century), and this openness had been growing exponentially since the eighteenth century because of travel and changes in technology, economy, and society. In the face of this accelerated change, the vernacular model provided a way to master the process: as we have seen in the case of Le Corbusier, it provided a conceptual structure for integrating the new inputs into the discipline of architecture and for broadening its vocabulary and responsibilities.[53]

CHAPTER SIX

The Vernacular, Memory, and Architecture

STANFORD ANDERSON

The term "vernacular architecture" is often used to refer to buildings, or rather, extended physical environments that are distant in time or space—places unfamiliar to modern societies. Distance allows these environments to be invested with idealized social commitments. This unification of idealized space and society can then be employed in a critique of modern societies.[1] A perceived close relationship of place and society is intrinsic to the notion of "the vernacular," but it is not necessary that this relationship be romanticized. This chapter argues that the vernacular persists in modern societies. Furthermore, even the most noted of modern architects have been known to draw upon the vernacular in the best of their works. Attention to the vernacular need not be a matter of nostalgia or of regressive social constructions. The vernacular need not be the enemy of the modern. Let us begin with an example.

Figure 6.1 shows houses in the market street of the Dutch town of Woudrichem. Under modern industrial conditions, even in the hands of modernists, vernacular traditions of building may be sustained. Most visitors to the Netherlands are struck by the distinctiveness of the typical houses, and thus by the urban fabric of the old centers of Dutch towns. Characteristically, these houses are of brick, in rows, with the gable end to the street; they are relatively small, but they have large windows directly at street level, with little if any separation from the street. Collectively, these houses yield a cityscape of remarkable intimacy and openness. Houses of this type were built without architects for centuries, certainly prominently from the Renaissance until the twentieth century, establishing a widely dispersed Dutch housing vernacular.

FIG. 6.1. Houses in market street, Woudrichem, Holland. Photograph by Stanford Anderson.

FIG. 6.2. J. M. Granpré Molière, Vreewijk, Rotterdam (1914–33). Photograph by Stanford Anderson.

In the early twentieth century, as Dutch architects pioneered in social housing for the emerging modern metropolis, the received type influenced their work significantly.[2] This tradition continued, with increased architectural and urban sophistication in the work of M. J. Granpré Molière (1883–1972), as in his famous Vreewijk community in Rotterdam (fig. 6.2). Granpré Molière was the conservative professor at the most important Dutch school of architecture, the Technical University in Delft, from 1924 to 1953. In his pedagogy and through the example of his work, such as Vreewijk, he championed tradition and resisted the then emergent international modern architecture. Still, one must give him his due. Today, eight decades after it was built, Vreewijk remains a highly successful, livable environment. The casual evidence of what one sees on the window sills, in the window dressing, and in the backyards of the current residents may be conservative and middle-class, but it appears in comfortable relation to an environment that is more valued today than at its inception.

Even architects of a distinctly modernist inclination established housing types that relied significantly on this tradition, as in the unassertive street ar-

FIG. 6.3. J. J. P. Oud, Kiefhoek housing estate, Rotterdam (1925–29). Photograph by Stanford Anderson.

chitecture with balconies and generous ground-floor windows by J. W. van der Weele on the Laan van Meerdervoort in The Hague (1927). Still more remarkable, much of the housing built in the interwar years by Dutch architects of such impeccable modernist credentials as J. J. P. Oud retained distinctive characteristics owing to the strong Dutch vernacular tradition, represented by his housing in the Kiefhoek housing estate, Rotterdam, dating from 1925–29 (fig. 6.3).

In the famous Weißenhofsiedlung in Stuttgart in 1927, a showcase for advanced modern architecture built under the direction of Ludwig Mies van der Rohe, two leading Dutch architects were represented, Oud and Mart Stam. It is notable that, even when working within such an experimental program and in another country, these Dutch modernists built row houses, though now with significantly altered organizations of space and function. It is of note that only the Dutch architects built row houses at the Weißenhof. Even this sketchy series of examples of Dutch domestic architecture reveals a recognizable tie, but also a progressively loosening tie, to a

Dutch vernacular tradition of house building. There is a loosening, though not a complete dissolution, of what I argue is the close relation of social and disciplinary memory in vernacular architecture—a close relationship, though not one that need be constructed in romantically idealistic terms. In this progression we do reach a point where one no longer speaks of vernacular architecture, but one still recognizes something indigenous to the place, an underlying "vernacular usage." The question of why the Dutch modernists performed in this way will be better addressed after some general considerations and the introduction of other examples.

What is at issue in relating the vernacular, memory, and modernism? In an earlier essay, I sought to understand what may be a special and close relationship between vernacular architecture and memory, what might be called "embodied memory."[3] A still earlier essay that was concerned with monumental architecture distinguished between "memory *through* architecture" and "memory *in* architecture." Put differently, a distinction was drawn between a "societal memory carried in architecture" as opposed to "the operation of memory within the discipline of architecture itself."[4] The former, let us call it *social memory* in architecture, was illustrated by, among other works, the medieval European copies of the Holy Sepulchre in Jerusalem (e.g., Santo Stefano in Bologna). Since such "copies" were quite different from one another, and from the original, it follows that the religiously generated recall of this holy site did not entail strict architectural norms. Social memory dominated architectural form and precedent.

On the other hand, *disciplinary memory* was illustrated by projects such as those of the so-called "Revolutionary architects" of eighteenth-century France—specifically those of Étienne Boullée. In such projects, recollection of significant precedents is at the same time more faithful formally and yet radically innovative in scale, organization, and meaning. Architecture here approaches an autonomous state. The argument of the earlier paper, however, invited other questions such as the following: Was (or is?) there a condition under which social and disciplinary memory are not separated? If so, under what conditions would social (or collective) memory and disciplinary memory diverge? In brief, my answers were these: first, what is commonly referred to as vernacular architecture represents at least a close cohesion of social and disciplinary memory; secondly, it is the advent of writing and history that invites the increasing distinction between these memory systems.

In looking to understand vernacular architecture, a first hypothesis is the one just stated: in vernacular architecture, social and disciplinary memory

are closely related. Yet the diversity of vernacular architecture accords with varying degrees of that relation of social and disciplinary memory—from a virtual fusion to a looser but still identifiable relation. Thirdly, these shifting degrees of relation, and what eventually may become a weak relation, accord with the passage from preliterate to literate societies. Finally, this passage is also a passage from societies dependent on memory alone to those with historical constructions. That is, in various societies, differences in the operation of memory accord with distinctions among vernacular architectures and between vernacular architecture and architecture that is more self-consciously conceived.

Vernacular Architecture: The Cohesion of Social and Disciplinary Memory

Take just one example from innumerable instances around the world, the Banni villages in the deserts of Gujarat (fig. 6.4) still preserve a distinctive building form that can be closely correlated with the social life of the people who inhabit them. Among the various aspects of this social life is the art of building itself, serving the maintenance of these structures, but also the construction of new units or compounds. Despite the presence from time immemorial of this art of building, like other customs in the social life of the Banni, it is very much a matter of the present. Until recently, and then from outside the community, there was no record of this building technology or its use other than in the actual buildings and the craft knowledge of the builders, passed from generation to generation. One must conceive that there have been changes in both the social life and the building technology of the Banni; yet such processes are necessarily lost in time. Innovation may continue to occur, but this too is experienced as a response to current conditions and then lost in the continuing presence of the artifacts. The widely admired vernacular architecture of many parts of the world, as often illustrated from the Greek islands, for example, would, until overridden by the radical changes of the twentieth century, accede to similar analyses that show a close relation of social and building programs.

The Relation of Collective Memory to History: Preliterate to Literate Society

What can be made of this theoretically? Considering the operation of memory in a society and its extension in time, we must distinguish between

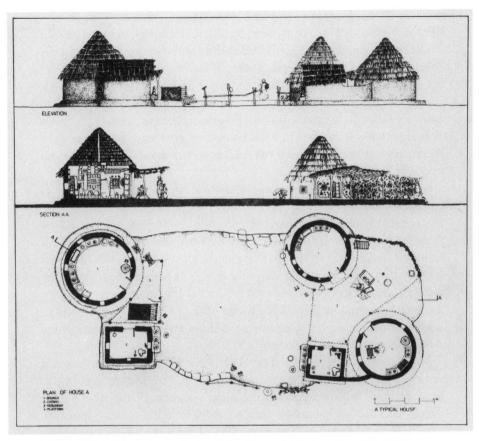

FIG. 6.4. Chief's house, Ludia village, Banni, Gujarat, India. Kulbushan Jain, *Mud Architecture of the Indian Desert* (Ahmedabad, 1992), fig. III. Plan, section, and elevation by Kulbushan Jain.

societies that possess only memory and those that confront memory with history. In an oral society, even if there is a dynamic leading to a collective understanding of the past, memory resides in individuals. The absence of records contributes to the modification of social memory and tradition from generation to generation. The past is not so much separate from, as subsumed in, the present. Studying preliterate societies, several authors note the insistent attention of these societies to the *present* moment and the distancing of the society from its past. In preliterate societies, cultural tradition is maintained in face-to-face communication and in the context of present issues. In such an oral society, *forgetting*, and even forgetting that

one forgets, is as important as memory. Jack Goody and Ian Watt observe that "the social function of memory—and of forgetting—can thus be seen as the final stage of what may be called the *homeostatic organization* of the cultural tradition in non-literate society."[5] Transformations of social practices or forms may or may not be noted at the time of the event, but are unlikely to remain in memory in the face of the perceived reinstatement of balance. Similarly, Jacques Le Goff observes that collective memory functions in oral societies according to what he calls a "generative reconstruction" that eliminates or transforms those parts of the tradition that are no longer operative.[6]

Under these conditions, social and disciplinary memories, only so recognized by an outsider, would both participate in this homeostatic process that constantly reestablishes the balance while also forgetting its difference from the past. The relation of these memories to one another may appear seamless. The making of the physical environment is at one with the social construction of the society; perhaps the builder is honored for demonstrable skills, but so too are others who are part of this attainment of balance through both maintenance and change. The generative reconstruction, aimed at maintaining a stable present, subsumes distinctions that only the external observer would perceive.

"Literate societies, on the other hand," write Goody and Watt, "cannot discard, absorb, or transmute the past in the same way. Instead, their members are faced with permanently recorded versions of the past and its beliefs; and because the past is thus set apart from the present, historical inquiry becomes possible. This in turn encourages skepticism; and skepticism, not only about the legendary past, but about received ideas about the universe as a whole. From here the next step is to see how to build up and to test alternative explanations; and out of this there arose the kind of logical, specialized, and cumulative intellectual tradition of sixth-century Ionia"[7]—and, of course, the intellectual traditions of our own day, both in the West and in other parts of the world. These are the preconditions for self-conscious forms of memory and for divergences of memory systems within a single culture. They are also the preconditions for memorialization; that is, assigning to built form the explicit role of maintaining memory.

Variations of Memory in Literate Societies

Consider now the variations and changes of memory in literate societies—still with attention to the production or reception of vernacular architecture. Goody and Watt are explicit that the nature of new historical societies varies with the form of language. Significant variations extend to our own day, perhaps in the relation of language and history, certainly in the societal apparatus constructed to facilitate or inhibit the writing of history and its concomitant critical role. Today, even among highly literate societies, there are still those that are relatively ahistorical. The distribution throughout the world of the concept of an archive—let alone of archives and museums themselves—is uneven. Preliterate societies, and also literate societies that have not given a prominent place to historical studies, differ greatly from the highly historicized societies of the West (and perhaps elsewhere) in respect to knowledge of the past and the relation of that knowledge to the present.[8]

One might remark that this differentiation is not only to be recognized by country or language area, but also by disciplines. Architecture has not been the most laggard of disciplines in the studied examination of its past. Yet the marketing of architectural drawings and the burgeoning of architectural archives and museums over the past two decades speaks to a significant change in the relation of history and artifacts, also in the West.[9] So-called vernacular architecture may be interestingly correlated with distinctions among societies as preliterate or literate within varying linguistic and memory systems—historic societies, that is, with varying levels or types of historic consciousness.

Sustained Vernacular Traditions Within Historical Societies

The Dutch examples cited above can be set into such a continuum of change within a vernacular tradition. Though perhaps not quite as strongly, much the same can be observed in English villages. In England, there is a stronger tradition of the free-standing house, a type that invites a turn in the argument, another route to modernism, conceived of by a figure already introduced in this volume—the German architect Hermann Muthesius.[10] Muthesius served from 1896 to 1903 as the "technical attaché" at the German embassy in London and was an assiduous student of the English architectural achievements of the late nineteenth century, especially in do-

F I G . 6.5. Richard Norman Shaw, housing, Bedford Park, U.K. (ca. 1875). Photo: Merrill Smith. Courtesy MIT Rotch Visual Collections.

mestic architecture, and the work of Ruskin and William Morris. He studied their churches, office buildings, apartment houses, and, especially, the English house. His three-volume work *Das Englische Haus*, published upon his return to Germany, is still the standard for scholarship on this important body of work.[11]

Muthesius was looking at the work of talented and developed architects, but he saw their achievement as intimately related to the English vernacular. Consider his enthusiastic and programmatic assessment of what was termed the Queen Anne style, so notably practiced by Richard Norman Shaw (fig. 6.5):

> [The new English domestic architecture] was nothing other than a rejection of architectural formalism in favor of a simple and natural, reasonable way of building. One brought nothing new to such a movement; everything had existed for centuries in the vernacular architecture of the small town and rural landscape . . . one found all that one desired and for which one thirsted: adaptation to needs and local conditions, unpretentiousness and honesty of feeling; the utmost coziness and comfort in the layout of rooms, color, an uncommonly attractive and painterly (but also reasonable) design, and an economy in building construction.

The new English domestic building art that developed on this basis has now produced valuable results. But it has also done more: it has spread the interest in and the understanding of domestic architecture to the entire people. It has created the only sure foundation for a new artistic culture: the artistic house. And as everyone connected with the Arts and Crafts movement in England certainly knows, it produced that for which everyone labored: the English house.[12] . . . [Germany can do what] once was done in England: return our vernacular building art to simplicity and naturalness, as is preserved in our old rural buildings; renounce every architectural trinket on and in our house; and introduce a sense of spatial warmth, color, natural layout, and sensible configuration. All this rather than continuing to be restrained by the chains of formalistic and academic architecture-mongering. The way in which the English achieved this goal, namely, by readapting vernacular and rural building motifs, promises us the richest harvest—precisely in Germany where the rural building manner of the past is clothed in a poetry and a wealth of sentiment that few old English buildings can match. If we restrict ourselves to the homegrown, and if each of us impartially follows his own individual artistic inclinations, then we shall soon have not only a reasonable but also a national, vernacular building art. Nationality in art need not be artificially bred. If one raises genuine people, we shall have a genuine art that for every individual with a sincere character can be nothing other than national. For every genuine person is a part of a genuine nationality.[13]

Muthesius's program has its roots in an aspiration for conventions shared by the entire society, and it is thus at base a social advocacy. Precisely for these reasons, he places the domestic interior and the house above all else in defining a new movement in architecture.[14] Muthesius sought to establish an indigenous German form of the new type of vernacular domestic architecture that was already well developed in England, but he wavered between the opportunities and difficulties of doing so. To the extent that this cultural work might depend on models in the vernacular of town and country, he considered Germany to have more and better models. Yet in Germany there was no culture of the house to compare with that of England. He lamented that Germans now characteristically lived in and moved among rental apartments. Consequently, they felt little or no concern for their surroundings, or that their dwellings be artistically designed. Nonetheless, Muthesius argued that "a change in our German artistic situation can only take its start in the German house, which essentially is yet to be created."[15]

Muthesius sought authenticity for architecture, both for its own integrity and as that which could win the common assent necessary for a general cultural advance. His book *Stilarchitektur und Baukunst* (1902), bears an epigram from William Morris: "Indeed, I have a hope that it will be from such necessary, unpretentious buildings that the new and genuine architec-

ture will spring, rather than from our experiments in conscious style more or less ambitious, or those for which the immortal Dickens has given us the never-to-be-forgotten adjective 'Architectooralooral.'" The proper models for a new and genuine architecture could only be "necessary, unpretentious buildings."[16] Such were the simple, *sachlich* burghers' houses of around 1800, "which could still be a model for our contemporary conditions."[17] Such also was the vernacular building art of town and country in a time and place where the nonmonumental was properly distinguished from the monumental.

In this advocacy, we may recognize, first, an appreciation for a received vernacular presumed to have the qualities of holding the environment and life itself in a harmonious relationship. If such a oneness was a thing of the past, or at least was slipping away, there was still the will to restore it. That restoration, it was argued, could only be effected by grasping closely what remained of the most recent presence of such a harmonious condition.

There is a romance in this program. We also know that it can lead to a cultural conservatism. With Muthesius and many others of this persuasion, this was a highly nationalist enterprise. For all the valued lessons of England, Germany would have to find its own way. The task was precisely to distinguish the German way of life from that of France. In the following decades and in other hands, such programs turned racist. However, I think none of these attributes—romanticism, conservatism, nationalism, or racism—cling necessarily to this enterprise. Consider again the Dutch examples introduced at the outset of this chapter. It is plausible to think that Granpré Molière was more successful in Muthesius's enterprise than Muthesius himself. Building for the higher levels of the industrializing German metropolis, Muthesius's work was notably marked by privilege and anglophilia. Granpré Molière's precedent was distinctly Dutch and, as housing, directly in the service of a collective. In accord with Dutch views during his lifetime, we can concede that his is a conservative path and marked by a national character. Yet, as already suggested, his work seems to deserve a more generous interpretation. Vreewijk is a notable exercise in city building, extended both in space and in time.

For all that the modernists saw themselves in contradistinction to Granpré Molière, much of their own housing work can be seen as a modernist extension of this same city-building tradition. The two Rotterdam examples introduced above and Oud's work at Kiefhoek maintain many of the traits of Dutch row houses—modest size, main dwelling area at street level and little removed from it, large windows that allow a view into, and often

through, the house. Oud and Stam's dwellings at the Weißenhofsiedlung are still row houses, seemingly because of this same city-building commitment. However, with an increasing commitment to international modernism, the interiors are innovative and more individualistic. Oud's Weißenhof row houses, for example, turn the relatively closed private areas of the house to the street and open the living spaces to a garden at the rear.

As in these examples, there is, then, a range of degrees of "vernacular usage" within highly literate and historical societies that extends from the relatively unselfconscious maintenance of housing and urban forms, through deliberate adaptations of the received vernacular types, to the adaptation of elements across time and space in explorations made possible by what I shall call the quasi-autonomy of architectural form. Even in highly literate and historical societies such as the Netherlands, there are traditions of dwelling type, of urban fabric, and even of architectural abstraction that represent interesting, often contributive, persistences of earlier sociocultural organization. Here I used the word "tradition." Within historic societies, I think it is tradition that continues to serve in the maintenance of a dynamic equilibrium in society. Increasingly, this will be "invented tradition,"[18] yet there are those conventions or traditions that form the substrate of any society—so pervasive that they are rarely brought to cognizance.

The historical concept of "mentalities" is particularly useful for understanding phenomena such as these. "The history of mentalities . . . is also a meeting point for opposing forces which are being brought into contact by the dynamics of contemporary historical research: the individual and the collective, the long-term and the everyday, the unconscious and the intentional, the structural and the conjectural, the marginal and the general," Jacques Le Goff observes.[19] This is an excellent catalogue of the concerns that must be represented in a study of traditional building practices (or what may be called "the vernacular") in historical societies.

A further step in the deployment of the vernacular in modern culture can be taken by emphasizing three points of this paper: first, vernacular architecture is often seen as an exemplar of a societal condition of wholeness; second, vernacular architecture can (should!) serve as a source for contemporary production that is judged particularly for its social contribution; and third, this enterprise is not only to be observed in architecture that is directly derivative from earlier examples. Reliance on what may, in fact, be learned from the vernacular appears, and appears most convincingly, in some of our most innovative architects. Consider Franceso Passanti's cogent essay in this volume on Le Corbusier. Charles-Édouard Jeanneret, the

young Le Corbusier, was trained in a regionalist Swiss art school. As a young man, in 1911, he made his now famous "voyage d'Orient."[20] Through the Balkans and Turkey, but also in his continued travels in the Mediterranean, Jeanneret paid close attention to the vernacular production of these regions. According to Passanti, Jeanneret sought the sites of a pure and natural man but also on this trip realized that these sites were even more vulnerable to change and loss than the environments of his own western European homeland. Solutions to the issues of modern change were not to be found directly in the vernacular, not even in the vernacular of places as yet less affected by modern change. Passanti observes that Jeanneret's notebooks from these travels record little of the architecture he encountered. Rather, he is impressed with the people and their relations to their artifacts. It was the attraction to such relations rather than the vernacular forms themselves that affected Le Corbusier's modernism. The account of the Banni given above and Le Corbusier's post–World War II fascination with vernacular architecture accord with this conviction about the closeness of people and their artifacts in these societal conditions.[21] In his own modern and Western setting, Le Corbusier sought the "found elements" of everyday life, not those conceived for aesthetic purposes. As in those times and places recognized to possess a vernacular tradition, this was a search for "forms not chosen but received."

We may recall, through Muthesius and others, the search for objects and environments perceived to be *sachlich*—factual, to the point, or pertinent—in their nature. Adolf Loos can be argued to have elevated this search both theoretically and in his architectural work.[22] He resisted formulaic modernisms precisely because he thought the modern vernacular surrounded him in modernizing cities such as his own Vienna. Muthesius, Loos, Oud, Le Corbusier, and others, each in his own way, held out the hope for a modern culture that would be as integral between life and form as the vernacular was conceived to be. With each step in this sequence of modern architects, we also take another step in the commitment of this integrated modern architecture, not to a direct assimilation of earlier forms, however admirable in their own right, but rather to a profound exploration of the conditions of its own modernity. In the work of Oud, there was still a tie to such *sachlich* matters as sound city building and, within the dwelling unit, a dominant attention to such generic issues as privacy, even as he radically altered that organization. With Le Corbusier, such issues might also be addressed, but the enterprise was lifted to a more abstract plane—one is as much confronted with the metaphoric account of our condition as with the altered condition itself.

If a significant relation of Le Corbusier to the vernacular can be established, and this in his most abstract works, it is no surprise that the same relation is found in the work of other notable modernists. "It is important to have established that [Alvar] Aalto's work was based on his own translation and development of vernacular inspiration, his 'natural variability of theme', rather than a direct copy of a vernacular model," Sarah Menin observes, for example.[23] Subtle readings of Le Corbusier have long since protected his work from the reductionism of his own famous dictum: "A house is a machine to live in." This subtlety also delivered him into the higher realms of abstraction and metaphor. One cannot deny Aalto his place in these realms, but one also distinguishes in his work the return to a more visceral relation of person and artifact, a more literal sense of relation to the vernacular. Aalto was not alone in this; Colin St. John Wilson built his critical career on this division within modern architecture. Aalto is particularly honored in Wilson's book *The Other Tradition of Modern Architecture*, but its subtitle is *The Uncompleted Project*.[24] Indeed, there are many well-received architects today who can be perceived as contributors to that project, among them Dimitris Antonakakis, Marlon Blackwell, Will Bruder, David Chipperfield, Sverre Fehn, Rick Joy, Ricardo Legoretta, Donlyn Lyndon, the late Samuel Mockbee, Glenn Murcutt, John and Patricia Patkau, Antoine Predock, Maurice Smith, and Lawrence Speck, to name only a few, of diverse orientation and some geographic distribution. That this "other tradition" finds value in the directly felt association of person and artifact does not diminish either the fact, or the intellectual and aesthetic demands, of the more remote appreciation of the vernacular in the work of a Le Corbusier or of our contemporaries who stand in that tradition.

Like Muthesius and others, Le Corbusier and Aalto saw the vernacular as a conceptual model for a natural relationship between society and its artifacts. While these architects, in their architectural work, each in his or her own way, could separate this enterprise from formal borrowings, the underlying ethos is the one that has been shared by many architects of varying persuasions—namely, again, that in the vernacular there is a natural relationship between society and its artifacts. Conversely, I think this perceived relationship is the way in which we have long recognized the traits by which we identify "the vernacular."

CHAPTER SEVEN

The Vernacular in Place and Time: Relocating History in Post-Soviet Cities

JOHN CZAPLICKA

This essay responds to the need to distinguish between the vernacular that historical geographers such as John Brinckerhoff Jackson have sought to recognize in the pervasive "sameness" of the modern American landscape and the very different vernacular to be found in the competing landscape of the Cold War Soviet East.[1] Whereas the landscape Jackson describes is predicated on the abstraction of the grid and the influence of a motorized culture, in the historical and geographical context of the former Eastern bloc, the idea and estimation of the modern and the vernacular cannot be separated from the experience of the authoritarian regimes that followed World War II or the context of a geopolitical competition with the capitalist states of the West.[2]

In this competition, the architecture of the Soviet area of influence became thoroughly politicized and in its modernity distinguished itself in many ways from modern architecture in the West, and yet, at the same time, it derived in part from Western models and from a similar, if belated, pattern of industrialization and the introduction of new building technologies and materials. Thus inevitably the modern in East and West bore certain similarities.[3] The main points of distinction involved related to the imposition of strictures by the state. Especially in the case of the Soviet Union, we see the Eastern modern configured, delimited, and transformed by the twists and turns of state ideology, by the introduction of a centralized mode of planning and construction, and by the mass production of building materials; and the Soviet modern in particular was starkly contingent on facts on the ground, such as the shortage of housing in a rigidly planned economy after the vast destruction of the world war.

In the field of architecture, this complex set of political and historical fac-

tors conspired to restrict the freedom of the architect, the plurality in architectural styles, and the expression of local distinctions. The emphasis and high valuation of an architecture demonstrating "socialist progress" led to a general negligence toward the architectural heritage representing a local idiom, which can be understood as one central element of the vernacular. With exceptions, socialist architecture tended to be unresponsive to the natural environment, local customs, and the built heritage of particular places or regions. Because the trajectory of the modern had to conform to the teleological perspective of the socialist state, derisive epithets such as "feudal," "bourgeois," and "capitalist" were directed at the historical substance that remained in the cities of the East after the ravages of war. Effectively, such remnants of the past and local heritage were *foreign* to the new political system and its goals.

Admittedly, there were varied reactions to the historical and vernacular architecture within the Eastern bloc, conditioned by degree to which each communist regime and its local extensions allowed local, national, and ethnic differences to be expressed during distinct periods of communist rule. One notes, for example, how attitudes to the architectural heritage and the role of historic preservation and reconstruction differed greatly between cities in the "regained territories" of Poland and cities subject to Soviet-Russian colonization, such as Riga or Tallinn. Still, despite these differences in attitude and permissiveness toward local and individual expression, architecture remained more or less a function of communist dogma and, above all, had to demonstrate the advantages of the new and ostentatiously modern socialist system.

With *glasnost*, the fall of the communist regimes in eastern Europe, and the dissolution of the Soviet Union came a revaluation of the version of "the modern" in architecture and urban design propagated by state-socialist regimes. In this changed and rapidly changing geopolitical environment, it was the local *historical* idiom in architecture that came to be acknowledged as the effective other of modern socialist architecture. Even before the fall of the eastern European state-socialist regimes, the traditional and retrospective aspect of the vernacular had become one point of resistance to the globalizing and colonizing tendencies implicit in the socialist project as a whole. For it served as a refuge and representation of particularist history, whether local, regional, national, or ethnic, which was an alternative history to the one propagated by the state.

As an antidote to socialist modernism, the function of the vernacular in this specific historical and geographic context was different than in the West and more political. The socialist modern to which it offered an implicit al-

ternative was, more often than not, formulated and regulated from afar and in a central governmental location, so that the form and substance of the architecture did not respond to differences in local environment and customs. Socialist modern architecture adhered rather to an abstract plan and vision fashioned in conformity with party precepts. The implementation of that abstraction had the effect of suppressing and neglecting local peculiarities in the built heritage, which after all belonged to the past and a nonprogressive era. Architecture was measured by its political correctness. The utopian perspective of the grand plan undermined local and regional distinctiveness by denying architecture its ability to convey a sense of place and a sense of history. In cities and towns such as Minsk or Kaliningrad (formerly Königsberg), which the devastation of war had left almost tabula rasa for the socialist architect, the implicit utopianism so characteristic of the modern movement as a whole, and so evident in the urban design of Ludwig Hilbersheimer and Le Corbusier, for example, came into play, albeit restricted by communist ideology.[4]

The postcommunist period, with its sense of historical loss and emphasis on the local and self-determination, turned the estimation of local architectural heritage on its head. The remaining historical substance of towns and cities that predated the communist era was revitalized and revalued; the old towns, once the object of neglect and derision became a focus of development, and the architecture of the socialist project was in turn ignored, neglected, and, in some cases, even demolished.[5] The historical substance itself became a representative means to reintegrate such cities as Riga, Vilnius, or L'viv into the geopolitical framework of a historical and contemporary "Europe," as well as a bridge to the particularist histories of religion, ethnicity, nation, region, and locality that had been suppressed under communist regimes. The modern architecture of socialist provenance became useless and a dispensable representation of a despised past in the turn to the West. The modernist dwellings of a communist "future" became despised reminders of a communist past.

What this radical pattern of historical revaluation suggests, and what the following essay means to underline, is the need to carefully contextualize the various conceptualizations of the modern and its sometime other, the vernacular, in a manner that allows for their historical, political, and geographical permutations in meaning and valuation. Recent revisionist debates about modernism have tended to focus largely on the victorious West, and on the postcolonial experience in former Western colonies, although occasionally touching on the relationship between authoritarian regimes and the modern (one thinks of Jeffrey Herf's contradictory formulation "re-

actionary modernism" in the case of Nazi Germany). This reconsideration needs to be expanded to include the particular setting(s) of eastern and central European and former Soviet cities, whose modernization process has been more fragmented and politicized.[6] A comparative reflection on the architecture and urban design of East and West could contribute to an understanding of the relationship of the modern and vernacular to the local and the global and to a contemporary articulation of the senses of place and time that flow from the configuration of the physical and architectural environment.

The architecture that resulted from the state-socialist project that dominated Europe east of the Elbe tended to exaggerate the uniformity and monotony often attributed to the modern in architecture and to become a utopian abstraction meant to stand *against* the local architectural heritage. In this chapter, an attempt is made to conceptualize the vernacular with respect to this heritage in the context of post-Soviet cities and to describe its relationship to the modern as it was articulated in them. I start from the premise that the vernacular is an idiom of architecture incorporating place-based characteristics, one informed by the customs and usages of the local population, the formation of a local or regional environment, and the availability of local materials. Under a political regime that centralizes authority and disallows free self-determination on the local level, such as state socialism, such a mode of expression is restricted by the prerogatives of the state. This local mode of expression is dynamic and not static, and in its political interpretations, it is quite often related to some imagination of ethnic or national essences.

The vernacular is formed in response to changing demographics, local materials and techniques, and social and economic relationships that evolve over time and are cultivated in a place. The conceptualization of the vernacular idiom in material culture related to post-Soviet cities that is proposed here finds this mode of expression in cumulative forms of place, as well as in the particularities of style and material, building type, technique, and urban design. Though the vernacular generally is of customary and local derivation, it may coincide with the modern in architecture and urban planning when a modern style, technique, or material used in building interrelates with a local environment and tradition (as was seldom the case under communist regimes), so that even in an understanding of the vernacular contingent on locality, local or regional variation in an international and modern style could also be deemed vernacular. Where the modern appears coextensive with a given natural environment and its customary built articulation, one could speak of a "vernacular modernism."

The vernacular is local and distinctive, and in its distinctiveness, it is congruent with place. This quality of the vernacular allows the local population to identify themselves in relation to a place and to the history of place. For the vernacular in its epistemological aspect transmits knowledge of a type of local history, the history of the human interaction with a particular environment. In the context of communist regimes, the vernacular represented the material presence of a historical alternative, for it rarely coincided with the socialist instantiation of the modern through architecture. In the postcommunist period, the vernacular is one element in the reconstitution of place-based identities.

Given the opposition of socialist modernism to local architectural expression, the concept of a "vernacular modernism" must seem derisive to longtime residents of post-Soviet or postcommunist cities. For the *ordinary* or *common* modernism of their everyday spaces largely consists of the poorly designed and constructed apartment blocks, factories, and government buildings of the socialist era, which defile whole regions and cities with a blight of monotony, structural dilapidation, and material decay. The poor quality and appearances of most socialist-dream architecture does little to inspire local pride and is rather the butt of local jokes. The nondescript character of such architecture can hardly be said to engender a sense of place. In fact, in describing their respective hometowns, most of the "locals" I have interviewed in cities like Gdansk, L'viv, Riga, and Vilnius tended to ignore such socialist incursions into the larger historical built environment, although a majority of them also inhabit such common structures. As a matter of course, most visitors to these cities ignore the dull, placeless settlements on the urban periphery that one sees on the way from the Vilnius airport, in driving the main road connecting Gdansk to Sopot and Gdynia, beyond the core area of L'viv, or along the Daugava driving north or south of Riga.[7]

People in Gdansk (formerly Danzig) spoke with pride about the totally reconstructed Old Town; about Oliwa, with its Cistercian monastery and beautiful church; about the renowned nineteenth-century seaside resort of Sopot, dotted with distinguished villas; and about Gdynia, the city and harbor the Poles built from scratch in the interwar years as an alternative to Danzig. Wrzeszcz, a district of Gdansk, had a high degree of recognition among the populace because of its quarter of turn-of-the-century villas or as the birthplace of the Nobel laureate Günther Grass. If expansive and monotonous modern settlements such as Przymorze and Zaspa were mentioned at all, it was generally to disparage them. I encountered this pattern of taking pride in one type of place and disparaging another in each of the

four cities I have chosen to study. Pride was taken in the heritage of place, and the disparagement focused on a version of modernity.

The reactions of those who reside in such postcommunist cities are understandable, given that most dwellings and offices built in the Soviet area of influence after the phase of monumental historicism under Stalin lack individuality and character. In fact, in all four cities one hears similar stories about confusions, about getting lost in such an areas, where everything looks the same. Those dense groups of uniform apartment blocks without landscaping and set apart on the edge of cities seem incursions into the distinct landscapes of eastern and central Europe. Their foreignness and abstract designs give them the character of colonial settlements. If the residents of Gdansk, L'viv, Riga, or Vilnius talk about this housing at all, it is to situate such buildings in the communist past, with little relation to their *own* history. After the dissolution of the Soviet Union and the end of the communist regimes, such structures have become monuments to almost fifty years of subjugation, to lost possibilities of development, and to the failure of a rootless utopian dream.

The ideological premises that fashioned such cityscapes and impelled the modernization of the Soviet state and its satellites not only worked toward eliminating class distinctions but also toward obliterating local, regional, ethnic, religious, and national ones. Mass housing, cheaply produced in great quantity, mirrored what might be called an ideology of increase in mass production. In Soviet travel guides to cities such as Riga, Vilnius, and L'viv, socialist progress expressed itself visually in images of lines of workers at machines, cans piled high on shelves, bottles of milk moving endlessly off production lines, and row after row of housing blocks. Only the photographs of precommunist architecture in such guidebooks distinguish one model settlement from another. For in using modern building technologies, modern materials and components, and employing elements of modern design associated with the "international style," the central authorities administering the Soviet realm filled production quotas for housing units and created architectural commonplaces that lacked variety in materials, style, composition, and building type.[8] The number of units was the chief measure of success, not the character of the building. Fulfilling planned production preceded any questions of quality or aesthetics.

The planned economies, industrialized production of building materials, and centralized decision-making processes resulted in a monumental uniformity that spread out into and over the landscape around cities without reference to the immediate natural or built environment. History that had accumulated in the material culture of a place over centuries was relegated

to a small and decaying part of the city. The *rayons* surrounding Soviet cities do not relate to the historic urban centers around which they are grouped, and only in rare cases, such as the towns of Eisenhüttenstadt in the former East Germany and Nowa Huta in Poland, do such settlements seem centered in themselves. Not unlike in the West, modernism's spatial, distributive, and architectural qualities disintegrated the urban fabric and obscured the historical "footprint"—in Aldo Rossi's words—that was a central component of urban identity.

If we were to apply the term "vernacular" devoid of its historical component to this context simply to indicate that which is "commonplace" or "ordinary" and relate it to pared-down, functional dwellings, then indeed those all pervasive Soviet-era apartment blocks, offices, and factories can be deemed a version of "vernacular modernism." Accepting that simple correlation between the commonplace and the vernacular, we might then modify John Brinkerhoff Jackson's deservedly famous dictum about the vernacular landscape being an "image of our common humanity"[9] to describe the Soviet vernacular landscape as the image of a common humanity regulated by an authoritarian state. Soviet building projects, which re-formed the landscapes of eastern and central Europe, convey more the ideology and workings of the state than the character of the people or the extant character of a place as it had been formed over time and through history.[10] This modernism is not vernacular but ideological.

Of course, we could understand the "vernacular" differently, and in a more restrictive sense, in eastern Europe. Drawing on Robert Riley's definition of "vernacular landscape" as "a human-made outdoor setting not of a type usually attributed to design professionals,"[11] it is possible to argue that only the small country houses, or dachas, built by "locals," often with scavenged materials, qualify as "vernacular" architecture under the Soviet regime.[12] Such architecture of the "private niche" existed apart from the pretensions and grand designs of the state.

But however we understand the vernacular, political ideology, a central planning authority, and a planned economy of scale all combined to impose a largely uniform character upon the locally diverse, historical-cultural landscapes east of the Elbe during the Cold War era.[13] This ideological stress, with its consequent negligence regarding inherited culture, threatened, weakened, and, in some cases, destroyed the distinctive identities of towns, cities, and regions that had developed through centuries of settlement and habitation.[14] The nonexistence of local self-government left the Communist Party and the central organization of state and industry in charge of configuring an abstract socialist future *against* the local heritage.[15] During the pe-

riod of *glasnost* and after the dissolution of the Soviet Union, it was thus exactly the attempt to retrieve this lost cultural heritage and source of identity that prompted historical reconstruction or preservation in many cities, towns, and localities. What local groups—including some of the first NGOs in the Soviet Union—sought to retrieve was at least a semblance of the distinct character and identity of place.[16] And it is exactly distinctiveness and identity that are, in my view, central to a broader understanding of the term "vernacular" as it might be applied to a built environment in the modern era.

Since around 1990, cities such as Kiev, Riga, and Vilnius have engaged in many projects of reconstruction, renovation, restoration, revitalization, and regeneration based on a shared concept of the *local* built heritage.[17] Building on and into an extant structural past and even expanding it further in the form of historical reconstructions—one thinks of the House of the Black Heads and Rathaus Square in Riga or the projected Lower Castle in Vilnius—serves the populations of these cities as a means both to overcome the Soviet past and to reassert their *own* histories (figs. 7.1–7.3). Local his-

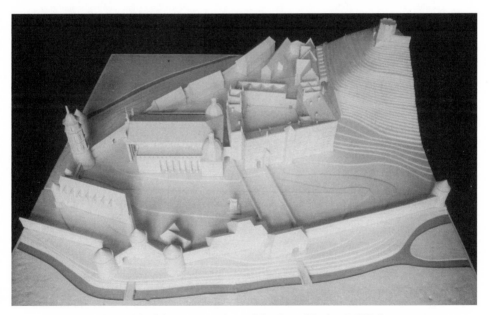

FIG. 7.1. A model of the Lower Palace of the Grand Dukes in Vilnius reconstructed by Napoleonas Kitkauskas. The Lower Palace complex includes and included buildings reflecting different architectural influences some of which, like the cathedral, are stylistic composites. Once reconstructed, the palace will complete a historical ensemble at the heart of the Lithuanian capital. Photograph by Jurgita Remeityte. Reproduced by kind permission.

FIGS. 7.2–7.3. Looking to the northeast and the southwest across Riga's Town Hall Square during its reconstruction. To the northeast, one sees the ongoing demolition of an ugly Soviet era building, which is being replaced by a modern reconstruction of the town hall that once stood at that site in this central location in Riga. To the southeast, one sees the newly reconstructed House of the Black Heads. The reconstituted square stands for—among other things—the reconstitution of a local and civic identity. Photographs by John Czaplicka.

tory relies on the distinctiveness of place embodied in a built heritage. In this cultural-political context, it is necessary to establish the clear relation of the term "vernacular" to place and time and not let it be defined solely with regard to the common and ordinary. First, in regard to place, vernacular architecture was both a product and determinant of place, in that it responds to the historical built environment and to the natural landscape, while at the same time changing them. Put another way, vernacular architecture informs and is informed by its physical context and location. This definition would tend to disqualify much of the "uninformed" Soviet construction.[18] Positing such a reciprocal relationship with the local natural and built environment, one could speak of the vernacular in architecture in terms of an *articulation of the local*, in that it displays knowledge of place and the shared knowledge of its inhabitants. This definition does not prescribe a particular style, whether modern, "folk," peasant, or historicizing, and would deemphasize the distinction between monumental-representative architecture and the "ordinary" architecture usually associated with the "vernacular."[19]

So understood, a vernacular idiom in architecture appears antithetical to the placelessness inherent in the *ideology* of modernism, which has global pretensions beyond the peculiar and common needs, beliefs, and customs of specific peoples. Both Soviet and more purely industrial or corporate architecture tend to neglect a basic responsiveness to the "local" characterizing the vernacular. Such an evident responsiveness is not limited to the folk, agricultural, peasant, village, or artisan structures gathered in theme parks on the edges of former Soviet cities such as L'viv and Riga. It can also be found in an innovative urban architecture that acknowledges the distinctive natural and cultural-historical character of places. The measure of the vernacular lies in the responsiveness of architecture to the climate and topography of a particular city or region, to the accumulated experience and history of its inhabitants, which is expressed in an extant material culture. As the famous Berkeley geographer Carl Sauer might have put it, vernacular architecture can be seen as adding to the distinctive "personality" of a place.

In various ways, architecture embodies or mediates the particulars of climate, topography, the technologies of a place or region, and the peculiar history and customs of local populations, both current and former. Whether in the tactile and visual characteristics of materials such as wood, natural stone, or brick, in the employment of distinctive building techniques (half-timber, stucco, specific bricklaying methods), in structural and design elements (arches, balconies, porches, and types and location of openings to the street), or in changes of scale and proportions, an architec-

ture that stands in a "conversant" relationship to a particular place and/or a particular population can be called "vernacular." Because vernacular architecture articulates the local, it often is or becomes an expression of cultural cohesion in place, whether place is defined as a region, a city, or a city district.[20] In an urban context, such architecture responds to the local built heritage of city districts as well as to the heritage of the city as a whole. If we emphasize the aspect of mediation, vernacular architecture functions as a local language of material and form that has evolved over time in relation to a place and its inhabitants.

The temporal aspect in this definition—the recognition of a particular heritage in place and the evolution of that heritage over time—distinguishes the vernacular from the all too common ideological renderings of "modernism" that claim universality while propagating revolution and disjuncture. Modernism of this ilk generates a discrete architecture of the drawing board and proposes a clean break with the past. In contrast, vernacular architecture is highly contextual and indeed explicitly derivative in many of its characteristics. The vernacular expresses itself in continuities rather than disjuncture, in gradual changes rather than sudden ones, and in patterns of distinction that rely on tradition rather than on a break with tradition.[21]

In postcommunist cities, vernacular architecture not only serves the purpose of lending distinction to place, thereby functioning as an antidote to the prevalent "placeless" socialist architecture, but also provides a point of reference for the history of cities before the period of communist rule. The relative valuation of local, historical, and vernacular architecture has thus risen greatly since the end of the communist regimes; this probably has to do as much with its aesthetic, structural, and material qualities as with the current tendency to denigrate anything associated with the Soviet era. During the late stages of the Soviet era, the recognition of the vernacular—that is, of the local architecture related to the history and traditions of a place—and its conservation served to help formulate a cultural and later political resistance to the dominance and patent insensitiveness of the communist regimes to everything local.

Thus even before the fall of the Soviet Union, activists in places such as Riga, Vilnius, and L'viv formed preservationist groups to restore and preserve the distinctive character of their cities. In Riga, local protesters sought to preserve a café located in a historic wooden building and attempted to halt the construction of a subway that would have cut through the center of the city. In Vilnius, the local preservation society prevented the building of

a parking garage in the center of the Old Town and a thoroughfare that was to cut through the center of the Old Town to provide a more direct route to the airport. In L'viv, the beginnings of the Ukrainian independence movement coincided with a new respect for that city's historical architecture, cemeteries, and monuments, expressed in the activities of local cultural groups who worked to preserve them.[22] In the decade after the fall of the Soviet Union, the work of preservationist groups in all three of the aforementioned cities gained them recognition from UNESCO, which declared them World Heritage Cities.[23] Such recognition came as a stark reaffirmation of their civic, regional, and European identities; according to the application, status as a "world city of cultural significance" depends on cultural distinctiveness.

The distinctiveness or peculiarity of vernacular architecture, once it is commonly recognized by a local population, may play a role in constituting and maintaining civic pride and place-based identities, whether they are locally, regionally, or even nationally defined. Considering the vernacular in these active senses, one could propose that this architecture of place provides one instrument in a set of cultural and political tools for the reconstitution of a civic identity and sense of belonging after the fall of communism.[24] The local architecture that I am calling "vernacular" lent character to these cities and had a peculiarly resonant relationship with the past.

It is obvious that this conception of the vernacular is neither sketched in the indelible ink of national or ethnic or peasant essences nor limited to a particular social class. It is, however, indelibly linked to the character of place and a concept of the "local." At the end of the Soviet period and especially after the introduction of glasnost in cities such as L'viv, Riga, and Vilnius, one saw the emergence of a new archaeology of the local that sought to recover aspects of history long suppressed under the communist regimes in Ukraine, Latvia, and Lithuania. An aspect of this archaeology entailed a new appreciation for historic preservation of local material culture as it had developed before the imposition of state-socialist rule, and with this came a new appreciation for vernacular architecture as I am defining it. This appreciation derived from the reevaluation of religious and bourgeois contributions to each city. Thus, for example, in Vilnius, Riga, and L'viv, the historic urban core took on new meaning, offering an image of the precommunist past and, to an extent, of a golden age before the coming of authoritarian rule. The residents of these and other former Soviet cities now in independent states conceive of themselves differently and draw upon their distinctive urban environments in doing so.

In the Soviet Union, Vilnius, Riga, and L'viv lay in the region of the vaguely defined "other" that was called the "near abroad" by Soviet citizens, who viewed these three cities quite simply as "European," and not Soviet or Russian, because they offered an image of difference generated in part by a distinctive historical architecture of place. The peculiar urban configurations of these cities in the near abroad offered a basis for historical reflection and, for their residents, self-reflection. Hanseatic and Jugendstil Riga, baroque Vilnius, and Habsburg L'viv had not been obliterated by war and only came fully into the Soviet sphere after World War II. One could hypothesize about the reasoning for the effect of this historical architecture on the understanding of these cities, seen as belonging to an "abroad" enclosed by the Soviet empire.

After the dissolution of that empire, the much sought after "return to Europe" found a ready-made vehicle in the architecture of these cities. How should one understand the extensive Jugendstil (German-style art nouveau) architecture of Riga, the panoply of baroque churches and Renaissance arcades in Vilnius, or the grand architecture of a provincial Habsburg capital like L'viv? Wasn't Jugendstil the fashionable style of a turn-of-the-century European bourgeoisie? Don't the baroque churches and Renaissance arcades in Vilnius display Catholic influences and the employment of Italian architects in the service of a European Counter-Reformation? Isn't L'viv's Habsburg heritage apparent in its administrative buildings and infrastructure such as train stations and hospitals? Doesn't such structural evidence situate these cities firmly within the western European cultural sphere?

The identity of place and the identity of people in place are embodied in such historical constellations. The people of a place may link themselves to a region or concept of Europe through the ability to distinguish the peculiar cultural influences and confluences on the formation of their hometowns. A mix of baroque, Renaissance, and neoclassical structures seems peculiar to Vilnius, whereas a pervasive, overwrought ornamentation characterizes Riga's Jugendstil, whose preponderance in that city's first modern suburbs sets it apart. Such peculiarities of a style or building type can also be seen as an element of a vernacular expression denied by the ideologues of universality. How Jugendstil differs from one city to the next is not only evident in terms of ornament. The number of stories of buildings in each city is different; the relationship of the façade to a broader or narrower street and the number and use of balconies differs.

The *Jugendstil* or National romantic apartment houses for the well-to-do of L'viv, Vilnius, or Riga are the national-romantic Jugendstil apartment

houses built for the well-to-do in L'viv, Vilnius, and Riga are, furthermore, the embodiment of an urban and "bourgeois" past denied or maligned by communist authorities. These dwellings represent the accomplishment of former citizens, their will to represent themselves as individuals, and an attempt to beautify the city. They are an expression of pride in self and place. The division and ornamentation of the façades, the ornate entryways, and stylish interior designs of such buildings represent a modern international style *in a distinctly local vein*. It would be too much here to try to describe the flamboyant and exaggerated Jugendstil ornamentation of many Riga buildings or to delineate the distinct influences of Carpathian or Latvian peasant architecture on the turn-of-the-century façades in cities such as L'viv, Riga, and Kraków. But local peculiarities can be distinguished. Jugendstil in Riga or L'viv is different from Jugendstil in Prague or Budapest, even if still part of the same international movement. Some of these distinctions relied on the use of designs by local architects.[25] The predominance of Jugendstil in Riga relates to a flourishing bourgeois community at the turn of the century who attempted to represent themselves in a "modern" vein, which has become very much part of the Riga vernacular—part of the city's identity. Tourist brochures and guidebooks call Riga a *Jugendstilmetropole*—an art nouveau metropolis.

This suggests that we might understand the vernacular also in a larger set of relations. The flowering of a bourgeois culture and a general prosperity throughout most of Europe led to the proliferation of certain styles around 1900; cities such as Vienna, Brussels, Barcelona, and Riga were marked strongly by an international turn-of-the-century style. The same could be said about the characteristic northern mannerist structures displaying the influence of the Netherlands and the Hanseatic League in cities such as Bruges, Gdansk, Lübeck, and Riga. Such structural resemblances have become very central in the identical composite of these cities—that is, to a degree, one identifies these cities through the presence of these styles of architecture and building types. The same could be said of the baroque churches that are so prominent in Vilnius's urban fabric. This style concretely relates the Lithuanian capital to Catholic and Counter-Reformation Europe and sets it starkly apart from the core areas of the former Soviet Union. The variation on and concentration of distinct architectural styles in a region or city are one element in a constellation of factors constituting an idiomatic architecture of place.[26] In Gdansk, one can see how the scale and style of adjacent postcommunist architecture has been influenced starkly by the postwar historical reconstruction of the city.

FIGS. 7.4–7.5. The changing street façade on the K. Valdemara iela and the Stabu iela in Riga. Four- to six-story historicizing Jugendstil apartment houses abut on nineteenth-century one- or two-story wooden structures, which once had garden plots behind them. Both structural types were included in the central historic preserve established when Riga was designated a World Heritage city by UNESCO. The radical change in scale, a mix of urban and suburban, is a local characteristic, which can be seen as an expression of the vernacular. Photographs by John Czaplicka, 2000.

The pattern of local distinction, however, has many other elements besides the preponderance, variation, or transmission of certain architectural styles and types. The configuration of architectural ensembles and use of materials are two other characteristic features. In certain quarters of the formerly Soviet cities of Riga, Tallinn, and Vilnius, wooden houses with courtyards are found interspersed among new buildings or in ensembles. This architecture characterizes the city through a display of local building techniques, ornamentation, and materials specific to the region, and at the same time it relates to folk traditions that are usually seen as local culture sub specie aeternitatis. It was the threatened destruction of one of these wooden structures in Riga that helped stir preservationist sentiment in the city during the Soviet period.

In Riga, once you move out of the Old Town into the area of Jugendstil and eclectic apartment houses, a singular street pattern peculiar to this city catches the eye. The street façade of four- to six-story apartment houses gives way abruptly to one-story wooden houses, often in the neoclassical style, built in the mid-ninteenth century (fig. 7.4–7.5). These wooden houses in Riga's inner suburbs that seem to break so abruptly into the modern street front lie within the city's UNESCO-designated historic preserve. The extant wooden architecture was one of the reasons for declaring Riga a World Heritage Site in 1996. This type of wooden urban architecture is characteristic of much of the Baltic region, but what distinguishes it in Riga is the manner in which it is combined with high-rise apartment houses, giving the streets of the suburbs their characteristic appearance and rhythm.[27]

Where the traditional wooden houses break into the street façade, they usually form ensembles, with inner courtyards that were once related to gardens. At some places in the Jugendstil district, one can walk into the courtyard of a six-story apartment house and still find the vestiges of a wooden building. Vilnius is comparable, with wooden architecture scattered through the city and a large tract of endangered wooden architecture in the Zverynas suburb, for example. Only in exceptional cases is this architecture being preserved.[28] Many of the wooden buildings in both cities are dilapidated, and they are disappearing under the pressures of capitalist investment, lack of a systematic enforcement of historic preservation laws, and municipal corruption or negligence. In Riga's Moscow suburb, an area that was largely composed of such examples of wooden architecture is being cleared because of such negligence.

The use of common or typical or historical building materials is another framework in which to consider the definition of a vernacular modernism.

In the study of material culture, the employment of distinct building materials and techniques within a clearly defined geographical area indicates the level of development and patterns of cultural influence, and it is sometimes associated with a place to the extent that we refer to these materials and techniques as "indigenous." As Akos Moravansky has noted, these indicators help define "material landscapes," both real and imaginary, and may even in part constitute the imagined geography of a region or nation.[29] The distinctive local character of cities often relies on similar patterns of association, and the history of cities might to some extent be written based on the use of construction techniques and materials.

Half-timbering, stucco in L'viv, wooden structures in Vilnius and Riga, bricks of a particular color, and building with common natural stone are part and parcel of vernacular expression. Red-brick gothic marks northern European and Hanseatic cities, and the yellow stucco of large public buildings in the cities of central Europe is sometimes understood as correlated with the Habsburg empire. In our contemporary global age, however, all types of materials are available everywhere, techniques are easily transferable, and central heating, air conditioning, and better insulation allow one to build independent of local climatic conditions. It is thus almost impossible to define an indigenous contemporary architecture with respect to materials and techniques.

Asking selected residents of my three cities about the indigenous materials and techniques that they associated with the architecture of their hometowns almost exclusively elicited references to their Old Towns, and at most to their nineteenth- and early twentieth-century expansions. Any discussion about a place-specificity as defined by materials focused on the "historical" city. Residents of all three cities referred to brick. In Gdansk, brick held a position of primary importance in defining the historical cityscape because of its extensive use in public buildings, major monuments, and landmarks for centuries. In Vilnius, however, brick specifically evoked the Gothic era before the baroque and neoclassical styles became predominant. Brick thus represented different time frames in these two cities. In Riga, beside "Hanseatic" brick, wood, a material still quite evident in Vilnius, Riga, Tallinn, and other cities of the northern and eastern Baltic, was especially mentioned. Perhaps most important in this sampling of material associations with hometowns and cultural landscapes drawn from interviews with residents of Gdansk, L'viv, Riga, and Vilnius is the fact that no one mentioned reinforced concrete, which was evidently unrelated to their sense of identity and place. And yet it is the widespread and unrefined

use of ferroconcrete throughout eastern and central Europe, especially in its prefabricated and mass-produced form, that has created most modern cityscapes in the region. Employed massively in these cities during the post-Stalinist period, ferroconcrete connotes, not only poor workmanship, brutal anonymity, and the communist era's failed concepts of communal housing, but the imposition of state and "foreign" authority.

These indications return us to a central question posed by the editors of this volume, whether "vernacular modern architecture" is not an oxymoron. If a relationship to the local is the essence of the vernacular, as I would argue, then in eastern and central Europe, there was a contradiction between Soviet modernism and the understanding of place, which can only be overcome when a new architecture begins to display sensitivity to nature, history, and the peoples who call the region home. In both Riga and Vilnius, the combination of architectural types and styles generates a characteristic cityscape informed by various periods of the city's history (figs. 7.6–7.7). The peculiarity of the historical composite is central in defining the individuality of each city. To say that few cities have the concentration of Jugendstil buildings that Riga displays and to note the unique juxtapositioning of high-rise and low-rise buildings of masonry and wood is to individuate the city. Its individual character, which can certainly be found in the distinctive silhouette of Riga's Old Town, also is expressed in the street patterns, the changes in scale, the rhythms of open and closed spaces, and the density of the city. The variation in these design elements is the result of successive stages in an individual urban history. They form an integral but variegated composite urban fabric. The conversations I had with residents of Riga in 1999 and 2001 about the identity and character of the city covered only the three aspects that are considered "historical" and that made Riga a World Heritage City: the Old Town, the ring of Jugendstil architecture, and wooden architecture. This composite was what was meant when one spoke of "the city." The socialist housing complexes and the modern ring of factories remained largely off the mental map, removed from any relationship with the city's identity. One might argue that the peculiar combination of form and material in this historical preserve constitute Riga's vernacular.

The vernacular is not only defined by a style, not just associated with one building type, one historical era, or one building technique or material, but expresses itself through multiple elements that are common to a place and combine there to make it distinctive. Extending this concept to the character of the built ensemble and the macrostructures of the city seems to fol-

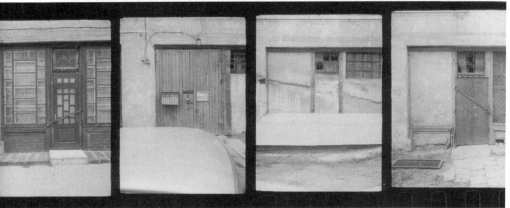

FIGS. 7.6–7.7. The extended courtyard at Pylimo 44 (Wall Street) in Vilnius, with the details of shop entrances. Vilnius has an old city of inner courtyards, streets that wind with the lay of the land, and two-story buildings. The scale and spatial articulation lend the city much of its characteristic "personality." It has a vernacular gestalt. Before World War II, this courtyard leading from one street to another was probably alive with small businesses. Photographs by Jurgita Remeityte. Reproduced by kind permission.

low logically and to be justified by the understanding of the city as a dwelling place and a locality—an understanding that may be outmoded in an era when the city resembles a system more than a home.

When I queried two of the original architects and engineers responsible for the rebuilding of Gdansk after World War II, they stressed to me how important it was to rebuild a historic street pattern, to keep the buildings in historical proportion to the street, and to reestablish the difference in scale between monumental churches and civic structures and merchant houses and warehouses. They were more concerned about getting this right than with the correct insertion of surviving ornamentation into the façades of the houses they were reconstructing. The spatial and proportional arrangement of the city according to a traditional hierarchy and to traditional patterns of use recall the origin and function of Gdansk as a harbor, warehouse, and marketplace. In Riga, many concerned planners and architects noted the need to relate the city to its harbor and riverfront, from which it had been cut off by the intrusion of a broad boulevard used for mass demonstrations in the Soviet period. In the same city, the reconstruction of the town hall square now taking place represents the felt need to reestablish the historic civic center of the Old Town. In L'viv, Vilnius, Riga, and Gdansk, there are plans for restoring the city's traditional density at places where war and communist planning created traffic arteries and empty squares. Such plans take into account how much of the sense of place depends on the structure and shape of a city and its relation to a natural topography. Perhaps even more than any single piece of architecture, this macrostructure conveys urban individuality and mediates history.

If we review the elements that are *common* to place and define it—such as particular materials, styles, scale, plan, and macrostructures—and understand them not as peculiarities of place in and of themselves but rather as an integrative constellation, one can begin to understand how a definition of the vernacular might lie in the relationship between the elements. In this conceptualization of the vernacular, the questions the idea of a "vernacular modernism" might raise all have to do with how and to what degree modernism integrates itself into a configuration of the local. The ideological modernism proposed by socialist regimes was set in opposition to the local and denied it in order to be rid of the ballast of history. Transposing this to conditions in the West, a similar denial of the vernacular and local takes place when architects or their sponsors build without reference to a local environment to "make a statement" or produce a "free-standing," autonomous work of art.

In identifying the vernacular of a region or a city, it seems advisable always to consider constellations of elements that lend a landscape or cityscape character or personality. The ensemble, configuration, and relationship of the built elements to a type of landscape—that is, combinations of elements seen together in a larger gestalt—generate a sense of place that transcends any single piece of architecture or single style. Given the cross-currents of culture that configure the complex fabric of cities, different epochal styles and forms are common to different places, and in their combination, they lend them distinction. It is through the combined qualities of the commonplace and distinctive that one can understand how a vernacular modernism could be conceived in a region where a version of modernism has generally been the vehicle and expression of placeless political abstraction. It would be a tragedy if the post–Soviet, postcommunist cities, with their new powers of self-determination, were now to fall prey to the placelessness of an ideologically driven architecture from the West or to nostalgic yearnings to reconstruct the lost past. Perhaps the new regionalism in Europe and the realization of belonging to Europe itself will allow the residents of these cities to configure their hometowns in a way that is true to their time and their place.

Critical Regionalism Revisited: Reflections on the Mediatory Potential of Built Form

KENNETH FRAMPTON

Critical regionalism would appear to be one of those formulations that has enjoyed a surprising longevity. Frederic Jameson makes this abundantly clear at the end of his book *The Seeds of Time* (1994) where he enters into a sensitive critique of the concept as the fulcrum of a potentially resistant culture. There are a number of passages in Jameson's appraisal when he is able to synthesize aspects of this hypothesis in a particularly revealing way. A single example will perhaps suffice. It occurs in that passage where, following my lead, he compares Tadao Ando's "self-enclosed modernity" to Jørn Utzon's Bagsvaerd Church, wherein the two architects are seen as adapting the same universal technology of reinforced concrete to totally different cultural ends. Thus where Utzon uses monolithic frame-and-shell construction to make a subtle synthesis between an oriental pagoda and a Nordic stave church, Ando casts his concrete into a top-lit prism constructed of load-bearing walls in order to engender a revitalized Japanese feeling for the interplay of light, material, and detail. Jameson points out how both examples "hold out the possibility of inventing some new relationship to the technological beyond nostalgic repudiation or mindless corporate celebration. If Critical Regionalism is to have any genuine content it will do so only on the strength of such invention and its capacity to 'enclose' or to re-open and transfigure the burden of the modern."

The prospect of transfiguring the modern transcends all those critical categories oscillating between the modern, the postmodern, and the anti-modern to leave us disarmed, as it were, before the relentless technoscientific modernization of our age. This being so, one is hard pressed to know how to situate oneself before the prospect of a vernacular modernism, par-

ticularly when the term comes to be applied across a fairly wide range of so-
cioanthropological–cum–art historical phenomena. Given that the Latin
terms *verna* and *modernus* both have their origins in the antique world some
five centuries before Christ, one becomes even more perplexed by the
provocative conjunction of these terms. While one may refer, as the editors
of this volume certainly do, to the widespread integration of agrarian building methods and materials into the unfolding trajectory of the modern
movement, going back certainly to William Morris's Red House of 1859 or
even further, by another century to Marie Antoinette's Hameau, discreetly
located as a rustic folly in the grounds of Versailles, one nonetheless remains
aware that, with the dissolution of agrarian building culture, the pre-aes-
thetic innocence of the vernacular, which could still be evoked by Adolf
Loos in 1910, now no longer presents itself as an option that is readily available.

One assumes that this is the polemical point of the term, namely, that the
vernacular cannot even be addressed today without subsuming it under the
aesthetic strategy of *modernism*. At the same time, instrumental reason continues to impose its machinations upon the world with no regard for the in-
tervening traces of a mediatory culture. However, it should be noted in this
respect that within the scope of the rationalized technology that is currently
at our disposal, the process of building remains stubbornly anachronistic in
character, above all because, notwithstanding the constant invention of new
light-weight materials, possessed of unprecedented advantageous properties, along with the development of an ever more sophisticated range of
electro-mechanical services, the insertion of a building into its site remains
as archaic as ever it was. It is surely this, plus the persistence of proprietal
rights, that enables building to resist its full commodification.

It may be argued that a critically resistant architecture is one that is totally opposed to rendering a building as a free-standing aesthetic object;
one that is akin to sculpture in terms of its figurative rhetoric. In light of
this, one remains convinced that the general environmental predicament in-
duced by the rapacity of "motopian" development can only be offset by according a priority to "landscape" both as a metaphor and as a literal device
for the ongoing modulation of the existing urbanized environment. It
should be self-evident by now that the megalopolis in all its vicarious forms
is on the verge of occupying the habitable surface of the entire earth. Thus
the *città diffusa* is potentially everywhere, and while there are no doubt
some vestiges left of preindustrial agrarian topography, we also know that
as far as maximized economic development is concerned, nothing is sacro-

sanct. It is symptomatic in this regard that the self-defeating, destructive pathos of mass tourism finds its corollary in the Disneyfication of the historic urban core. While building in the midst of a traditional urban context is largely a matter of sustaining the grain of the existing fabric, building on "Greenfield" sites inevitably runs the risk of adding one more arbitrary object to the endless proliferation of such objects. Against this regard there remains the critical possibility of extending the earthwork of a building (i.e., the foundations) in such a way that the structure becomes integrated into the landscape and vice versa.

Roofwork and Earthwork

In many so-called primitive building cultures, the roofwork and the earthwork are brought together in such an intimate way as to eliminate the need for any kind of vertical enclosure. At the same time as far as our received notions of the vernacular are concerned, it is obvious that the roof has to be pitched, if traditional cultural conventions are to be respected. This norm prevails as a sign of "dwelling" in the ubiquitous suburbia that constitutes the residential fabric of the average megalopolis. One hardly needs to add that the modernist flat roof was always a violation of this traditional iconography. We need only to recall the Aryan roof of the Heimatstil in the Third Reich to understand the full measure of this time-honored prejudice. It is surely significant, in this regard, that a regionally oriented modern architecture has often entailed making a particularly noticeable play with the form of the roof, as we find this say in the late 1940s and early 1950s in the work of such architects as Jørn Utzon, Alvar Aalto, Hans Scharoun, and even Le Corbusier, not to mention more recent organic works designed by John and Patricia Patkau of Vancouver, or let us say the corrugated, metal "outback" roofs that would grace the domestic work of the Australian architect Glenn Murcutt in the 1970s. Clearly, the oversailing roof has certain advantages from the point of view of sustainability. I am alluding to its innate capacity to provide shade, to protect walls and above all of course to dispose of rainfall and snow. In any event in the pre-industrial vernacular, the roof, whether flat or pitched, was always apparently a direct consequence of the climate in which the building happened to be situated. Thus along with the influence of local craft methods invariably bestowed upon the work its specific "placelike" character.

One may argue that in tectonic terms both the roofwork and the earthwork are crucial factors from the point of view of engendering sectional

profiles and topographic boundaries that are capable of standing against the space-endlessness of the "value-free," megalopolitan domain. It would be demagogic, however, to conclude from this that flat roofs have no possible critical cultural capacity.

Mauer and Wand

The German words *Mauer* and *Wand*, which may, I believe, be used all but interchangeably in translating the English "wall," clearly allude to two tectonically opposite methods for the enclosure of space, and in this opposition, there surely resides a potentially infinite range of expression as far as spatial enclosure is concerned. Where the one assumes those opaque, heavyweight, load-bearing characteristics that we necessarily associate with the earthwork, the other has a relatively lightweight, screenlike character, possibly even translucent or transparent, one that may be readily affiliated with a load-bearing structural frame and with the roofwork that such a frame invariably supports. It should be self-evident that this already presents a kind of irreducible tectonic articulation that may be orchestrated in countless ways so as to express distinctly different and highly layered cultural connotations, as a kind of infinite poetic potential arising out of tradition, including by now the all but infinite tradition of the "new," which is perhaps one of the most inescapably postmodern effects of our time. This tectonic *poiēsis*, as it were, should in no way be at variance with the project of cultivating a sustainable building culture that in its full potential would by definition be resistant to the global nemesis of environmental pollution. Here, of course, many time-honored factors come back into play: the old constraints of landfall, wind, watershed, and the trajectory of the sun. Beyond these constant limitations arising out of the site, there lies an all but infinite range of relative permeability, irrespective of the basic tectonic character of the wall. I am alluding of course to the way in which fenestration may be positioned, inflected, shaded, and so on, irrespective of whether the openings are pierced or made an integral part of a lightweight membrane.

Center and Periphery

As far as architecture is concerned, the limitations of the mediatory stem perhaps from the experiential "distancing" that necessarily accompanies its representation in terms of photography and film. The camera unavoidably reduces architecture to the perspectival image, that is to say to an exclu-

sively visual phenomenon that is by definition removed from our everyday tactile-cum-spatial experience of built form. However, we also need to acknowledge a certain measure of mediatory ambivalence owing to the universal proliferation and distribution of images, for while the mediatory facilitates consumerist fashion and stimulates desire, it has, at the same time, been beneficial in its capacity to disseminate information in such a way as to overcome the long-standing schism between center and periphery—between the dominance of the one and the subservience of the other. This is particularly evident in contemporary architecture, where some of the most sophisticated work realized today is being produced in countries that are variously distanced from the traditional centers of cultural power and influence—in countries such as Japan, Australia, India, Finland, Spain, Portugal, Norway, Ireland, and in many different regions of the South American continent. It is ironic that the very system that pushes the cult of the "star" architect should also provide for its antithesis; that is to say, for the generation of quality work all over the world, so much so that one of the paradoxes of critical regionalism as a cultural hypothesis is that it tends toward the spontaneous cultivation of a kind of hybrid "world culture" continually open to further enrichment and development.

At the same time, it is necessary to recognize the limits of architecture as a métier; above all perhaps the fact that however much advanced techno-scientific methods may be employed in its realization, it is no more an applied science than it is a form of fine art. Despite the ubiquitous triumph of technological modernization, the practice of architecture is still to be more properly regarded as a craft, one that, at its full range, is dedicated to the significant mediation of the environment. In this respect, it is always as much an ontological presence and an embodiment of societal value in spatial terms, as it is an abstract or symbolic representation. Hence, it is doubtful whether it can ever be appropriately rendered as "fine art writ large." Unlike literature, music, painting, and sculpture, or even theater, photography, and film, architecture cannot legitimately aspire to any kind of cultural autonomy, since it is too intimately involved with the processes of everyday life and with what Jürgen Habermas calls the unfinished modern project; in a word, with what Marshall Berman has identified as the pastoral, as opposed to the counterpastoral of the formalist neo–avant garde. It should, in fact, be contextual in respect of the culture of the lifeworld rather than preemptive.

Notes

Hüppauf and Umbach: Introduction

The editors of this book gratefully acknowledge the support of several academic institutions and funding bodies. The conference at which the plan for this book first emerged was generously sponsored by New York University's Deutsches Haus. Research and editorial work for this project also benefited from the generous support of the British Academy, the Arts and Humanities Research Board (AHRB), the Leverhulme Trust, the University of Manchester, and the Institució Catalana de Recerca i Estudis Avançats (ICREA).

1.   Hilde Heynen, *Architecture and Modernity: A Critique* (London, 1999), argues that modernism in architecture is the aesthetic expression of the animating principles of modernization. Such views draw upon an earlier definition of modernity as proposed by classical modernization theorists, who highlighted aspects such as "rationalization," disenchantment, social mobility, and fragmentation as distinctive features. The most widely cited formulation of modernization theory is the five-stage model developed by Walt Whitman Rostow, *The Stages of Economic Growth: A Non-Communist Manifesto* (Cambridge, 1960). See also Philip Abrams, *Historical Sociology* (Ithaca, N.Y., 1982), esp. chap. 5, 108–46, and, more critically, and *Directions of Change: Modernization Theory, Research, and Realities*, ed. Mustafa O. Attir, Burkart Holzner, and Zdenek Suda (Boulder, Colo., 1981). The Cold War politics behind modernization theory are the subject of Nils Gilman, *Mandarins of the Future: Modernization Theory in Cold War America* (Baltimore, 2003). An interesting attempt to incorporate some of these challenges into the modernization model is Hans Ulrich Wehler, *Modernisierungstheorie und Geschichte* (Göttingen, 1975). On the misunderstanding and mythologizing of "functionalism" as an icon of modernism, see Stanford Anderson, "The Fiction of Function," *Assemblage* 2 (1986): 19–31.

2.   A fuller definition of our take on the "vernacular" will be mapped out on the following pages. It is important to emphasize here, however, that we use the term to refer to a sense of place. In this, our view differs from that of John Brinckerhoff Jackson, *Discovering the Vernacular Landscape* (New Haven, 1984), for whom the

vernacular denotes a universal idiom of popular (versus high) culture, with no, or at least no necessary, pattern of local, individual or other variation.

3. On the etymology of modernity, see Matei Calinescu, "Modernity, Modernism, Modernisation: Variations on Modern Themes," in *Turn of the Century: Modernism and Modernity in Literature and the Arts*, ed. C. Berg, F. Durieux, and G. Lernout (New York, 1995), 33–52.

4. Göran Therborn, *European Modernity and Beyond: The Trajectory of European Societies, 1945–2000* (Thousand Oaks, Calif., 1995), 4.

5. E. P. Thompson, "Time, Work-Discipline and Industrial Capitalism," *Past and Present*, no. 38 (1967): 56–97. This classical study has been much scrutinized and criticized since, e.g., by David S. Landes, *Revolution in Time: Clocks and the Making of the Modern World* (1983; rev. ed., Cambridge, Mass., 2000). Cf. also Paul Glennie and Nigel Thrift, "The Spaces of Clock Time," in *The Social in Question: New Bearings in History and the Social Sciences*, ed. Patrick Joyce (London, 2002), 151–74.

6. Reinhart Koselleck, *Vergangene Zukunft: Zur Semantik geschichtlicher Zeiten* (Frankfurt a/M, 1979). This hypothesis has been criticized by Wolfgang Ernst Becker, *Zeit der Revolution!—Revolution der Zeit? Zeiterfahrungen in Deutschland in der Ära der Revolutionen, 1789—1848/49* (Göttingen, 1999).

7. A rich documentation of evidence for the role of speed and movement in modernist aesthetics and thought is provided in *The Weimar Republic Sourcebook*, ed. Anton Kaes, Martin Jay, and Edward Dimendberg (Berkeley, 1994).

8. Stephen Kern, *The Culture of Time and Space, 1880–1918* (Cambridge, Mass., 1983).

9. Richard Sennett, *The Fall of Public Man* (1977; reprint, New York, 1992).

10. An interesting collection of essays presenting the case for a reinstatement of domesticity in the discourse of modernism is *Not At Home: The Suppression of Domesticity in Modern Art and Architecture*, ed. Christopher Reed (London, 1996).

11. Jürgen Habermas, *The Structural Transformation of the Public Sphere*, trans. Thomas Burger (Cambridge, 1992).

12. On modernization theory, see Rostow, *Stages of Economic Growth*; Abrams, *Historical Sociology*; and *Directions of Change: Modernization Theory*, ed. Attir et al. An excellent survey of the connection between modernization and nation-building is *Becoming National: A Reader*, ed. Geoff Eley and Ronald Grigor Suny (New York, 1996).

13. Eugen Weber, *Peasants into Frenchmen: The Modernization of Rural France, 1870–1914* (London, 1979).

14. A conceptual discussion of the meaning of modernity outside its Western context, in locations ranging from nineteenth-century Bengal to contemporary Morocco, is provided by *Questions of Modernity*, ed. Timothy Mitchell (Minneapolis, 2000). A similar problematic is the subject of Arjun Appadurai, *Modernity at Large: Cultural Dimensions of Globalization* (Minneapolis, 1996). Both provide excellent introductions to a growing literature on postcolonial challenges to Western ideal of modernity too extensive to be surveyed here.

15. A useful summary of this debate is provided by Susan Stanford Friedman, "Definition Excursions: The Meanings of Modern, Modernity, Modernism," *Modernism/Modernity* 8, 3 (2001): 493–513.

16. Scott Lash and Jonathan Friedman, "Subjectivity and Modernity's Other," in *Modernity and Identity*, ed. id. (Oxford, 1992), 1.

17. Bruno Latour, *Nous n'avons jamais été modernes* (Paris, 1991), trans. Catherine Porter as *We Have Never Been Modern* (Cambridge, Mass., 1993).

18. Postmodernism, or more specifically, texts such as Jean-François Lyotard, *The Postmodern Condition: A Report on Knowledge*, trans. Geoff Bennington and Brian Massumi (Minneapolis, 1984), have inspired a range of attempts to reconceptualize the modern. In the United States, one of the most important forums for this debate is the journal *Modernism/Modernity*, published by the Johns Hopkins University Press since 1994. Its editors state: "The success of modernism was so great that we all feel ourselves to be latecomers: postmodernism is the term now invoked to assert an epochal shift away from our parents' perspective." Lawrence Rainey and Robert von Hallberg, "Editorial—Introduction," *Modernism/Modernity* 1, 1 (1994): 1–3, quotation from 1. An excellent overview that pays particular attention to the French and German contribution to this debate is *Wege aus der Moderne: Schlüsseltexte der Postmoderne-Diskussion*, ed. Wolfgang Welsch (Weinheim, 1988).

19. Marshall Berman, *All That Is Solid Melts into Air: The Experience of Modernity* (New York, 1982).

20. This approach is represented by Eric Rothstein, "Broaching a Cultural Login of Modernity," *Modern Languages Quarterly* 61, 2 (2000): 359–94. Bernard Yack, *The Fetishism of Modernities: Epochal Self-Consciousness in Contemporary Social and Political Thought* (Notre Dame, Ind., 1997), argues that postmodernists have fetishized modernity in such a way as to obscure the very feature to which they first drew our attention, namely, its heterogeneity.

21. Francis Fukuyama, *The End of History and the Last Man* (London, 1992). For the debate on Fukuyama, see *After History? Francis Fukuyama and His Critics*, ed. Timothy Burns (London, 1994), and *Has History Ended? Fukuyama, Marx, Modernity*, ed. Christopher Bertram and Andrew Chitty (Brookfield, Vt., 1994).

22. According to James C. Scott, "high-modernist ideology" was one of four elements that, in a "pernicious combination," caused "the most tragic episodes of state-initiated social engineering" (Scott, *Seeing Like a State: How Certain Schemes to Improve the Human Condition Have Failed* [New Haven, 1998], 4).

23. The category of "Heroic Modernism" is developed by Charles Jencks, *Modern Movements in Architecture* (Harmondsworth, U.K., 1985). The label refers to classical modernism in its most radical, uncompromising, and triumphalist mode. Yet it is confusing in that the term "heroic" suggests that modernism's chief characteristic, the triumph of abstraction, can be likened to something that is by definition idiosyncratic: the "heroism" of an individual.

24. Astrudas Eysteinsson, *The Concept of Modernism* (Ithaca, N.Y., 1990) is a useful overview of modernism as a cultural movement.

25. Sarah Goldhagen, "Coda: Reconceptualizing the Modern," in *Anxious Modernisms: Experimentation in Postwar Architectural Culture*, ed. id. (Cambridge, Mass., 2000), 301–25, quotation from 303. This reading is defined as an alternative to interpretations of modernism as "style," which, she argues, "constitute a reification of the forms of modernism into modernism itself" (ibid.).

26. Matei Calinescu, *Five Faces of Modernity: Modernism, Avant-Garde, Deca-*

dence, Kitsch, Postmodernism (Durham, N.C., 1987), challenges the notion that modernism is simply a cultural expression of modernity, interpreting it, rather, as a cultural strategy to combat the effects of modernization. See also Y. Vadé, "Modernisme ou Modernité?" in *Turn of the Century: Modernism and Modernity in Literature and the Arts*, ed. C. Berg, F. Durieux, and G. Lernout (New York, 1995), 53–65. Similarly, for Peter Bürger, *Das Altern der Moderne: Schriften zur bildenden Kunst* (Frankfurt a/M, 2001), and *Theorie der Avantgarde* (3d rev. ed., Frankfurt a/M, 1981), the "critical gap" between modernism and modernity is the ultimate measure for distinguishing between true (radical, oppositional) and false (conformist) modernism.

27. See, e.g., Michel Foucault, "Space, Knowledge and Power" in *Rethinking Architecture: A Reader in Cultural Theory*, ed. Neil Leach (London, 1997), 367–79. Foucault's *Discipline and Punish: The Birth of the Prison* (New York, 1995) is a classic case study.

28. Michel Foucault, "Governmentality," in *The Foucault Effect: Studies in Governmentality*, ed. Graham Burchell, Colin Gordon, and Peter Miller (Chicago, 1991), 87–104.

29. Chris Otter "Making Liberalism Durable: Vision and Civility in the Late Victorian City," *Social History* 27, 1 (January 2002): 1–15, quotation from 3.

30. A seminal example is Patrick Joyce, *The Rule of Freedom: Liberalism and the Modern City* (New York, 2003).

31. Patrick Joyce "The Return of History: Postmodernism and the Politics of Academic History in Britain," *Past and Present*, no. 158 (February 1998): 207–35. Fritz Stern's warnings have lost none of their pertinence over the years.

32. Michel Foucault, *Naissance de la clinique: Une Archéologie du regard médical* (Paris, 1963), trans. A. M. Sheridan Smith as *The Birth of the Clinic: An Archeology of Medical Perception* (1973; London, 1973).

33. The most extreme version of this skepticism is Richard Evans, *In Defence of History* (London, 1997), which links postmodernism to Holocaust denial. A useful genealogy of Evans's own methodological trajectory is provided in the introduction to his *Rethinking German History: Nineteenth-Century Germany and the Origins of the Third Reich* (London, 1987).

34. See, e.g., T. J. Jackson Lears, *No Place of Grace: Antimodernism and the Transformation of American Culture, 1880–1920* (Chicago, 1983). A similar tendency, albeit with a more critical twist, characterized the recent exhibition project that led to the publication of *Die Lebensreform: Entwürfe zur Neugestaltung von Leben und Kunst um 1900*, ed. Kai Buchholz, Rita Latocha, Hilke Peckmann, and Klaus Wolbert, 2 vols. (Darmstadt, 2001).

35. The literature on the relationship between local, regional and national languages in relation to English as the language of globalization is growing rapidly. It is also divided by dramatic conceptual rifts, for example between functional approaches, as exemplified by David Crystal, and critical approaches centered on the notion of cultural imperialism, as in the writings of Robert Phillipson. For useful surveys of these, see Ian Buruma, "The Road to Babel," *New York Review of Books,* May 2001, 23–26, and *Globalization and the Future of German*, ed. Andreas Gardt and Bernd Hüppauf (New York, 2004).

36. See, e.g., David Harvey, *The Condition of Postmodernity: An Enquiry into the Origins of Cultural Change* (Oxford, 1989), and David Ley, "Modernism, Postmodernism and the Struggle for Place," in *The Power of Place*, ed. John A. Agnew and James S. Duncan (Winchester, Mass., 1989), 44–65.

37. An outstanding example of this genre is Dipesh Chakrabarty, *Provincializing Europe: Postcolonial Thought and Historical Difference* (Princeton, 2000).

38. *Transactions, Transgressions, Transformations: American Culture in Western Europe and Japan*, ed. Heide Fehrenbach and Ute Poiger (New York, 2000), xxxvi. Cf. also *Consuming Tradition, Manufacturing Heritage: Global Norms and Urban Forms in the Age of Tourism*, ed. Nezar Alsayyad (London, 2001).

39. Cf. John Brinckerhoff Jackson, *Discovering the Vernacular Landscape* (New Haven, 1984).

40. The centrality of globalization to political debates of the later nineteenth century is discussed by Carl Strickwerda, "The World at the Crossroads: The World Economy and International Relations in Two Eras of Globalization, 1890–1914 and 1989 to the Present" (working paper, University of Kansas); Hans Pohl, *Aufbruch der Weltwirtschaft: Geschichte der Weltwirtschaft von der Mitte des 19. Jahrhunderts bis zum Ersten Weltkrieg* (Stuttgart, 1989); and Maiken Umbach, "Made in Germany," in *Deutsche Erinnerungsorte*, ed. Hagen Schulze and Etienne François, vol. 2 (Munich, 2001).

41. For an example of a leftist critique of the pervasiveness of the *Heimat* ideal in German culture, leading to "borders of exclusions," see Peter Blickle, *Heimat: A Critical Theory of the German Idea of Homeland* (Rochester, N.Y., 2002). David Midgley, "Los von Berlin! Anti-Urbanism as Counter-Culture in Early Twentieth-Century Germany," in *Counter-Cultures in Germany and Central Europe: From Sturm und Drang to Baader-Meinhof*, ed. Steve Giles and Maike Oergel (Oxford, 2003), 121–36, interrogates the alleged association between the *Heimat* movement and the political right, recovering some of its less obvious progressive potentials without whitewashing the history of this problematic ideal.

42. N. Bormann, *Paul Schultze Naumburg, 1869–1949: Maler, Publizist, Architekt, vom Kulturreformer der Jahrhundertwende zum Kulturpolitiker im Dritten Reich* (Essen, 1989).

43. The *Sonderweg* concept, which inspired an enormous debate in its own time, has been irrevocably refuted by Geoff Eley and David Blackbourn's seminal study *The Peculiarities of German History* (Oxford, 1984). This had profound implications for many fields of historical research. In regard to the German concept of *Heimat*, it enabled the emergence of a range of anti-teleological reappraisals, the most important of which are William R. Rollins, *A Greener Vision of Home: Cultural Politics and Environmental Reform in the German Heimatschutz Movement, 1904–1918* (Ann Arbor, Mich., 1997), and Jennifer Jenkins, *Provincial Modernity: Local Culture and Liberal Politics in Fin-de-Siècle Hamburg* (Ithaca, N.Y., 2003).

44. D. Kramer, "Die politische und ökonomische Funktionalisierung von Heimat im deutschen Imperialismus und Faschismus," *Diskurs* 6–7 (1973): 3–22, and D. von Reeken, *Heimatbewegung, Kulturpolitik und Nationalsozialismus: Die Geschichte der "Ostfriesischen Landschaft," 1918–1949* (Aurich, Germany, 1995); J. A. Williams, "The Chords of the German Soul Are Tuned to Nature: The Movement

to Preserve the Natural Heimat from Kaiserreich to the Third Reich," *Central European History* 29, 3 (1996): 339–84. Specifically on the role of *Heimat* in National Socialism, see Otto Thomae, *Die Propaganda-Maschinerie: Bildende Kunst und Öffentlichkeitsarbeit im Dritten Reich* (Berlin, 1978).

45. Michael Hardt and Antonio Negri, *Empire* (Cambridge, Mass., 2000); see also Manuel Castells, *The Information Age. Society and Culture*, 3 vols. (Oxford, 1996–98).

46. Foucault, *Discipline and Punish*.

47. Celia Applegate, *A Nation of Provincials: The German Idea of Heimat* (Berkeley, 1990).

48. The most important examples of this rapidly expanding new literature are Alon Confino, *The Nation as a Local Metaphor: Württemberg, Imperial Germany and National Memory, 1871–1918* (Chapel Hill, N.C., 1997); Jenkins, *Provincial Modernity*; Georg Kunz, *Verortete Geschichte: Regionales Geschichtsbewusstsein in den deutschen Historischen Vereinen des neunzehnten Jahrhunderts* (Göttingen, 2000); Arjun Appadurai, *Modernity at Large: Cultural Dimensions of Globalization* (Minneapolis, 1996), esp. section on "The Production of Locality," 178–99.

49. Nikolaus Pevsner, *Pioneers of Modern Design: From William Morris to Walter Gropius* (1949; rev ed., Harmondsworth, U.K., 1975).

50. Elizabeth Boa and Rachel Palfreyman, *Heimat: A German Dream: Regional Loyalties and National Identity in German Culture, 1890–1990* (Oxford, 2000), point out that *Heimat* is increasingly used in the English language, too. For an example of such a transfer to the American context, see Bert Lachner, *Heimat North America: English and German* (Glen Ellyn, Ill., 1997).

51. Bertrand A. Goldgar, *Walpole and the Wits: The Relation of Politics to Literature, 1722–1742* (Lincoln, Neb., 1976).

52. The literature on the politics of the English garden is vast, so only a few crucial studies can be cited here. On Stowe and Chiswick, see G. B. Clarke, "Grecian Taste and Gothic virtue: Lord Cobham's Gardening Programme and Its Iconography," *Apollo* 97 (June 1973): 566–71, and Richard Hewlings, "Chiswick House and Gardens: Appearance and Meaning," in *Lord Burlington. Art, Architecture and Life*, ed. T. Barnard and J. Clark (London, 1995), 1–149. Exemplary studies on the use of this model in American and European Enlightenment culture are Malcolm Kelsall, "Vitruvian Man and the Iconography of the Opposition: Lord Burlington's Chiswick and Jefferson's Monticello," *British Journal for Eighteenth-Century Studies* 18, 1 (Spring 1995): 1–17, and Maiken Umbach, *Federalism and Enlightenment in Germany, 1740–1806* (Rio Grande, Ohio, 2000).

53. The phrase "Satanic mills" from William Blake's famous anthem "Jerusalem" was later adopted by Karl Marx and became part of the anti-modernist paradox in socialist thought.

54. An excellent introduction to the "modernist" faction arising from the English Arts and Crafts movement, who used the London Underground to propagate their design ideas, is Michael T. Saler, *The Avant-Garde in Interwar England* (Oxford, 1999).

55. Schumacher's work was famously "rediscovered" by the pioneering work of Vittorio Magnago Lampugnani and Romana Schneider in their edited volume

Moderne Architektur in Deutschland 1900 bis 1950: Reform und Tradition (Stuttgart, 1992); see also *Fritz Schumacher: Reformkultur und Moderne,* ed. Hartmut Frank (Stuttgart, 1994). It was recently discussed as a part of a seminal study on the role of vernacular motifs in modern art by Jenkins, *Provincial Modernity,* esp. 261–93.

56. Ernst Bloch, *Das Prinzip Hoffnung,* 3 vols. (1954; Frankfurt a/M, 1959); trans. Neville Plaice, Stephen Plaice, and Paul Knight as *The Principle of Hope,* 3 vols. (Cambridge, Mass., 1986).

57. Theodor W. Adorno, "Blochs Spuren," in id., *Noten zur Literatur,* vol. 2 (Frankfurt a/M, 1961), 131.

58. Among the popular authors of this aspect of Jewish renaissance in the early twentieth century were Scholem Alejchem and Shalom Ash.

59. *New Heimat,* exhibition catalogue, ed. Karl-Heinz Kohl and Nikolaus Schaffhausen (New York, 2001).

60. Gilles Deleuze and Felix Guattari, *Anti-Oedipus: Capitalism and Schizophrenia* (Minneapolis, 1983).

61. Stephen Toulmin, *Cosmopolis: The Hidden Agenda of Modernity* (New York, 1990).

62. Robert B. Pippin, *Modernism as a Philosophical Problem: On the Dissatisfactions of European High Culture* (2d ed., Oxford, 1999).

63. The term is borrowed from cultural historian Wilhelm Heinrich Riehl, who pioneered an ethnographic approach to history. See Riehl, *Die bürgerliche Gesellschaft* (Stuttgart, 1853), and id., *Land und Leute* (Stuttgart, 1855), 132–217.

64. Bloch, *Prinzip Hoffnung,* vol. 1: 19.

65. The term "critical regionalism" was originally coined by the architectural theorists Alexander Tzonis and Liane Lefaivre, in *Tropical Architecture: Critical Regionalism in the Age of Globalization,* ed. Alexander Tzonis, Liane Lefaivre, and Bruno Stagno (New York: Wiley-Academic, 2001), but it is more prominently associated with Kenneth Frampton's writings, such as "Towards a Critical Regionalism: Six Points for an Architecture of Resistance," in *Postmodern Culture,* ed. H. Foster (London, 1985), 16–30, and "Critical Regionalism: Modern Architecture and Cultural Identity," in id., *Modern Architecture: A Critical History* (rev ed., London, 1992), 314–27. Frampton's paradigm has since inspired several, at times critical, investigations into contemporary architectural regionalisms, such as a dedicated special issue on "Critical Regionalism" in *Arcade: The Journal for Architecture and Design in the Northwest* 16, no. 4 (1998).

66. Frederic Jameson, *The Seeds of Time* (New York, 1994).

1. Bacon: Modernism and the Vernacular at the Museum of Modern Art, New York

1. This chapter is a revised version of a paper I presented at the Ninth Annual Deerfield-Wellesley Symposium in American Culture, "The Past in the Present: How Museums Interpret History," November 1, 2002. I wish to thank the symposium organizers, Jessica Neuwirth and James F. O'Gorman, and Francesco Passanti, Maiken Umbach, and Philip Walsh for their critical reading of a draft of the manuscript. Their insights and suggestions have strengthened this essay.

2. For an analysis of the culture of the "present" in the formation of modernism, see William H. Jordy, "The Symbolic Essence of Modern European Architecture of the Twenties and Its Continuing Influence," *Journal of the Society of Architectural Historians* 22 (October 1963): 177–87.

3. The Museum of Modern Art first exhibited Demuth's *My Egypt* in 1929 at the exhibition "Paintings by Nineteen Living Americans." Alfred H. Barr Jr., *Paintings by Nineteen Living Americans* (New York: Museum of Modern Art, 1929), 17, 19, cat. no. 13. The Modern first exhibited Shahn's work in 1930 at "An Exhibition of Work of 46 Painters and Sculptors under 35 Years of Age." See Alfred H. Barr Jr., *An Exhibition of Work of 46 Painters and Sculptors under 35 Years of Age* (New York: Museum of Modern Art, 1930), 10. In 1932, the Modern exhibited a large panel (oil and tempera on canvas) of *The Passion of Sacco and Vanzetti* at its exhibition "Murals by American Painters and Photographers." *Murals by American Painters and Photographers* (New York: Museum of Modern Art, 1932), n.p.

4. A model and a photograph of the Villa Savoye and a photograph of the de Mandrot House were featured in the Le Corbusier section of the "Modern Architecture: International Exhibition" in 1932. See *Modern Architecture: International Exhibition* (New York: Museum of Modern Art, 1932), 87–88. These works were included in Le Corbusier's solo exhibition at the Modern in 1935, "The Recent Work of Le Corbusier." See Henry-Russell Hitchcock Jr., *Le Corbusier*, "Exhibition Arranged by the Department of Architecture of The Museum of Modern Art" (New York: Museum of Modern Art, 1935), n.p. On the importance of folk and vernacular influences in the work of Le Corbusier, see Chapter 5 in this volume.

5. Paul Sachs, "Address at Tenth Anniversary Ceremonies," May 1939, as quoted in Helaine Ruth Messer, "MOMA: Museum in Search on an Image" (Ph.D. diss., Columbia University, 1979), 4.

6. *Journal of the Meetings of the Board of Regents of the University of the State of New York* (Albany: University of the State of New York, 1929), 464–65. In 1931, an "absolute charter" replaced its provisional one. See *Journal of the Meetings of the Board of Regents of the University of the State of New York* (Albany: University of the State of New York, 1931), 160.

7. Alfred H. Barr Jr., "Why the Museum of Modern Art was Founded," in *The Museum of Modern Art, New York* (undated report, submitted at the meeting of the Board of Trustees of the Museum of Modern Art on November 12, 1936), 4 (Rockefeller Family archives, R.G. 2, OMR, Cultural Interests, box 22, Rockefeller Archive Center). See also Alfred H. Barr Jr., "Modern & 'Modern,'" *Art Digest* 8 (August 1, 1934): 6, reprinted in id., *Defining Modern Art: Selected Writings of Alfred H. Barr, Jr.*, ed. Irving Sandler and Amy Newman (New York: Abrams, 1986), 82–83.

8. For an analysis of the institution's political structure, see Messer, "MOMA: Museum in Search on an Image."

9. Barr endorsed the view of Henri Verne, director of the National Museums of France: "In that mutual understanding and appreciation which are achieved with such difficulty by modern democracies mutual knowledge and mutual respect are essential. The intelligent appreciation of the art of each can contribute to this spirit. Art teaches us not to love, through false pride and ignorance, exclusively that which

resembles us. It teaches us rather to love, by a great effort of intelligence and sensibility, that which is different from us." See Barr, "Why the Museum of Modern Art Was Founded."

10. Abby Aldrich Rockefeller was the wife of John D. Rockefeller Jr., whose family fortune derived from the Standard Oil Company. Unmarried, Lillie (Lizzie) Bliss was the daughter of a textile manufacturer and merchant. Mary Sullivan was the wife of Cornelius J. Sullivan, a lawyer who collected rare books and paintings. See Russell Lynes, *Good Old Modern: An Intimate Portrait of the Museum of Modern Art* (New York: Atheneum, 1973), 3–18; Alfred H. Barr Jr., *Painting and Sculpture in the Museum of Modern Art, 1929–1967* (New York: Museum of Modern Art, 1977), 620–21; Messer, "MOMA: Museum in Search of an Image"; Sam Hunter, "Introduction," in *The Museum of Modern Art, New York* (New York: Museum of Modern Art, 1984), 9–12; Sybil Gordon Kantor, *Alfred H. Barr, Jr., and the Intellectual Origins of the Museum of Modern Art* (Cambridge, Mass.: MIT Press, 2002), 190–95. See also *New Criterion* (Summer 1987), special issue devoted to Alfred H. Barr Jr. and the Museum of Modern Art; Aline B. Saarinen, *The Proud Possessors* (New York: Museum of Modern Art, 1958), 344–95.

11. Holger Cahill, "The Reminiscences of Holger Cahill" (transcript of interviews conducted by the Oral History Research Office of Columbia University, 1957), 194 (hereafter cited as Cahill interviews).

12. Rockefeller was especially drawn to contemporary American art because she felt that it held more meaning for young audiences than other forms of art. See Lynes, *Good Old Modern*, 5; Bernice Kert, *Abby Aldrich Rockefeller: The Woman in the Family* (New York: Random House, 1993), 139, 186, 217, 220, 255, 274–75, 297–98, 322–23; Kantor, *Alfred H. Barr, Jr.*, 191–97.

13. Lynes, *Good Old Modern*, 6–8, 49–50, 168. On the Bliss collection and the terms of the bequest, see Alfred H. Barr Jr., *The Lillie Bliss Collection* (New York: Museum of Modern Art, 1934), and Barr, *Painting and Sculpture in the Museum of Modern Art, 1929–1967*, 621.

14. For Barr's wide-ranging view of modernism and the traditions that shaped the early history of the institution, as well as his appointment as instructor at Harvard, see Kantor, *Alfred H. Barr, Jr.*, 51, 61.

15. On Barr's formalism, see Kantor, *Alfred H. Barr, Jr.*, xix, xxi, 38, 42–43, 77–80, 141, 328, 330, 335.

16. According to Kantor, Barr was listed as a seminar participant but not registered in the course. He was then an instructor. See *Alfred H. Barr, Jr.*, 61.

17. Lincoln Kirstein, Edward M. M. Warburg, and John Walker III, three Harvard undergraduates, founded the Harvard Society for Contemporary Art in December 1928. Paul Sachs served on its board of trustees, as did Edward Forbes, director of the Fogg Art Museum. In the fall of 1927, the first issue of *Hound & Horn* appeared. Although the journal and the organization were separate enterprises, they shared much of the same leadership, including Kirstein, who governed both—intellectually as well as financially. Nicholas Fox Weber, *Patron Saints* (New York: Alfred A. Knopf, 1992), 3–132; Kantor, *Alfred H. Barr, Jr.*, 140–45. See also Lincoln Kirstein, *Mosaic: Memoirs* (New York: Farrar, Straus, and Giroux, 1994), 101–12, 159–86.

18. Lynes, *Good Old Modern*, 24; Kantor, *Alfred H. Barr, Jr.*, 197–210, 415n25.

19. As a Princeton student, Barr visited the Metropolitan's exhibition of modern French painting in 1921. Kantor, *Alfred H. Barr, Jr.*, 30, 108. In the belief that the Metropolitan Museum of Art should encourage applied arts, it brought modernism to public attention in 1917 with a series of exhibitions entitled "Art in Industry." Its subsequent exhibitions "The Architect and the Industrial Arts" in 1929 and "Contemporary American Industrial Art" in 1934 brought new commercially available design to public attention. See Robert A. M. Stern, Gregory Gilmartin, and Thomas Mellins, *New York 1930* (New York: Rizzoli, 1987), 338–41, 345, 350–52.

20. Barr, "Why the Museum of Modern Art Was Founded," 4. On the European perception of America, associated with the concept of *américanisme*, see *Américanisme et modernité*, ed. J.-L. Cohen and H. Damisch (Paris: EHESS and Flammarion, 1993); Jean-Louis Cohen, *Scenes of the World to Come: European Architecture and the American Challenge, 1893–1960* (Paris and Montréal: Flammarion and Canadian Centre for Architecture, 1995); and Mardges Bacon, *Le Corbusier in America: Travels in the Land of the Timid* (Cambridge, Mass.: MIT Press, 2001), xiii–xviii, 6.

21. [Alan Blackburn] "Present Status and Future Direction of the Museum of Modern Art: Confidential Report to the Executive Committee" (1933), 2–6 (Rockefeller Family archives, R.G. 2 OMR, Cultural Interests, box 20, folder 197, Rockefeller Archive Center).

22. On modernism as an open-ended concept, see Marshall Berman, *All That Is Solid Melts into Air* (New York: Penguin Books, 1982).

23. Quoted in Barr, *Painting and Sculpture in the Museum of Modern Art, 1929–1967*, 622; see Kirk Varnedoe, "The Evolving Torpedo: Changing Ideas of the Collection of Painting and Sculpture of The Museum of Modern Art," in *The Museum of Modern Art at Mid-Century: Continuity and Change* (New York: Museum of Modern Art, 1995), 20; see also Kantor, *Alfred H. Barr, Jr.*, 366–67.

24. Alfred H. Barr Jr., *First Loan Exhibition: Cézanne, Gauguin, Seurat, van Gogh* (New York: Museum of Modern Art, 1929).

25. Alfred H. Barr Jr., "Foreword," in id., *Paintings by Nineteen Living Americans*, 9–10. The Modern distinguished its shows of contemporary art from Whitney's annual exhibitions because it allowed each artist to be represented by several canvases, rather than just one. Patterson Sims, *Whitney Museum of American Art: Selected Works from the Permanent Collection* (New York: Whitney Museum of Modern Art, 1985), 11. For a brief history of Gertrude Vanderbilt Whitney's exhibitions in her Studio Building on Eighth Street from 1904 and the Whitney Studio Club from 1914, see Juliana R. Force, "Foreword," and Hermon More, "Introduction," in *Whitney Museum of American Art: Catalogue of the Collection* (New York: Whitney Museum of Modern Art, 1931), 7–9; Lynes, *Good Old Modern*, 69.

26. Barr, "Foreword," in id., *Paintings by Nineteen Living Americans*; "New Museum Names 19 Artists for Exhibition," *Herald Tribune* (December 11, 1929), 9–103; "The Art Galleries: Nineteen Who Are Living," *New Yorker* 5 (December 21, 1929), 72. Museum of Modern Art Archives, New York: Public Information Scrapbooks, Museum of Modern Art, New York, reel 5055, frame 89 (Archives of American Art, Smithsonian Institution).

27. Patricia Hills, *Modern Art in the USA: Issues and Controversies of the 20th Century* (Upper Saddle River, N.J.: Prentice Hall, 2001), 177–78.

28. Barr, *Paintings by Nineteen Living Americans*; Terence Dewsnap, "Paintings by Nineteen Living Americans," in *Nineteen Americans: A Tribute to Alfred H. Barr, Jr.* (New York: Forum Gallery, 1990), 10–18.

29. "The Art Galleries: Nineteen Who Are Living," 72. The Whitney Museum of American Art acquired Demuth's *My Egypt* in 1931. See Sims, *Whitney Museum of American Art: Selected Works from the Permanent Collection*, 61.

30. Alfred H. Barr Jr., *Painting in Paris from American Collections* (New York: Museum of Modern Art, 1930), 31–32, cat. no. 47 .

31. Alfred H. Barr Jr., *Cubism and Abstract Art* (New York: Museum of Modern Art, 1936).

32. On Barr's use of charts and diagrams, see Kantor, *Alfred H. Barr, Jr.*, 21–26, 325–28, 334, 366–67. On the use of the diagram in architectural publications and the discursive relationships that it promoted within the discipline of architecture, see Hyungmin Pai, *The Portfolio and the Diagram: Architecture, Discourse, and Modernity in America* (Cambridge, Mass.: MIT Press, 2002).

33. Barr, *An Exhibition of Work of 46 Painters and Sculptors under 35 Years of Age*.

34. On modernism as a shared language, see Berman, *All That Is Solid Melts into Air*, 161–62.

35. For an analysis of the distinctions between popular (and academic) and folk in material culture, see Henry Glassie, *Pattern in the Material Folk Culture of the Eastern United States* (Philadelphia: University of Pennsylvania Press, 1968), 33.

36. Alfred H. Barr Jr., "Introduction," in *Paintings from the Museum of Modern Art* (New York: The Metropolitan Museum of Art, 1956), n.p., as quoted by Irving Sandler, "Introduction" in Barr, *Defining Modern Art*, ed. Sandler and Newman, 13, 245 n29.

37. Lincoln Kirstein, "A Memoir: The Education," *Raritan* 2 (Winter 1983): 45, as quoted in Kantor, *Alfred H. Barr, Jr.*, 234, 425n181.

38. As Kantor suggests, the "founding fathers at Princeton hoped that aesthetic considerations would play an important role in the design of objects of everyday life." See *Alfred H. Barr, Jr.*, 34. On Morey's influence on Barr's understanding of style, see Kantor, *Alfred H. Barr, Jr.*, 20–21; see also Sandler, "Introduction" in Barr, *Defining Modern Art*, ed. Sandler and Newman, 8

39. Alfred H. Barr Jr., "A Modern Art Questionnaire," *Vanity Fair* (August 1927), reprinted in Barr, *Defining Modern Art*, ed. Sandler and Newman, 56–61.

40. On Barr's 1927–28 tour, see Rona Roob, "Alfred H. Barr, Jr.: A Chronicle of the Years 1902–1929," *New Criterion* (Summer 1987), special issue devoted to Alfred H. Barr Jr., and the Museum of Modern Art, 13–16 (hereafter cited as "Barr Chronicle"); see also Kantor, *Alfred H. Barr, Jr.*, 146–86.

41. Roob documents a visit by Barr to the Weißenhofsiedlung in Stuttgart in March 1928, but Barr later recalled to Hitchcock that he had not visited it until 1933. See Roob, "Barr Chronicle," 16; Henry Russel [*sic*] Hitchcock, "Le Corbusier and the United States," *Zodiac* 16 (1966): 9.

42. Kantor, *Alfred H. Barr, Jr.*, 155.

43. Barr's diary records his meetings with El Lissitzky, Rodchenko, Ginzburg, Tatlin, and Tretyakov, among others, see Barr, "Russian Diary 1927–28," *October* 7 (Winter 1978): 7–50, reprinted in id., *Defining Modern Art*, ed. Sandler and Newman, 103–37.

44. Barr, "Russian Diary 1927–28," 46, reprinted in id., *Defining Modern Art*, ed. Sandler and Newman, 133.

45. Kantor, *Alfred H. Barr, Jr.*, 237.

46. Alfred H. Barr Jr., "In 1930," in *Sixth Loan Exhibition, New York, May 1930: Winslow Homer, Albert P. Ryder, Thomas Eakins*, with essays by Frank Jewett Mather Jr., Bryson Burroughs, and Lloyd Goodrich (New York: Museum of Modern Art, 1930), 6–7.

47. Alfred H. Barr Jr., *A Brief Survey of Modern Painting* (New York: Museum of Modern Art, 1934), 5. Lloyd Goodrich concurs with Barr. Goodrich records that Eakins studied under Jean-Léon Gérôme at the École des Beaux-Arts in Paris from 1866 to 1869, was introduced to the work of Ribera and Velasquez in Spain, and undoubtedly admired Rembrandt, but he concludes that "these were not so much influences as temperamental coincidences." Lloyd Goodrich, "Thomas Eakins," in *Sixth Loan Exhibition*, 18–19, 29.

48. In another essay, Barr denounced the "American imitation" of contemporary French painting. See Alfred H. Barr Jr., "Otto Dix," *Arts* 17 (January 1931): 251, reprinted in id., *Defining Modern Art*, ed. Sandler and Newman, 153.

49. Alfred H. Barr Jr., "Edward Hopper," *Edward Hopper Retrospective Exhibition* (New York: Museum of Modern Art, 1933), 12–15, cat. no. 24.

50. Alfred H. Barr Jr., *Painting and Sculpture in the Museum of Modern Art* (New York: Museum of Modern Art, 1942), quoted in Dorothy C. Miller, "Foreword and Acknowledgments," in *American Realists and Magic Realists*, ed. id. and Alfred H. Barr Jr. (New York: Museum of Modern Art, 1943), 5.

51. For the work of the Mexican sculptor Fides Elizando, the Spanish painter Francisco Borès, the Mexican painter Miguel Covarrubias, Hokeah, a painter identified as a "Kiowa Indian," and Oqwa Pi and Awa Tsireh, each called a "Pueblo Indian," see Barr, *Exhibition of Work of 46 Painters and Sculptors under 35 Years of Age*, 4, 7–11.

52. In Moscow, Barr purchased a charcoal drawing from Rivera. Barr, "Russian Diary 1927–28," 47, reprinted in id., *Defining Modern Art*, ed. Sandler and Newman, 134.

53. Frances Flynn Paine, *Diego Rivera* (New York: Museum of Modern Art, 1931).

54. See Alfred H. Barr Jr., biographical notes in *Painting and Sculpture from Sixteen American Cities* (New York: Museum of Modern Art, 1933), and id., *Exhibition of Work of 46 Painters and Sculptors under 35 Years of Age*. Horace Pippin exhibited four paintings in the 1938 exhibition. See Dorothy C. Miller, "Horace Pippin," in *Masters of Popular Painting: Modern Primitives of Europe and America* (New York: Museum of Modern Art, 1938), 125–26. See also Kantor, *Alfred H. Barr, Jr.*, xxi.

55. See, e.g., Meyer Schapiro, "Race, Nationality and Art," *Art Front* 2 (March 1936), 10–12; reprinted in Hills, *Modern Art in the USA*, 136–39.

56. *Second Annual Report, The Harvard Society for Contemporary Art* (1930–31), n.p.

57. For the two exhibitions scheduled for 1932–33, Barr recommended Lloyd Goodrich for the American show and Holger Cahill for the American primitive exhibition consisting of Rockefeller's collection, for which he had already prepared a

catalogue. Abby Aldrich Rockefeller, letter to Alfred H. Barr Jr., June 28, 1932. Alfred H. Barr Jr. Papers, Museum of Modern Art Archives, New York, reel 2164, frames 116–18 (Archives of American Art, Smithsonian Institution).

58. According to Russell Lynes, a "nerve specialist" recommended that Barr take a year of rest. See Lynes, *Good Old Modern*, 103; see also Kantor, *Alfred H. Barr, Jr.*, 155, 354–55.

59. Abby Aldrich Rockefeller recommended Cahill for the position. Cahill interviews, 214, 228. *Bulletin of the Museum of Modern Art* 1 (June 1933), n.p.

60. One additional work came from Cahill's collection. Cahill interviews, 216. Holger Cahill, *American Folk Art: The Art of the Common Man in America, 1750–1900* (New York: Museum of Modern Art, 1932); see also Kert, *Abby Aldrich Rockefeller*, 322–23.

61. See Holger Cahill, "American Resources in the Arts" (speech delivered at the John Dewey Eightieth Birthday Celebration, October 1939), reprinted in *Art for the Millions: Essays from the 1930s by Artists and Administrators of the WPA Federal Art Project*, ed. Francis V. O'Connor (Boston: New York Graphic Society, 1973), and Hills, *Modern Art in the USA*, 119–21. Cahill expressed similar thoughts in his catalogue for the Museum of Modern Art's exhibition "New Horizons in American Art" in 1936. Holger Cahill, *New Horizons in American Art* (New York: Museum of Modern Art, 1936), 9–41.

62. Paul Rosenfeld, "Art, Bread Lines and a Museum," *Nation* 132 (February 11, 1931): 160.

63. Roob, "Barr Chronicle," 17. The Roob transcription reads "erotic forms." Kantor amends this to read "exotic forms"; see *Alfred H. Barr, Jr.*, 189.

64. Barr, "Foreword," in *First Loan Exhibition: Cézanne, Gauguin, Seurat, van Gogh*, 11.

65. At Goodyear's insistence, Cahill in his catalogue essay qualified the claim suggested by the exhibition title: "There is no intention here to insist that ancient American art is a major source of modern art. Nor is it intended to suggest that American artists should turn to it as the source of native expression. It is intended, simply, to show the high quality of ancient American art, and to indicate that its influence is present in modern art in the work of painters and sculptors some of whom have been unconscious of its influence, while others have accepted or sought it quite consciously." Holger Cahill, *American Sources of Modern Art* (New York: Museum of Modern Art, 1933), 5. See Lynes, *Good Old Modern*, 107.

66. Cahill, *American Sources of Modern Art*, 6–8. According to Cahill, "the interest in the Aztec type, those heavy figures and all that sort of thing which you see in Rivera and others—they got that from Paris, you know. They didn't dig that up by themselves. The interest in that sort of thing, that originated in Paris and Munich and Dresden, affected them, and affected these American artists." Cahill interviews, 195.

67. Alfred H. Barr Jr., ed., *Modern Works of Art: Fifth Anniversary Exhibition* (New York: Museum of Modern Art, 1934), 19, cat. no. 167.

68. Cahill, *American Sources of Modern Art*, 30, 32, cat. nos. 21 and 41.

69. James Johnson Sweeney, "The Art of Negro Africa," in *African Negro Art*, ed. id. (New York: Museum of Modern Art, 1935), 11–21.

70. Alfred H. Barr Jr., *Prehistoric Rock Pictures in Europe and Africa: From material in the Archives of the Research Institute for the Morphology of Civilization, Frankfurt-on-Main* (New York: Museum of Modern Art, 1937).

71. Roob, "Barr Chronicle," 14. See also Kantor, *Alfred H. Barr, Jr.*, 155–61, and *Bauhaus, 1919–28*, ed. Herbert Bayer, Walter Gropius, and Ise Gropius (New York: Museum of Modern Art, 1938).

72. Alfred H. Barr Jr., "A New Art Museum" (1929), as quoted in Barr, *Painting and Sculpture in the Museum of Modern Art, 1929–1967*, 620.

73. Barr exhibited Kirchner's *The Street* in the 1931 exhibition "Modern German Painting and Sculpture." See Alfred H. Barr Jr., *Modern German Painting and Sculpture* (New York: Museum of Modern Art, 1931), 25–26, cat. no. 38. The Museum of Modern Art Film Library held screenings of *The Cabinet of Dr. Caligari*.

74. "The Founding of the Film Library," *Bulletin of the Museum of Modern Art* 3 (November 1935).

75. "Advance [exhibition] Schedule 1933–1934," *Bulletin of the Museum of Modern Art* 1 (October 1933); Philip Johnson, "History of Machine Art," and [Alfred H. Barr Jr.,] "Foreword," in *Machine Art* (New York: Museum of Modern Art, 1934); "Machine Art," *Bulletin of the Museum of Modern Art* 1 (November 1933), n.p.

76. Francesco Passanti offers this definition of *Sachlichkeit* in "The Vernacular, Modernism, and Le Corbusier," *Journal of the Society of Architectural Historians* 56 (December 1997): 442–45, 448–49n18. On *Sachlichkeit*, see esp. Stanford Anderson, "Introduction," in Hermann Muthesius, *Style-Architecture and Building-Art: Transformations of Architecture in the Nineteenth Century and Its Present Condition* (Santa Monica, Calif.: Getty Center for the History of Art and the Humanities, 1994), trans. Anderson, 5, 38n10.

77. These exhibitions included "Objects: 1900 and Today" (1933), "Useful Household Objects Under $5" (1938), and "Useful Objects of American Design Under $10" (1939).

78. William H. Jordy, "Four Approaches to Regionalism in the Visual Arts of the 1930s" in *The Study of American Culture: Contemporary Conflicts*, ed. Luther S. Luedtke (Deland, Fla.: Everett Edwards, 1977), 32.

79. Cahill identified Benton's painting "Aggression" (1920) in the catalogue for the 1932 exhibition as "one of five panels illustrating American history"; *American Painting and Sculpture, 1862–1932* (New York: Museum of Modern Art, 1932), 25, cat. no. 4; Barr, "Modern Works of Art," in *Modern Works of Art: Fifth Anniversary Exhibition*, ed. id., 16. In 1929, Barr included Thomas Benton's name on one of his working lists for the exhibition "Paintings by Nineteen Living Americans." See *Nineteen Americans: A Tribute to Alfred H. Barr, Jr.*, 17. In 1930, Barr invited Benton to show his work in the exhibition "Painting and Sculpture by Living Americans," but the artist declined because he was then engaged in mural painting; see Alfred H. Barr Jr., "Foreword," in *Painting and Sculpture by Living Americans* (New York: Museum of Modern Art, 1930), 5. In 1933, the Modern exhibited Grant Wood's painting *Woman with Plant (Portrait of the Artist's Mother)*; see Barr, *Painting and Sculpture from Sixteen American Cities* (New York: Museum of Modern Art, 1933), n.p., cat. no. 36. Benton's *Homestead* (1934) and Grant Wood's *Daughters of Revolution* (1932)

were exhibited in *Modern Works of Art: Fifth Anniversary Exhibition*, ed. id., 25–26, 34, cat. nos. 37, 153.

80. On the exhibition "Tennessee Valley Authority—Architecture and Design," see *Bulletin of the Museum of Modern Art* 8 (April–May 1941): 8–9. On TVA as an example of regional planning, see Jordy, "Four Approaches to Regionalism in the Visual Arts of the 1930s," 32–40.

81. Jordy, "Four Approaches to Regionalism in the Visual Arts of the 1930s," 35. See William Stott, *Documentary Expression and Thirties America* (New York: Oxford University Press, 1973).

82. The Modern's Film Library held screenings of John Ford's *The Grapes of Wrath*. By 1942, the museum had acquired ten or more prints of Dorothea Lange; see John Szarkowski, "Photography," in *The Museum of Modern Art, New York* (New York: Harry N. Abrams, 1984), 464.

83. Lincoln Kirstein donated the photographs on view in the Architecture Room, November 16, 1933, to January 1, 1934. See Lynes, *Good Old Modern*, 155–56; Lincoln Kirstein, "Walker Evans' Photographs of Victorian Architecture," *Bulletin of the Museum of Modern Art* 1 (December 1933), n.p. In 1938, the Modern held a second Evans exhibition, "Walker Evans: American Photographs."

84. On Barr's didactic wall texts, see Kantor, *Alfred H. Barr, Jr.*, 73, 188, 359. Barr, "Russian Diary 1927–28," 46, reprinted in id., *Defining Modern Art*, ed. Sandler and Newman, 133. Typically, Museum of Modern Art paperback catalogues sold for $1 or $2.

85. Alfred H. Barr Jr., "Foreword," in *Modern Architecture: International Exhibition*, 14–16. Jere Abbott, for example, employed the term "International Style" in his account of their trip to Russia in 1928; see "Notes from a Soviet Diary," *Hound & Horn* 2 (Spring 1929): 263. On the origin of the term "International Style," see Kantor, *Alfred H. Barr, Jr.*, 167, 292–93, 408n76, 439n65; see also Riley, *The International Style: Exhibition 15 and the Museum of Modern Art* (New York: Rizzoli, 1992), 89–93, and Henry-Russell Hitchcock Jr. and Philip Johnson, *The International Style: Architecture Since 1922* (New York: W. W. Norton, 1932).

86. Letter, Lewis Mumford to Frank Lloyd Wright, February 6, 1932; as quoted in Robert Wojtowicz, *Lewis Mumford and American Modernism* (New York: Cambridge University Press, 1996), 94, 181n91.

87. Barr, "Foreword," in *Modern Architecture: International Exhibition*, 15.

88. Lewis Mumford, letter to Catherine K. Bauer [Wurster], February 9, 1931, Mumford Papers, folder 6345; as quoted in Wojtowicz, *Lewis Mumford and American Modernism*, 92, 180n83.

89. Lewis Mumford, *Sticks and Stones: A Study of American Architecture and Civilization* (New York: Houghton Mifflin, 1924), and id., *The Brown Decades: A Study of the Arts in America, 1865–1895* (New York: Harcourt, Brace, 1931; 2d rev. ed., 1971).

90. [Henry-Russell Hitchcock Jr.,] *Exhibition of Early Modern Architecture, Chicago, 1870–1910* (New York: Museum of Modern Art, 1933; 2d rev. ed., 1940). The first edition of the catalogue was stenciled, which indicates a limited press run.

91. Hitchcock, *International Style: Architecture Since 1922*, 25; Henry-Russell Hitchcock Jr., "Henry Hobson Richardson: The Development of the Skyscraper,"

in *Art in America in Modern Times*, ed. Holger Cahill and Alfred H. Barr Jr. (New York: Reynal and Hitchcock, 1934), 63–67.

92. Henry-Russell Hitchcock Jr., *The Architecture of H. H. Richardson and His Times* (New York: Museum of Modern Art, 1936), 164.

93. For a more comprehensive analysis, see Bacon, *Le Corbusier in America*, 6–8.

94. Jere Abbott, "Four Photographs," *Hound & Horn* 1 (September 1927), opposite page 36.

95. Barr cited F. C. Lutze as "engineer and chief designer" of the Necco factory, who, he wrote, "has achieved architecture positively by manipulation of proportions and masses, and by the restrained use of handsomer materials than were structurally necessary; negatively by the utmost economy in decorative motive and by the frank acknowledgment of utilitarian necessity both in plan and elevation." His article also included a photograph by F. L. Fales. Alfred H. Barr Jr., "The Necco Factory," *Arts* 13 (May 1928): 292–95, reprinted in id., *Defining Modern Art*, ed. Sandler and Newman, 62–66.

96. Henry-Russell Hitchcock Jr., *The Urban Vernacular of the Thirties, Forties and Fifties: American Cities Before the Civil War* (Wesleyan University Architectural Exhibitions, 1934). In 1993, two former Wesleyan students remounted the exhibition, accompanied by a catalogue reproducing Abbott's photographs, which Hitchcock's abbreviated catalogue of 1934 had not. Janine A. Mileaf, *Constructing Modernism: Berenice Abbott and Henry-Russell Hitchcock* (Middletown, Conn.: Wesleyan University, 1993); see also my review essay, "Constructing Modernism: Berenice Abbott and Henry-Russell Hitchcock," Davison Art Center, Wesleyan University 28 October–10 December 1993, *Journal of the Society of Architectural Historians* 53 (June 1994): 232–34.

97. Hitchcock, *Urban Vernacular of the Thirties, Forties and Fifties*, 2, 7, 8.

98. Henry-Russell Hitchcock Jr., "The Architectural Future in America," *Architectural Review* 82 (July 1937): 2.

99. For an analysis of pastiche in Goodwin and Stone's design for the Museum of Modern Art, see Bacon, *Le Corbusier in America*, 284–87.

100. William H. Jordy, "The International Style in the 1930s," *Journal of the Society of Architectural Historians* 24 (March 1965): 10–14.

101. Barr and Abbott visited Sergei Tretyakov, a founder of the Russian journals *Lef* and *Novyi Lef*, in his apartment in the Dom Gostrak building. Alfred H. Barr Jr., "Notes on Russian Architecture," *Arts* 15 (February 1929): 105, pl. 105; Abbott, "Notes from a Soviet Diary," 263. See also Kantor, *Alfred H. Barr, Jr.*, 166–69.

102. Henry-Russell Hitchcock Jr., "Frank Lloyd Wright," in *Modern Architecture: International Exhibition*, 36. See also Henry-Russell Hitchcock Jr., "Wright and the International Style," in *Art in America in Modern Times*, ed. Cahill and Barr, 70–72.

103. Lewis Mumford, "Organic Architecture," in "The Sky Line," *New Yorker* 8 (February 27, 1932): 45–46.

104. John McAndrew, "Architecture in the United States," in *Trois siècles d'art aux États-Unis, Musée du Jeu de Paume, Paris* (Paris, 1938), 69–77. McAndrew published a revised version of the essay "Architecture in the United States" in *Bulletin of the Museum of Modern Art* 6 (February 1939): 1–12.

105. *Built in USA—1932–1944*, ed. Elizabeth Mock (New York: Museum of Modern Art, 1944), 13–14.

106. Henry-Russell Hitchcock Jr., "Richard J. Neutra," in *Modern Architecture: International Exhibition*, 158.

107. Alan R. Michelson, "William Wurster Chronology," in *An Everyday Modernism: The Houses of William Wurster*, ed. Marc Treib (Berkeley: University of California Press, 1995), 227.

108. John McAndrew, *A New House by Frank Lloyd Wright on Bear Run, Pennsylvania* (New York, 1938).

109. John McAndrew, "Foreword," in *Aalto: Architecture and Furniture* (New York: Museum of Modern Art, 1938), 5–6.

110. On the concept of critical regionalism, see Alexander Tzonis and Liane Lefaivre, "The Grid and the Pathway: An Introduction to the Work of Dimitris and Susana Antonakakis," *Architecture in Greece* no. 15 (1981): 164–78; Kenneth Frampton, "Prospects for a Critical Regionalism," in *Perspecta* 20 (1983): 147–62.

111. Carol Aronovici, "Housing and Architecture," *Bulletin of the Museum of Modern Art* 2 (October 1934): 2–3; G. Lyman Paine Jr., "Outline of the Exhibition of Slum Clearance and Low-Cost Housing of the City of New York," in *America Can't Have Housing*, ed. Carol Aronovici (New York: Museum of Modern Art, 1934), 75–78.

112. Catherine Bauer, "House and Cities," in *Art in America in Modern Times*, ed. Cahill and Barr, 80.

113. Frederick Gutheim and John McAndrew, "Houses and Housing," in *Art in Our Time: Tenth Anniversary Exhibition* (New York: Museum of Modern Art, 1939), 288–331.

114. McAndrew, "Architecture in the United States," in *Trois siècles*, 76–77; id., "Architecture in the United States," *Bulletin*, 11–12.

2. Saler: At Home in the Ironic Imagination

1. Max Weber, "Science as a Vocation," in *From Max Weber: Essays in Sociology*, ed. H. H. Gerth and C. Wright Mills (New York, 1958), 155; Max Weber, *The Protestant Ethic and the Spirit of Capitalism*, trans. Talcott Parsons (New York, 2001), 181.

2. Michel Surya, *Georges Bataille: An Intellectual Biography*, trans. Krzysztof Fijalkowski and Michael Richardson (New York, 2002), 515n23.

3. H. Stuart Hughes, *Consciousness and Society: The Reorientation of European Social Thought, 1890–1930* (New York, 1958); J. W. Burrow, *The Crisis of Reason: European Thought, 1848–1914* (New Haven, 2000).

4. Recent studies have begun to explore interesting points of convergence that have been obscured by this discourse. See, e.g., Edward A. Tiryakian, "Dialectics of Modernity: Reenchantment and Dedifferentiation as Counterprocesses," in *Social Change and Modernity*, ed. Hans Haferkamp and Neil J. Smelser (Berkeley, 1992), 78–93; James Cook, *The Arts of Deception: Playing with Fraud in the Age of Barnum* (Cambridge, Mass., 2001); Simon During, *Modern Enchantments: The Cultural Power of Secular Magic* (Cambridge, Mass., 2002). For a similar point of view dis-

cussed in terms of contemporary political theory, see Jane Bennett, *The Enchantment of Modern Life: Attachments, Crossings, and Ethics* (Princeton, 2001).

5. I am adopting this term from the title of a contemporary review of Haggard's *She*: Augustus Moore, "Rider Haggard and 'The New School of Romance,'" *Time,* May 1887, 513–24.

6. The phrase "secondary worlds" is taken from J. R. R. Tolkien's discussion of fantasy literature, as discussed later in this chapter.

7. Roland Barthes, *The Rustle of Language*, trans. Richard Howard (New York, 1986), 141–48.

8. Richard Rorty, *Times Literary Supplement,* December 3, 1999, 11.

9. S. T. Coleridge, *Biographia Literaria*, ed. J. Shawcross, 2 vols. (Oxford, 1967), 6.

10. Concepts that have a family resemblance to the "ironic imagination" have been adumbrated by Neil Harris as the "operational aesthetic," James Cook as "artful deception," Joshua Landy as "Lucid Self-Delusion," and Simon During as both "secular magic" and the "magical assemblage." See Neil Harris, *Humbug: The Life of P. T. Barnum* (Boston, 1973); Cook, *Arts of Deception*; Joshua Landy, "The Cruel Gift: Lucid Self-Delusion in French Literature and German Philosophy, 1851–1914" (Ph.D. diss., Dept. of Comparative Literature, Princeton University, 1997); Simon During, *Modern Enchantments: The Cultural Power of Secular Magic* (Cambridge, Mass., 2002).

11. Michael North, *Reading 1922: A Return to the Scene of the Modern* (New York, 1999), 206; 208.

12. For a consideration of the spectrum of metafictions, see Robert Alter, *Partial Magic: The Novel as a Self-Conscious Genre* (Berkeley, 1975).

13. Dan Clore, "Fake *Necronomicons*," www.geocities.com/SoHo/9879/necfake.htm (accessed February 11, 2005). See also his "The Lurker on the Threshold of Interpretation: Hoax *Necronomicons* and Paratextual Noise," www.geocities.com/SoHo/9879/lurker.htm (accessed February 11, 2005).

14. It is true that the "romantic irony" expressed by Fichte and some other romantic writers in the early nineteenth century shared a similar concern for human finitude and contingency, but this was nevertheless cast within an overarching metaphysical framework. See Anne K. Mellor, *English Romantic Irony* (Cambridge, Mass., 1980).

15. See Richard D. Altick, *The English Common Reader: A Social History of the Mass Reading Public, 1800–1900* (Chicago, 1957), 99–140; Patrick Brantlinger, *The Reading Lesson: The Threat of Mass Literacy in Nineteenth-Century British Fiction* (Bloomington, Ind., 1998), 1–2.

16. For interesting explorations of brief vogues for fictional characters in the eighteenth and nineteenth centuries, see James Grantham Turner, "Novel Panic: Picture and Performance in the Reception of Richardson's *Pamela*," *Representations* 48 (Fall, 1994): 70–96; Peter Bailey, "Ally Sloper's Half-Holiday: Comic Art in the 1880's," in id., *Popular Culture and Performance in the Victorian City* (Cambridge, 1998), 47–79; and A. O. Scott, "A Hunger for Fantasy, an Empire to Feed It," *New York Times,* June 16, 2001, §2, 26.

17. Among the numerous monographic length "biographies" of Sherlock Holmes are T. S. Blakeney, *Sherlock Holmes: Fact or Fiction* (London, 1932); Vincent

Starrett, *The Private Life of Sherlock Holmes* (New York, 1933); and W. S. Baring-Gould, *Sherlock Holmes of Baker Street: A Life of the World's First Consulting Detective* (New York, 1962). Following the early example of Holmes scholarship, innumerable biographies and concordances have appeared devoted to fictional worlds and characters, from Doc Savage and Tarzan to *Star Trek* and *The X-Files.* Two useful surveys (themselves indicative of the twentieth-century interest in secondary worlds of the imagination) are Alberto Manguel and Gianni Guadalupi, *The Dictionary of Imaginary Places* (New York, 2000) and David Pringle, *Imaginary People: A Who's Who of Modern Fictional Characters* (New York, 1987).

18. Peter Bailey, "The Victorian Middle Class and the Problem of Leisure," in id., *Popular Culture and Performance,* 13–29.

19. Humphrey Carpenter, *Secret Gardens: The Golden Age of Children's Literature* (Boston, 1985).

20. Vanessa Schwartz, *Spectacular Realities: Early Mass Culture in Fin-de-siècle Paris* (Berkeley, 1998).

21. Cook, *Arts of Deception.*

22. Nicholas Daly *Modernism, Romance and the Fin de siècle: Popular Fiction and British Culture, 1880–1914* (Cambridge, 1999), 22–36, argues that late nineteenth-century romance should be seen as an attribute of modernism.

23. Quoted in Edward Salmon, *Juvenile Literature As It Is* (London, 1888), 105.

24. Symbolist poets did not necessarily conceive of their art as anti-modern or opposed to the findings of contemporary science, but they were critical of positivism and did not work within the rationalist worldview in the way that New Romance authors did. See Richard Candida Smith, *Mallarmé's Children: Symbolism and the Renewal of Experience* (Berkeley, 1999).

25. J. R. R. Tolkien, *Tree and Leaf* (Boston, 1989), 45, 49, 51.

26. Humphrey Carpenter, *J. R. R. Tolkien: A Biography* (Boston, 2000), 198–99.

27. "Welcome Faces in the Family Album," *Sunday Times* (London), July 15, 2001, $5, 9.

28. A. O. Scott, "A Hunger for Fantasy, and an Empire to Feed It," *New York Times,* June 16, 2002, $2, 1, 26.

29. Arjun Appadurai, *Modernity at Large: Cultural Dimensions of Globalization* (Minneapolis, 1997), 53–54.

30. Laura Chrisman, *Rereading the Imperial Romance: British Imperialism and South African Resistance in Haggard, Schreiner, and Plaatje* (Oxford, 2000); Wendy Katz, *Rider Haggard and the Fiction of Empire: A Critical Study of British Imperial Fiction* (Cambridge, 1987).

31. Daniel Karlin does offer an insightful interpretation of Haggard's use of humor and burlesque in *She.* Daniel Karlin, "Introduction," *She* (New York, 1991), vii–xxxi.

32. Robert Lindner, *The Fifty-Minute Hour: A Collection of True Psychoanalytic Tales* (1955; New York, 1966), 197–98.

33. The *OED,* for example, lists as meanings of "enchant": ". . . to hold spellbound; in a bad sense, to delude, befool," as well as to "delight, enrapture."

34. Ernst Bloch, *The Principle of Hope,* 3 vols., trans. Neville Plaice, Stephen Plaice, and Paul Knight (Cambridge, Mass., 1986), 1: 3.

35. Ernst Bloch, *Literary Essays* (Stanford, 1998), 169.

36. Anonymous [Andrew Lang], *He* (London, 1887), n.p.

37. Quoted in Peter Berresford Ellis, *H. Rider Haggard: A Voice from the Infinite* (London, 1978), 119.

38. Quoted in Morton Cohen, *Rider Haggard: His Life and Works* (London, 1960), 117.

39. Some critics have argued that the "New Romance" was a reaction against realism and return to the Gothic (e.g., Brantlinger, *Reading Lesson*, 171, 209). But, as Nicholas Daly notes in his rebuttal to this line of argument, this was not how contemporary critics envisaged the genre (Daly, *Modernism, Romance and the Fin de siècle,* 12), a finding my own research supports.

40. Anon., "The Fall of Fiction," *Fortnightly Review* 44 (September 1, 1888): 333.

41. Cohen,, 102, 116.

42. Anon., "Modern Men," *Scots Observer* (April 27, 1889): 631–32.

43. Anon., "The Old Saloon," *Contemporary Review*, February 1887, 303.

44. Andrew Lang, "Realism and Romance," *Contemporary Review* 52 (November 1887): 683.

45. Anon., "Modern Marvels," *Spectator*, October 17, 1885, 1365.

46. Anon., "The Fall of Fiction," *Fortnightly Review* 44 (September 1, 1888): 324–36.

47. H. Rider Haggard, *The Days of My Life* (London, 1926), 2: 90–91.

48. Robert Louis Stevenson, "A Gossip on Romance," in *The Lantern-Bearers and Other Essays* (New York, 1988), 179.

49. Cook, *Arts of Deception,* 17–19.

50. Harris, *Humbug,* 69–88.

51. Haggard, *Days,* 1: 242.

52. Richard Lancelyn Green, ed., *The Sherlock Holmes Letters* (Iowa: University of Iowa Press, 1987), 28.

53. Lang, "Realism and Romance," 689.

54. Neil Harris, "Iconography and Intellectual History: The Halftone Effect," in *Cultural Excursions: Marketing Appetites and Cultural Tastes in Modern America* (Chicago, 1990), 304–17.

55. Robert Louis Stevenson, "Treasure Island," in id., *My First Book* (London, 1897), 307–8.

56. Ibid., 308.

57. Harris, "Iconography and Intellectual History," 307.

58. Cohen, *Rider Haggard,* 91; Ellis, *H. Rider Haggard,* 112.

59. Haggard, *Days,* 1: 242.

60. For a discussion on how photography was used as evidence by the Victorians, see Jennifer Tucker, "Photography as Witness, Detective, and Imposter: Visual Representation in Victorian Science," in *Victorian Science in Context*, ed. Bernard Lightman (Chicago, 1997), 378–408.

61. Ellis, *H. Rider Haggard,* 108.

62. H. Rider Haggard, *She*, ed. Karlin, 3.

63. Ibid., 10.

64. Ellis, *H. Rider Haggard,* 109.

65. Anonymous [Andrew Lang], *He* (London, 1887), 15.

66. Ibid., 29.

67. Joseph M. Brown, *Astynanax* (New York, 1907), xi.

68. Arthur Conan Doyle, *The Annotated Lost World*, annotated by Roy Pilot and Alvin Rodin (Indianapolis, 1996), 252.

69. Rudyard Kipling, *With the Night Mail: A Story of 2000 A.D. (Together with Extracts from the Contemporary Magazine in Which It Appeared* (New York, 1909), 70.

70. Ibid., 39.

71. Ibid., n.p.

72. Arthur C. Clarke has noted that while science fiction should be technically accurate, "accuracy should not be too much of a fetish, for it is often the spirit rather than the letter that counts. Thus Verne's [novels] are still enjoyable, not only because Verne was a first-rate storyteller, but because he was imbued with the excitement of science and could communicate this to his readers." Arthur C. Clarke, *Greetings, Carbon-Based Bipeds! A Vision of the Twentieth Century as It Happened*, ed. Ian. T. Macauley (London, 2000), 247.

73. The "reading revolution" thesis and its critics is discussed in Stephen Colclough, "Recovering the Reader: Commonplace Books and Diaries as Sources of Reading Experience," *Publishing History* 44 (Fall 1998): 5–37.

74. Private correspondence from Mike Ashley, a historian of popular fiction magazines in America and Britain, August 29, 2002.

75. Quoted in Peter Berresford Ellis, *The Last Adventurer: The Life of Talbot Mundy, 1879–1940* (West Kingston, R.I., 1984), 160.

76. Quoted in *The Baker Street Reader: Cornerstone Writings About Sherlock Holmes*, ed. Phillip Shreffler (Westport, Conn., 1984), 5.

77. For one study on how a sense of community was established at the national level through a shared mass culture, see D. L. LeMahieu, *A Culture for Democracy* (New York, 1988).

78. Lindner, *Fifty-Minute Hour,* 200.

79. Ibid., 199.

80. Clarke, *Greetings, Carbon-Based Bipeds!* 248.

3. Hüppauf: Spaces of the Vernacular

1. See *Grosstadt: Soziologische Stichworte*, ed. Hartmut Häussermann (Opladen, 2002), s.v. "Urbanität."

2. See, e.g., Wolfgang Essbach, *Die Junghegelianer: Soziologie einer Intellektuellengruppe* (Munich, 1988), and id., "Radikalismus und Modernität bei Jünger und Bloch, Lukács und Schmitt," in *Intellektuellendiskurse in der Weimarer Republik*, ed. Manfred Gangel and Gérard Raulet (Frankfurt a/M, 1994), 145–59.

3. Dina Smith, "The Narrative Limits of the Global Guggenheim," *Mosaic*, 35, 4 (December 2002): 98.

4. Niklas Luhmann, *Die Gesellschaft der Gesellschaft* (Frankfurt a/M, 1997), 809.

5. It is equally correct to argue that globalization spells the end of any meaningful notion of space, because it destroys every boundary and renders the distinc-

tion between inside and outside meaningless. The literature on the subject is grow-
ing at an enormous pace. Among recent publications are Robert Went, "Globaliza-
tion in the Perspective of Imperialism," *Science and Society* 66, 4 (2002–3): 473–97;
David Harvey, *Spaces of Capita: Towards a Critical Geography* (New York, 2001);
James Petras and Henry Veltmeyer, *Globalization Unmasked: Imperialism in the 21st
Century* (London, 2001); and Saskia Sassen, *Globalization and Its Discontents* (New
York, 1998). Niklas Luhmann, "Temporalisierung von Komplexität: Zur Semantik
neuzeitlicher Zeitbegriffe," in id., *Gesellschaftsstruktur und Semantik: Studien zur
Wissenssoziologie der modernen Gesellschaft* (Frankfurt a/M, 1993), 235–300, offers a
theoretically elaborated discussion of temporality as the prime category of moder-
nity.

6. Celia Applegate, *A Nation of Provincials: The German Idea of Heimat* (Berkeley, 1990), was among the first to liberate the notion of *Heimat* from nostalgic emo-
tions and link it to social and emotional needs produced by industrialization and
modernity.

7. The view that the English language has no equivalent and that *Heimat* cannot be translated is widespread. See, e.g., Christopher J. Wickham, *Constructing
Heimat in Postwar Germany: Longing and Belonging* (Lewiston, N.Y., 1999), 4.

8. A comprehensive history of the word is provided by Carola Müller, "Der
Heimatbegriff: Versuch einer Anthologie," in *Wesen und Wandel der Heimatliter-
atur*, ed. Karl Konrad Polheim (Bern, 1989), 207–63.

9. In 1997, Luhmann, *Gesellschaft der Gesellschaft*, 168, observed the paradox that
the ever-expanding international networks also produce a growing desire for local
identification and neighborhood.

10. For a short and critical overview of events and current research literature, see
Winfried Nerdinger, "Modernisierung-Bauhaus-Nationalsozialismus," in *Bauhaus-
Moderne im Nationalsozialismus: Zwischen Anbiederung und Verfolgung*, ed. id. (Mu-
nich, 1993), 9–23.

11. However, Georg Simmel sharpened a generation's perception of the small
and the insignificant. "Idealism had alienated the German mind from the touch of
the concrete . . . and it would be productive to entice it to listen to things [*in die
Sachen hineinlauschen*]," Siegfried Kracauer wrote ("Philosophische Brocken," in
Berliner Nebeneinander: Ausgewählte Feuilletons, 1930–33, ed. Andreas Volk [Zurich,
1996], 205). Similarities and overlaps with the later Heidegger's philosophy of "the
thing" would warrant close scrutiny.

12. "The position that an epoch occupies in the historical process can be determined more strikingly from an analysis of its inconspicuous surface-level expressions than from that epoch's judgement about itself," Siegfried Kracauer wrote in
1920. "The surface-level expressions, by virtue of their unconscious nature, provide
unmediated access to the fundamental substance of the state of things" (Kracauer,
The Mass Ornament: Weimar Essays, ed. Thomas Y. Levin [Cambridge, 1995], 75).

13. Despite Bloch's emphasis on Hegel's dialectics, Jürgen Habermas calls him
a "Marxist Schelling" (Habermas, "Ernst Bloch: Ein marxistischer Schelling," in id.,
Philosophisch-politische Profile (Frankfurt a/M, 1971), 147–67.

14. Siegfried Kracauer published small feuilletons in the *Frankfurter Zeitung* on

unrelated and capricious spaces such as the hotel lobby, the underpass, the unemployment office, the bar, a dancing hall, etc. See id., *Berliner Nebeneinander*, ed. Volk; *Schriften*, ed. Inka Mülder-Bach (Frankfurt a/M, 1990), vol. 5, chs. 1–3.

15. Theodor W. Adorno, "Zum Charakter von Blochs Terminologie," in *Materialien zu Ernst Blochs Prinzip Hoffnung*, ed. Burghart Schmidt (Frankfurt a/M, 1978), 77

16. Siegfried Kraucauer remarks in a highly critical review of Bloch's book on Thomas Müntzer ("Prophetentum: Ernst Bloch's Thomas Müntzer als Theologe der Revolution," in Kraucauer, *Schriften*, ed. Mülder-Bach, 5.1: *Aufsätze, 1915–36*) that "Müntzer becomes a mask and history a mere pretext" for Bloch's millenarianism (196). He discovers unresolved intrinsic contradictions: "Bloch does not care the least about reality. . . . His learned syncretism is incompatible with his magic conjuring of the end . . . the miracle comes by decree, the leap turns into a process and we happily arrive at a dialectics of history with Hegel and Marx" (201).

17. This was shared with other thinkers of his time. "Spatial images are the dreams of society," Kracauer wrote. "Wherever the hieroglyphics of any spatial image is deciphered, there the basis of social reality presents itself." See David Frisby, *Fragments of Modernity: Theories of Modernity in the Work of Simmel, Kracauer, and Benjamin* (Cambridge, Mass., 1986), 109–86.

18. Bloch borrowed the term *Ungleichzeitigkeit* from the art historian Wilhelm Pinder, who used it in his theory of generations. For a detailed discussion of Bloch's interpretation of "untimely contradiction" in opposition to National Socialist attempts to appropriate the term and link it to the Third Reich, see Gunter Scholtz, *Zwischen Wissenschaftsanspruch und Orientierungsbedürfnis:. Zu Grundlage und Wandel der Geisteswissenschaften* (Frankfurt a/M, 1991), 358–85.

19. Ernst Bloch, *Das Prinzip Hoffnung*, 3 vols. (1954; Frankfurt a/M, 1959); trans. Neville Plaice, Stephen Plaice, and Paul Knight as *The Principle of Hope*, 3 vols. (Cambridge, Mass., 1986).

20. See Helmut Plessner, *Grenzen der Gemeinschaft: Eine Kritik des sozialen Radikalismus* (Bonn, 1924; new ed., Frankfurt a/M, 2002), trans. Andrew Wallace as *The Limits of Community: A Critique of Social Radicalism* (Amherst, N.Y., 1999).

21. Immanuel Kant, Mutmasslicher Anfang der Menschengeschichte, in: Kant, *Werke*, ed. Wilhelm Weischedel, vol. 9, 1: *Schriften zur Anthropologie, Geschichtsphilosophie, Politik und Pädagogik* (Wiesbaden, 1964), 85–104.

22. See Bloch, *Prinzip Hoffnung*, vol. 1: 19.

23. Applegate, *Nation of Provincials*, 19.

24. Theodor W. Adorno, "Blochs Spuren," in id., *Noten zur Literatur II* (Frankfurt a/M, 1961), 131.

25. "Auch aus nichts wird etwas," Bloch writes. "Aber es muss in ihm zugleich angelegt sein. So lässt sich keinem etwas geben, was er nicht vorher hat. Mindestens als Wunsch hat" (Bloch, *Subjekt-Objekt: Erläuterungen zu Hegel* [Berlin, 1951; rev. ed., Frankfurt a/M, 1962], 17). This corresponds to the romantic ideal of the absolutely free being as the grounding idea of all philosophy. See, e.g., *Mythologie der Vernunft: Hegels "ältestes Systemprogramm" des deutschen Idealismus*, ed. Christoph Jamme and Helmut Schneider (Frankfurt a/M, 1984), 11: "die erste Idee ist natür-

lich d[ie] Vorst[ellung] von mir selbst, als einem absolut freien Wesen. Mit dem freyen, selbstbewussten Wesen tritt zugleich eine ganze Welt aus dem Nichts hervor—die einzig wahre und gedenkbare Schöpfung aus Nichts."

26. Ernst Bloch, *Tübinger Einleitung in die Philosophie* (Frankfurt a/M, 1963), 1: 122.

27. Traditionally *Heimat* is identified with rural spaces. From the early nineteenth century, an urban environment was considered hostile to the experience of *Heimat*: the city threatens the very basis of *Heimat* because it has no soil for putting down roots.

28. In her analysis of the *Heimat* literature, *Der territoriale Mensch* (1972), Ina-Maria Greverus avoids the term because of its vagueness and substitutes an ethnographical vocabulary (50f.).

29. Mack Walker has written a political and social history and prehistory of the German *Kleinstadt* which he appropriately calls the "home town." Walker's *German Home Towns: Community, State, and General Estates, 1648–1871* (Ithaca, N.Y., 1971) is not concerned with the cultural significance of the *Kleinstadt* as a symbolic construction, but with its political history. He places its beginning after 1648 and sees the end of its history as a result of the creation of a unified nation in 1871. His aim is to "work toward a sociopolitical typology to replace traditional ones" (6), which are incapable, he argues, of grasping the specificity and importance of the unique phenomenon of the *Kleinstadt*.

30. Ibid., 18.

31. The *Kleinstadt* has to be distinguished from the residential town built in the wake of the Thirty Years' War, which gave expression to the idea of absolutism that subjected urban space and the subjects living in it to the centralizing forces of a political system centered on a prince and his residence. Compared to the order of the centers of absolute states, the *Kleinstadt* had no planned structure. Its ("organic") disorder had its painters and photographers, who produced an imaginary world, a *Kleinstadt* of the soul or the mind. There is an iconographic history that, through illustrations in schoolbooks and collections of fairy tales and short fictional prose, lasted well into the twentieth century. Apart from this popular and often trivial but influential imagery, serious artists also contributed to the creation of the image of the specifically German, Dutch, or Danish town. Its best-known representative is certainly Carl Spitzweg, who, despite his great skills and talent and the influence of Delacroix and other painters whose works he studied in Paris, London, and Brussels, never escaped the mediocrity of a Biedermeier idyll. Other painters such as Moritz von Schwind, Carl Blechen, Christian Friedrich Gille, and Carl Rottmann (whose early "dramatic" oil paintings, rather than his polished later style, made a remarkable contribution to the imagery of the *Kleinstadt*) succeeded in avoiding the fake sweetness of their *sujet* by representing the particular historical, architectural, and social conditions of towns of their epoch.

32. On the ordering of German medieval towns, see *Die Stadt des Mittelalters*, ed. Carl Haase, 3 vols. (Darmstadt, 1969–73); Karl Gruber, *Die Gestalt der deutschen Stadt: Ihr Wandel aus der geistigen Ordnung der Zeiten* (Munich, 1977); P. Zucker, *Entwicklung des Stadtbildes: Die Stadt als Form* (Munich, 1923); and Cord Meckseper, *Kleine Kunstgeschichte der deutschen Stadt im Mittelalter* (Darmstadt, 1982).

33. Until the middle of the nineteenth century, big cities had preserved spaces that had resisted change and were enclaves reminiscent of the medieval origin of the modern city. They can well be interpreted as a form of a *Kleinstadt* within the city. They were no longer considered safe and up to hygienic standards, but rather a breeding ground for poverty and social unrest. City planners in Paris, London, and elsewhere who made the decision to eradicate these quarters were well aware of the radical change in the architectural and mental structure of the city resulting from the definitive elimination of these *Kleinstadt* quarters, and, as a result, months before the demolition began, professional photographers were commissioned to document the buildings, streets, and the street life for remembrance in future times.

34. Franco Moretti, *Atlas of the European Novel, 1800–1900* (New York, 1998), 165. Moretti is certainly correct in his rejection of Bakhtin's assertion about the decentering impact of novelistic writing , which cannot be sustained even by focusing on the Russian novel of the nineteenth century.

35. Ibid., 120.

36. Ibid., 122.

37. Bettina Arnim, *Dies Buch gehört dem König; des Königbuchs erster Band* (Berlin: Arnim's Verlag, 1852).

38. Kenneth Clark, "Provincialism," in id., *Moments of Vision and Other Essays* (New York, 1981), 50–62; quotation, 51. Clark goes on to develop a sophisticated argument about the independent mind of the modern provincial artist.

39. Luhmann, *Gesellschaft der Gesellschaft*, 667.

40. The cultural historian Wilhelm Heinrich Riehl's term "individualized country" clearly resonates with Kenneth Frampton's "critical regionalism" and, in certain respects, can be read as a complementary precursor to it. Riehl pioneered an ethnographic approach to history (Viktor Geramb called it *Anthropogeographie*, in *Von Volkstun und Heimat: Gedanken zum Neuaufbau*, 2d ed. [Graz: U. Moser, 1922]). He distinguished between the north and the south of Germany, which, under the political rule of Prussia and Austria respectively had turned into centralized country, whereas the area geographically and politically located in between these power centers developed into multicentered space with local identities. Among the weaknesses of his approach is the opposition he creates between two opposing forces, the forces of retardation (*Beharrung*) and dynamic forces (*Bewegung*). In contrast to Frampton's emphasis on aspects of mobility and critique inherent in regionalism, Riehl's preference for persistence created an obstacle for the perception of the contradictory character of modern society that succeeded in integrating dynamics and retardation to a complex system. See Riehl, *Die bürgerliche Gesellschaft* (Stuttgart, 1853), and, *Land und Leute* (Stuttgart, 1855), 132–217.

41. The foremost example of the self-assured *Kleinstadt* as an intellectual and artistic ex-centric center was Weimar. Among the numerous publications on the "Musentempel," there are very few that deal with spatial aspects in the Weimar myth. Most common are variants of the history of ideas paradigm. An early attempt to write a cultural history in terms of a modern definition of material culture, following Raymond Williams, is Walter H. Bruford, *Culture and Society in Classical Weimar, 1775–1805* (Cambridge, 1962); more recent is the popular Peter Merseburger, *Mythos Weimar: Zwischen Geist und Macht* (Stuttgart, 1998; 3d ed., 1999). The first

publication that combined images, including photography, and texts in an attempt to capture the atmosphere of Weimar as a place was a small book by the Goethe admirer Wilhelm Bode, *Damals in Weimar* (Leipzig 1912; facs. reprint, Weimar, 1991). Moretti's emphasis on the metropolis as the center that defines standards and norms with general validity makes this very clear.

42. "Die handvoll trübseliger Kleinbürger im Parterre des weimarischen Theaterschuppens waren kein Volk," Heinrich von Treitschke wrote. "Es fehlte den Deutschen überhaupt, wie Goethe klagte, eine Nationalkultur" ("Die goldenen Tage von Weimar," in id., *Bilder aus der deutschen Geschichte* [Leipzig, 1911], 2: 1–25; quotation, 11). Treitschke associated the multitude of theaters in decentralized Germany with "anarchy, which, alas, also offered the spell of unlimited freedom" (12).

43. Gerd Theile, "The Weimar Myth: From City of the Arts to Global Village," in *Unwrapping Goethe's Weimar: Essays in Cultural Studies and Local Knowledge*, ed. Burkhard Henke, Susanne Kord, and Simon Richter (Rochester, N.Y., 2000), 310–27, writes: "Innovative nineteenth-century literary and arts movements connected with names such as Poe, de Quincy, and Baudelaire created artificial paradises to which Germany offered its own dream in stone: Weimar as the city of the arts." Later, several travelogues of the nineteenth century conjured up a Biedermeier idyll for which Heinrich Laube's *Reise durch das Biedermeier* (1834–37) was the model. This was a portrait of the *Kleinstadt* already in a state of decline.

44. Alon Confino, *The Nation as a Local Metaphor: Württemberg, Imperial Germany and National Memory, 1871–1918* (Chapel Hill, N.C., 1997), creates a hierarchy and interprets *Heimat* as an auxiliary tool for the overriding objective of nation building.

45. Maiken Umbach, "The Politics of Sentimentality and the German Fürstenbund, 1779–1785," *Historical Journal* 41 (1998): 679–704, specifically refers to Goethe's political concept in the context of tensions between Berlin's politics of centralization and Weimar's counter position. The essay is a fine example of the productivity of exploring unusual sources, such as literary prose, or the stylistic interpretation of words and phrases from diaries and letters, for the interpretation of political history. Her political interpretation of friendship creates a strong contrast to the reading suggested in my essay.

46. Cf. *The Transfer and Transformation of Ideas and Material Culture*, ed. Peter J. Hugill and D. Bruce Dickson (College Station, Texas, 1988), esp. Torsten Hägerstrand, "Some Unexplored Problems in the Modeling of Culture Transfer and Transformation of Ideas and Material Culture."

47. The underlying idea of a *politics of friendship* in the eighteenth century is ill conceived of as an extension of previous models of friendship in Roman antiquity or the Renaissance. They are not compatible with the cultural condition of the period around 1800 when passion and emotion were rediscovered and legitimized in opposition to the concept of the man of reason. A political definition of friendship involves sacrificing a rich literary and emotional genealogy for the sake of an abstract political or philosophical category.

48. An example is the Tafelrunde, or "roundtable," in the Wittumspalais of the duchess of Saxony-Weimar-Eisenach, Anna Amalia (1739–1807), which is well

known through Georg Melchior Kraus's 1795 painting of it. See www.biblint.de/goethe_tafelrunde_kraus.html (accessed February 11, 2005).

49. From the late seventeenth century on, intensive letter writing was the sphere of scholars, poets, and merchants, all of whom in Germany were closely associated with the culture of towns and not, in contrast to France and England, with city life. Wilfried Barner, in his essay "Gelehrte Freundschaft im 18. Jahrhundert: Zu ihren traditionalen Voraussetzungen," in *Frauenfreundschaft, Männerfreundschaft: Literarische Diskurse im 18. Jahrhundert*, ed. Wolfram Mauser and Barbara Becker-Cantarino (Tübingen, 1991), 23–45, discusses the cultural significance of this broad movement. Maiken Umbach adds an unexpected group to these authors of letters, the ruling princes of German states. She emphasizes the terminology of "friendship," which, she argues, gained a political dimension. In recent years, a considerable number of books and articles have explored the political dimension of friendship, including Jacques Derrida's famous *Politiques de l'amitié* (Paris, 1994), trans. George Collins as *Politics of Friendship* (New York, 1997). However, the eighteenth-century cult of friendship is misread when viewed principally as a means for achieving political aims. Rather, the cult of sentimentality was so pervasive that even aristocratic rulers and politicians felt the need to couch their political statements in the language of friendship.

50. Anne-Louise-Germaine de Staël (1766–1817), Madame de Staël, *De l'Allemagne* (Paris Novelle Édition 1879), 79–80.

51. Ibid., 119.

52. The period of philosophical and literary innovation around 1800 was linked to the hometown in ways that, despite deep changes, can be observed again in the early twentieth century, when Weimar once again became the focal point of an innovative movement in the arts, architecture, and literature. Creative minds such as Harry Graf Kessler and Henry van de Velde chose Weimar as the site for their experiments. Yet this was the swan song of the *Kleinstadt*, a last moment of creativity before its final collapse.

53. Gottfried Keller, *Der Grüne Heinrich*, in id., *Sämtliche Werke und ausgewählte Briefe*, ed. Clemens Heselhaus (Munich, 1958), 9–11.

54. The Weimar exhibition "Aufstieg und Fall der Moderne" (1999–2000), presented the early beginnings and clearly demonstrated the importance of this anti-center. Darmstadt's "Mathildenhöhe" would be another example.

55. Thomas Bernhard has produced a haunting and aesthetically most persuasive representation of and attack on this sick idyll (*Frost*, 1964); other examples are Franz Innerhofer (*Schöne Tage*, 1974), Josef Haslinger (*Der Tod des Kleinhäuslers Ignaz Hajek*, 1985) and dramas by Franz Xaver Kroetz, Rainer Werner Fassbinder, Martin Sperr, and Elfriede Jellinek.

56. Words like *Heimtücke* (malice or treachery) and *heimsuchen* (to infest or haunt) make use of the reversal of the term *Heim* into its opposite.

57. Theories of globalization continue analyzing the present on a macro level, offering explanations of the process through highly generalized concepts. Within this framework, the demise of the *Kleinstadt* was not the struggle of a politics and culture of place. Recent debates, following Henri Lefèbvre's celebrated thesis of

capitalism's strategy of survival through the "production of space" in *La Survie du capitalisme: La Ré-production des rapports de production* (Paris, 1973) have focused on the organization and reorganization of territorial divisions of power and labor by creating dynamic spaces of production and the accumulation of capital. Current geographical reconstructions and reorganizations of spatial distribution of labor and capital and their concentration in a small number of big cities can be interpreted as the latest continuation of an ongoing process that once led to the eclipse of the *Kleinstadt* after 1900. In a world of expanding capitalism, the emerging global system of the early twentieth century simply had no room for the luxury of a space characterized by obstinacy and retardation. Its demise might be called a domestic colonization of "unproductive" space. For these theories, the vernacular is but a small footnote. For recent publications, see n. 5 above; and see also Saskia Sassen, *The Global City: New York, London, Tokyo* (Princeton, 2001), and Robert Went, *The Enigma of Globalization: A Journey to a New Stage of Capitalism* (New York, 2002).

58. Manfred Riedel refers to Nietzsche's influence on the early Bloch. But it is precisely the utopian dimension in Bloch's thought, referred to by Riedel, that marks the sharp difference between their respective conceptions of present and future. Manfred Riedel, *Tradition und Utopie: Ernst Blochs Philosophie im Licht unserer geschichtlichen Denkerfahrung* (Frankfurt a/M, 1994), 268ff.

59. Bloch, *Prinzip Hoffnung*, 22f.

60. Among recent attempts to reinterpret Bloch's concept of history and politics, see Riedel, *Tradition und Utopie*; also *Not Yet: Reconsidering Ernst Bloch*, ed. Jamie Owen Daniel and Tom Moylan (New York, 1997).

61. Foucault also uses the metaphor of hollow spaces left behind by the exit of the gods. He thinks of a third alternative by drawing attention to space's power of opposition to scientific discourse reduced to an endless stream of words in a modern culture devoid of meaning and purpose. Michel Foucault, *Naissance de la clinique: Une Archéologie du regard médical* (Paris, 1963), trans. A. M. Sheridan Smith as *The Birth of the Clinic: An Archeology of Medical Perception* (London, 1973), 179.

62. Bloch, *Prinzip Hoffnung*, vol. 2: 807.

4. Umbach: The Deutscher Werkbund, Globalization, and the Invention of Modern Vernaculars

The author wishes to thank the British Academy, the Arts and Humanities Research Board (AHRB), the Leverhulme Trust, and the Institució Catalana de Reecerca i Estudis Avançats (ICREA) for their generous support at different stages of this research.

1. According to Kevin H. O'Rourke and Jeff G. Williamson, "When Did Globalization Begin?" *NBER Working Papers* No. W7632 (April 2000), the nineteenth century witnessed "a very big globalization bang." Globalization is here defined as trade expansion driven by the integration of markets between trading economies. The takeoff began around 1830 in the agricultural sector; the market for manufactured goods followed suit a few decades later.

2. These features have been regarded as cornerstones of the modernization process ever since modernization theory was first formulated in the classic five-stage

model developed by Walt Whitman Rostow, *The Stages of Economic Growth: A Non-Communist Manifesto* (Cambridge, 1960). They persist in the more critical interpretations of Hans Ulrich Wehler, *Modernisierungstheorie und Geschichte* (Göttingen, 1975); *Directions of Change: Modernization Theory, Research, and Realities*, ed. Mustafa O. Attir, Burkart Holzner, and Zdenek Suda (Boulder, Colo., 1981); and Philip Abrams, *Historical Sociology* (Ithaca, N.Y., 1982), esp. chap. 5, 108–46. An excellent survey of the connection between modernization and nation-building is *Becoming National: A Reader*, ed. Geoff Eley and Ronald Grigor Suny (New York, 1996). The debate about the onset of globalization is outlined later in this chapter.

3. Wilhelmine Germany's relative modernity—or lack thereof—has been the subject of an intense and ongoing historiographical debate since the so-called "Fischer Controversy." In the 1970s, a series of studies, initiated by Karl Dietrich Bracher (see, e.g., his *Das deutsche Dilemma: Leidenswege der politischen Emanzipation* [Munich, 1971], trans. Richard Barry as *The German Dilemma: The Throes of Political Emancipation* [London, 1974]), focused on Germany's exceptionalism and "misdevelopment," understood in terms of a "blocked modernization." Hans-Ulrich Wehler's *Das deutsche Kaiserreich, 1871–1918* (Göttingen, 1973) is today the best-known example for this approach. Wehler has restated the position in more recent publications, such as "The German Double Revolution and the Sonderweg, 1848–79," in *The Problem of Revolution in Germany, 1789–1989*, ed. Reinhard Rürup (Oxford, 2000). The late 1970s and the 1980s saw the publication of a wave of critical responses, arguing for the heuristic value of studying German history between 1871 and 1914 as a period in its own right. Most notable among these are David Blackbourn and Geoff Eley, *The Peculiarities of German History: Bourgeois Society and Politics in Nineteenth-Century Germany* (New York, 1984); Richard Evans, *Rethinking German History: Nineteenth-Century Germany and the Origins of the Third Reich* (London, 1987); and, more recently, Geoff Eley, "Introduction I: Is There a History of the Kaiserreich?" and "German History and the Contradictions of Modernity: The Bourgeoisie, the State, and the Mastery of Reform," in *Society, Culture, and the State in Germany, 1870–1930*, ed. id. (Ann Arbor, Mich., 1997), 1–42, 67–103. Recent cultural history has further promoted this reassessment. Studies such as Kevin Repp, *Reformers, Critics, and the Paths of German Modernity: Anti-Politics and the Search for Alternatives, 1890–1914* (Cambridge, Mass., 2000), firmly locate this period of German history within an analytical framework of modernity; the same author's *Berlin Moderns: Art, Politics, and Commercial Culture in Fin-de-Siècle Berlin* (forthcoming) even appropriates the classical Weimar label "laboratory of modernity" for Germany's Wilhelmine years. See also Volker Berghahn, "The German Empire, 1871–1914: Reflections in the Direction of Recent Research," and Margaret L. Anderson, "Reply to Volker Berghahn," *Central European History*, 35, 1 (2002): 75–82 and 83–90; and James Retallack, "Ideas into Politics: Meanings of Stasis in Wilhelmine Germany," in *Wilhelminism and Its Legacies: German Modernities, Imperialism and the Meanings of Reform, 1890–1930* ed. id. and Geoff Eley (New York, 2003), 235–52. Much recent research concentrates on the role of the locality as a site for progressive reform. See e.g. Jennifer Jenkins, *Provincial Modernity: Local Culture and Liberal Politics in Fin-de-Siècle Hamburg* (Ithaca, N.Y., 2003); Jan Palmowski, *Urban Liberalism in Imperial Germany: Frankfurt am Main, 1866–1914* (Oxford, 1999), and

id., "Mediating the Nation: Liberalism and the Polity in Nineteenth-Century Germany," *German History*, 19, 4 (2001), 573–98, which provides an excellent survey of recent studies of liberalism in its local settings.

4. *The Globalization Syndrome: Transformation and Resistance*, ed. James H. Mittelman (Princeton, 2000), and Jan Aart Scholte, *Globalization: A Critical Introduction* (New York, 2000), provide summaries of the current state of the debate.

5. See, e.g., Wil Hout, *Capitalism and the Third World: Development, Dependence and the World System* (Brookfield, Vt., 1993), and *Capitalism and Colonial Production*, ed. Hamza Alavi (London, 1982). Useful critical surveys of the debate over "dependency theory" are *Dependency Theory: A Critical Reassessment*, ed. Dudley Seers (London, 1981); Ronald H. Chilcote, *Dependency and Marxism: Toward a Resolution of the Debate* (Boulder, Colo., 1982); Magnus Blomström and Björn Hettne, *Development Theory in Transition: The Dependency Debate and Beyond: Third World Responses* (London, 1984); and Baidyanath N. Ghosh, *Dependency Theory Revisited* (Aldershot, Hants, U.K., 2001).

6. This trend was famously diagnosed by Paul Ricoeur, "Universal Civilization and National Cultures" in id., *History and Truth*, trans. Charles A. Kelbley (Evanston, 1965), 271–284. The debate about the cultural implications of globalization has since sparked a vast literature. Seminal studies include Arjun Appadurai, *Modernity at Large: Cultural Dimensions of Globalization* (Minneapolis, 1996); *Questions of Modernity*, ed. Timothy Mitchell (Minneapolis, 2000); and *Consuming Tradition, Manufacturing Heritage: Global Norms and Urban Forms in the Age of Tourism*, ed. Nezar Alsayyad (London, 2001).

7. Niall Ferguson, "Globalization and Gunboats: The Costs and Benefits of the British Empire Revisited" (working paper, Oxford University, 2002).

8. Harold James, *The End of Globalization: Lessons from the Great Depression* (Cambridge, Mass., 2001). On globalization in the later nineteenth century, see *Historical Foundations of Globalization*, ed. James Foreman-Peck (Northampton, Mass., 1998); Carl Strickwerda, "The World at the Crossroads: The World Economy and International Relations in Two Eras of Globalization, 1890–1914 and 1989 to the Present" (working paper, University of Kansas); Hans Pohl, *Aufbruch der Weltwirtschaft: Geschichte der Weltwirtschaft von der Mitte des 19. Jahrhunderts bis zum Ersten Weltkrieg* (Stuttgart, 1989); and Maiken Umbach, "Made in Germany," in *Deutsche Erinnerungsorte*, ed. Hagen Schulze and Etienne François (Munich, 2001), 2: 405–38.

9. See O'Rourke and Williamson, "When Did Globalization Begin?"

10. Bjarne Stoklund, "The Role of International Exhibitions in the Construction of National Cultures in the Nineteenth Century," *Etnologia: European Journal of Ethnology* 24, 1 (1994): 35–44; Bernhard Rieger, "Envisioning the Future: British and German reactions to the Paris World Fair in 1900," in *Meanings of Modernity: Britain from the Late-Victorian Era to World War II*, ed. id. and Martin Daunton (New York, 2001), 145–65; and Winfried Kretschmer, *Geschichte der Weltausstellungen* (Frankfurt a/M, 1999); Werner Plum, *World Exhibitions in the Nineteenth Century: Pageants of Social and Political Change*, trans. Lux Furtmüller (Bonn–Bad Godesberg, 1977); Evelyn Kroker, *Die Weltausstellungen im 19. Jahrhundert* (Göttingen, 1975).

11. Joachim Radkau, "Die Wilhelminische Ära als nervöses Zeitalter, oder: Die Nerven als Netz zwischen Tempo und Körpergeschichte," *Geschichte und Gesellschaft* 20, 2 (1994): 211–41. As cultural history expands beyond studies of intellectual "heroes" such as Oscar Wilde or Thomas Mann, nervousness and related paradigms are gradually replacing the notion of "decadence" as a label for the entire epoch. Others have redefined the term "decadence" to embrace sociopsychological phenomena, e.g., Bertrand Taithe, *Defeated Flesh: Welfare, Warfare and the Making of Modern France* (Manchester, 1999).

12. Celia Applegate, *A Nation of Provincials: The German Idea of Heimat* (Berkeley, 1990).

13. Alon Confino, *The Nation as a Local Metaphor: Württemberg, Imperial Germany and National Memory 1871–1918* (Chapel Hill, N.C., 1997); Jenkins, *Provincial Modernity*; Georg Kunz, *Verortete Geschichte: Regionales Geschichtsbewusstsein in den deutschen Historischen Vereinen des neunzehnten Jahrhunderts* (Göttingen, 2000); and Appadurai, *Modernity at Large*, esp. section on "The Production of Locality," 178–99.

14. William R. Rollins, *A Greener Vision of Home: Cultural Politics and Environmental Reform in the German Heimatschutz Movement, 1904–1918* (Ann Arbor, Mich., 1997), and David Midgley, "Los von Berlin! Anti-Urbanism as Counter-Culture in Early Twentieth-Century Germany," in *Counter-Cultures in Germany and Central Europe: From Sturm und Drang to Baader-Meinhof,* ed. Steve Giles and Maike Oergel (Oxford, 2003), 121–36.

15. Typical examples amongst primarily historical studies of the *Heimat* idea are *Antimodernismus und Reform: Zur Geschichte der deutschen Heimatbewegung*, ed. Edeltraut Klueting (Darmstadt, 1991), and W. Hartung, *Konservative Zivilisationskritik und regionale Identität am Beispiel der niedersächsischen Heimatbewegung 1895 bis 1919* (Hannover, 1991).

16. The German idea of *Heimat* is portrayed as proto- and/or pro-fascist in D. Kramer, "Die politische und ökonomische Funktionalisierung von Heimat im deutschen Imperialismus und Faschismus," *Diskurs* 6–7 (1973): 3–22; David von Reeken, *Heimatbewegung, Kulturpolitik und Nationalsozialismus: Die Geschichte der "Ostfriesischen Landschaft," 1918–1949* (Aurich, Germany, 1995); and J. A. Williams, "The Chords of the German Soul Are Tuned to Nature: The Movement to Preserve the Natural Heimat from Kaiserreich to the Third Reich," *Central European History* 29, 3 (1996): 339–84.

17. N. Bormann, *Paul Schultze-Naumburg, 1869–1949: Maler, Publizist, Architekt, vom Kulturreformer der Jahrhundertwende zum Kulturpolitiker im Dritten Reich* (Essen, 1989).

18. On *Heimat* and war, cf. Confino, *Nation as a Local Metaphor*; Jeffery Verhey, *The Spirit of 1914: Militarism, Myth and Mobilization in Germany* (Cambridge, 2000); Bernd Ziemann, *Front und Heimat: Ländliche Kriegserfahrungen im südlichen Bayern 1914–1923* (Essen, 1997); Aribert Reimann, *Der große Krieg der Sprachen: Untersuchungen zur historischen Semantik in Deutschland und England zur Zeit des Ersten Weltkriegs* (Essen, 2000).

19. Hermann Muthesius, "Die Bedeutung des Kunstgewerbes" (lecture at the Handelshochschule, Berlin, 1907), reprinted in Die Neue Sammlung, Staatliches

Museum für angewandte Kunst, *Zwischen Kunst und Industrie, Der Deutsche Werkbund*), exhibition catalogue, ed. W. Fischer (1975; rev. ed., Stuttgart, 1987), 39–55; quotation, 49.

20. Between 1907 and 1926, Muthesius published over 600 articles and reviews in 60 different newspapers and journals and gave countless public speeches and lectures, thus establishing himself as the leading critic of contemporary arts and crafts, architecture, and industrial design in Germany. Muthesius's writings are preserved in his *Nachlass* in the Werkbund Archiv Berlin (www.werkbundarchiv-berlin.de [accessed February 12, 2005]). A representative sample has been published by Hans-Joachim Hubrich, *Hermann Muthesius: Die Schriften zu Architektur, Kunstgewerbe, Industrie in der "Neuen Bewegung"* (Berlin, 1981). The best critical monograph on Muthesius is Fedor Roth, *Hermann Muthesius und die Idee der harmonischen Kultur: Kultur als Einheit des künstlerischen Stils in allen Lebensäußerungen eines Volkes* (Berlin, 2001), which strikes a balance between attempts to integrate Muthesius into a teleology of triumphant modernism, and those who see him as a precursor of the fascist reaction. J. V. Maciuka, "Hermann Muthesius and the Reform of German Architecture, Arts and Crafts, 1890–1914" (Ph.D. diss., University of California, Berkeley, 1998) sees Muthesius, and the Werkbund in general, as exemplifying the role of the Prussian state in promoting modern functionalism. Frederic J. Schwartz, *The Werkbund: Design Theory and Mass Culture Before the First World War* (New Haven, 1996), agrees with the modernist interpretation, yet criticizes this quality as symptomatic of art selling out to the capitalist system. By contrast, Werner Oechslin, "Politisches, allzu Politisches . . . : "Nietzschelinge", der "Wille zur Kunst" und der Deutsche Werkbund vor 1914," in *Architektur als politische Kultur*, ed. Hermann Hipp and Ernst Seidl (Berlin, 1996), 151–90, regards the role of Muthesius in the Werkbund as part of a dark prehistory of modernism, with fascist affinities.

21. Born in 1861, Muthesius read philosophy and art history at Berlin University, before he went on to the Technical University to study architecture and engineering. He graduated as a doctor of engineering sciences in 1887 and joined an architectural practice before becoming a member of the Prussian civil service, where he started his career in the office overseeing building schemes in Prussia. On Muthesius's life, cf. Julius Posener's many writings, such as the "Hermann Muthesius" entry in *Architect's Yearbook* 10 (1962): 45–61; *Anfänge des Funktionalismus: Von Arts and Crafts zum Deutschen Werkbund* (Berlin, 1964); and *From Schinckel to Bauhaus: Five Lectures on the Growth of Modern German Architecture*, Architectural Association Papers, no. 5 (London, 1972).

22. Hermann Muthesius, *Die Zukunft der deutschen Form*, Der Deutsche Krieg: Politische Flugschriften, no. 50, ed. E. Jäckh (Berlin, 1915), 36.

23. *Deutsche Geschichte*, ed. Hans-Joachim Bartmuss et al., vol. 2 (Berlin, 1975), 785.

24. Cf. D. Head, *"Made in Germany," The Corporate Identity of a Nation* (London, 1992), and Umbach, "Made in Germany" (cited n. 8 above), 405–18.

25. Andrew Bonnell, "Cheap and Nasty: German Goods, Socialism, and the 1876 Philadelphia World Fair," *International Review of Social History* 46 (2001): 207–26.

26. R. G. Hirschmann, "Made in Germany—Rolle und Bedeutung aus

deutscher Sicht," in *Dokumentation "Made in Germany": Deutsche Qualität auf dem Prüfstand*, Achter deutscher Quality Circle Kongress (Mannheim, 1989), 7–16.

27. E. E. Williams, *"Made in Germany"* (1897; reprint, Brighton, U.K., 1973).

28. The persistence of artisanal attitudes to labor among the German working-class movement, with a concomitant emphasis on "quality work," is discussed in Bonnell, "Cheap and Nasty," and T. Welskopp, *Das Banner der Brüderlichkeit: Die deutsche Sozialdemokratie vom Vormärz bis zum Sozialistengesetz* (Bonn, 2000).

29. The economic imperative for quality work as a means to improve the German balance of trade was the subject of numerous studies at the time, such as those of the Institut für exakte Wirtschaftsforschung at Rostock University in a series of publications directed by Johannes Buschmann; by Heinrich Waentig, professor of economics and history at Berlin and Munich; and, of course, by Friedrich Naumann, e.g., his *Neudeutsche Wirtschaftspolitik* (Berlin, 1906).

30. This point is particularly emphasized by Maciuka, "Hermann Muthesius and the Reform of German Architecture," who sees German modernism as a brainchild of Prussian bureaucrats.

31. The classic English-language introduction remains Joan Campbell, *The German Werkbund: The Politics of Reform in the Applied Arts* (Princeton, 1978), esp. 3–81 on the pre-1914 era. Other seminal works include id., *Joy of Work, German Work* (Princeton, 1989); Posener, *Anfänge des Funktionalismus*; Stefan Muthesius, *Das englische Vorbild: Eine Studie zu den deutschen Reformbewegungen in Architektur, Wohnbau und Kunstgewerbe im späten 19. Jahrhundert* (Munich, 1974); Mark Jarzombek, "The Kunstgewerbe, the Werkbund and the Aesthetics of Culture in the Wilhelmine Period," *Journal of the Society of Architectural Historians* 53, 1 (March 1994): 7–19; K. Junghanns, *Der Deutsche Werkbund: Sein erstes Jahrzehnt* (Berlin, 1982); and Schwartz, *Werkbund*.

32. Among the founding members of the Werkbund, only two men, both architects first and foremost, established independent careers as designers. Richard Riemerschmid became well known for his design of simple vernacular furniture and household objects, many of which were produced in the new reform manufactures, notably the Deutsche Werkstätten für Handwerkskunst. His design work is documented in Winfried Nerdinger, *Richard Riemerschmid vom Jugendstil zum Werkbund: Werke und Dokumente* (Munich, 1982). The case of Peter Behrens is more famous, but also highly unusual: Behrens became chief designer for the AEG electricity works; in this capacity, he not only designed several famous industrial buildings, such as the turbine hall, but also several lines of company products, as well as the accompanying advertising campaigns and the firm's logo. While most classical studies, such as Stanford Anderson, *Peter Behrens and a New Architecture for the Twentieth Century* (Cambridge, Mass., 2000), see Behrens primarily as an architect, several monographs, articles, and collections consider his design oeuvre in total, notably Alan Windsor, *Peter Behrens: Architect and Designer, 1868–1940* (London, 1981); *Industriekultur: Peter Behrens und die AEG 1907–14*, ed. Tilman Buddensieg and H. Rogge (Berlin, 1980); Frederic J. Schwartz, "Commodity Signs: Peter Behrens, the AEG, and the Trademark: His Designs for German Allgemeine Elektricitäts-Gesellschaft," *Journal of Design History* 9, 3 (1996): 153–84; Giovanni Anceschi, "The First Corporate Image: Peter Behrens and the AEG," *Domus*, no. 605 (1980): 32–34;

and *Peter Behrens: "Wer aber will sagen, was Schönheit sei?" Grafik, Produktgestaltung, Architektur*, ed. Hans Georg Pfeiffer (Düsseldorf, 1990).

33. The collection is documented in "Moderne Formgebung, 1900–1914: Die Mustersammlung des Deutschen Werkbundes," in *Das Schöne und der Alltag: Die Anfänge des modernen Designs, 1900–1914*, ed. Michael Fehr, Sabine Röder and Gerhard Storck (Cologne, 1997), 10–305.

34. The classic study remains George L. Mosse, *The Nationalization of the Masses: Political Symbolism and Mass Movements in Germany from the Napoleonic Wars through the Third Reich* (New York, 1975).

35. Recent years have seen a proliferation of publications on specific momuments. Most follow the format developed in Charlotte Tacke's magisterial study *Denkmal im sozialen Raum: Nationale Symbole in Deutschland und Frankreich im 19. Jahrhundert* (Göttingen, 1995).

36. Hermann Muthesius, "Die moderne Bewegung," in *Speemanns goldenes Buch der Kunst* (Berlin, 1901), n.p., para. nos. 1029–60, quotation from no. 1032. Cf. also id., "John Ruskin," *Centralblatt der Bauverwaltung* 7 (27 January 1900): 43. For a discussion of Ruskin's and Morris's constitutive roles in English modernism during the interwar period, see M. T. Saler, *The Avant-Garde in Inter-War England: Medieval Modernism and the London Underground* (Oxford, 1999), esp. 10–24.

37. *The Lamp of Memory: Ruskin, Tradition, and Architecture*, ed. Michael Wheeler and Nigel Whiteley (Manchester, 1992).

38. Useful introductions to vernacular themes in the Arts and Crafts movement are: Peter Davey, *Arts and Crafts Architecture* (1980; new ed., London, 1995); Malcolm Haslam, *Arts and Crafts* (London, 1988); Gillian Naylor, *The Arts and Crafts Movement: A Study of Its Sources, Ideals and Influence on Design Theory* (London, 1971); Elizabeth Cumming and Wendy Kaplan, *The Arts and Crafts Movement* (London, 1991); *Encyclopedia of Arts and Crafts: The International Arts Movement, 1850–1920*, ed. Wendy Kaplan (London, 1989); André Chaves, *Intentionality and Arts and Crafts Decoration* (Pasadena, Calif., 1996); Lionel Lambourne, *Utopian Craftsmen: The Arts and Crafts Movement from the Cotswolds to Chicago* (London, 1980). On the architectural dimension of the Arts and Crafts movement, see James Macauley, Wendy Hitchmough, and Edward R. Bosley, *Arts and Crafts Houses II: Charles Rennie Mackintosh, Hill House, C. F. A. Voysey, The Homestead, Greene and Greene, Gamble House* (London, 1999).

39. In 1860, Ruskin defined good taste as the essence of social morality. In 1880, his pupil William Morris took up that theme by suggesting that ugliness was but an outward sign of the moral decay of modern industrial Britain. See *New Approaches to Ruskin: Thirteen Essays*, ed. Robert Hewison (London, 1981), and Peter Stansky, *William Morris, C. R. Ashbee and the Arts and Crafts* (London, 1984).

40. Cf. Eileen Boris, *Art and Labor: Ruskin, Morris, and the Craftsman Ideal in America* (Philadelphia, 1986).

41. They operated on an extremely small scale, and the goods they produced were far too expensive to sell to the masses. In fact, Morris's largest orders came from the church, the aristocracy, and the court. See Peter Stansky, *Redesigning the World: William Morris, the 1880s, and the Arts and Crafts* (Princeton, 1985), and Linda

Marilyn Austin, *The Practical Ruskin: Economics and Audience in the Late Work* (Baltimore, 1991).

42. Hermann Schwabe, "Die Förderung der Kunst-Industrie in England und der Stand dieser Frage in Deutschland: Für Staat und Industrie, Gemeinden, Schul- und Vereinsleben," 1866, quoted from Monika Franke, "Entstehungsgeschichte des Königlichen Kunstgewerbemuseums in Berlin," in *Packeis und Preßglas: Von der Kunstgewerbebewegung zum Deutschen Werkbund*, ed. Werkbund-Archiv (Berlin, 1987), 174–85; quotation, 174.

43. The point was later elaborated by Friedrich Naumann, "Kunst und Volkswirtschaft: Vortrag im Auftrag des Deutschen Werkbundes" (1912), in id., *Werke*, 6 vols. (Cologne, 1964), vol. 6, *Ästhetische Schriften*, ed. H. Ladendorf, 331–50.

44. N. Rooke, *The Craftsman and Education for Industry: Four Lectures*, Arts and Crafts Exhibition Society (London, 1935); quotation, 57.

45. There is an unfortunate tendency in some recent historiography to divorce the Werkbund's history from its international context, and portray it as part of a German Sonderweg leading straight to Auschwitz's infamous motto "Arbeit macht frei." See, e.g., Holger Schatz and Andrea Woeldike, "Deutsche Arbeit und eleminatorischer Anti-Semitismus: Über die sozio-ökonomische Bedingtheit einer kulturellen Tradition," in *Die Fratze der eigenen Geschichte: Von der Goldhagen-Debatte zum Jugoslawien-Krieg*, ed. Jürgen Elsässer and Andrei S. Markovits (Berlin, 1999), 103–23. A much less teleological version of this argument, but still maintaining that the idea of "joy in work" was a particularly German invention is Campbell, *Joy of Work, German Work*.

46. Saler, *Avant-Garde in Inter-War England*, 61–91.

47. A classical exposition of the theme was Muthesius's speech at the Werkbund conference in Cologne in 1914, quoted in Neue Sammlung, *Zwischen Kunst und Industrie*, 112. Cf. also his collected essays in Hubrich, *Hermann Muthesius*. The idea of *Typisierung*, or typification, is a leitmotif in Muthesius's writings, public and private, both before and after World War I.

48. Hermann Muthesius, *Das Englische Haus: Entwicklungen, Bedingungen, Anlage, Aufbau, Einrichtung und Innenraum*, 3 vols. (Berlin, 1904–5; 2d rev. ed., 1908–11).

49. Muthesius, "Bedeutung des Kunstgewerbes," 45.

50. This theory was formulated concisely by Thomas Crow, "I'll take the high road, you take the low road," *Artforum* 29:5 (1991): 104–7. Most canonical examples of interwar modernism did indeed set out to undermine older forms of domestic life in an attempt at social engineering through aesthetics. Two examples can serve to illustrate this point. The first relates to the debate about different kitchen designs. In the early twentieth century, May and Lihotzky based their famous "Frankfurt kitchen" on scientific motion studies, likening the job of a housewife to that of a worker in a modern Fordist plant. Opponents, such as Meitninger (designer of the "Munich kitchen"), argued that work and living areas should be closely integrated, defining the role of the housewife as a social one. See Lore Kramer, "Rationalisierung des Haushalts und Frauenfrage: Die Frankfurter Küche und zeitgenössische Kritik," in *Ernst May und das neue Frankfurt, 1925–1930*, ed. Heinrich Klotz (Be-

rlin, 1986), 77–84; and Leif Jerram, "Buildings, Spaces, Politics: Munich City Council and the Management of Modernity" (Ph.D. diss., Manchester 2001), esp. chap. 3. The second example of anti-domesticity in modernist architecture are socialist attempts to create a "new man" through the manipulation of living space. See Victor Buchli, *An Archaeology of Socialism* (Oxford, 1999); Vladimir Paperny, "Men, Women and the Living Space," in *Russian Housing in the Modern Age: Design and Social History*, ed. William Brumfield and Blair Ruble (Cambridge, 1993), 149–70; *Socialist Modern: New Perspectives on East German Cultural History*, ed. Paul Betts and Katherine Pence; and *Style and Socialism: Modernity and Material Culture in Post-War Eastern Europe*, ed. David Crowley and Susan Reid (New York, 2001).

51. An interesting collection of essays that presents a multifaceted view of the role of domesticity in modernism is *Not at Home: The Suppression of Domesticity in Modern Art and Architecture*, ed. Christopher Reed (London, 1996). For an etymological discussion of the term "vernacular" and its Latin root *verna*, which translates as "born into or belonging to a household," see the Introduction to this volume.

52. Iain Boyd Whyte has written persuasively about the problems inherent in the "functionalist" master-narrative. Focusing on Bruno Taut—who diverged from functionalism not in terms of a vernacular but in terms of an expressionist or "Activist" idiom—he writes: "To maintain the Functionalist succession, which ran from the Crystal Palace to the International Movement, the early historians of the modern movement tried to isolate the Expressionist phase and extract it from the clear path of progress. . . . [Yet] the Activist interlude made an important contribution to this tradition. It was based on the assumption that the *geistig* architect could reform and remodel society and could produce harmony and happiness. . . . The belief in an all-seeing and all-healing architecture was fundamental to the [entire] modern movement." Iain Boyd Whyte, *Bruno Taut and the Architecture of Activism* (Cambridge, 1982), 223–24. On the complex and often misunderstood trajectory of "functionalism" in the days of the Werkbund, see Stanford Anderson, "The Fiction of Function," *Assemblage* 2 (1986): 19–31.

53. Hermann Muthesius, *Englische Haus*, quoted from Hubrich, *Hermann Muthesius*, 43.

54. Friedrich Naumann, "Der Industriestaat" (1909), in id., *Werke*, vol. 3, *Politische Schriften*, 42–70.

55. Hermann Muthesius, *Der Kunstwart* 17 (1904): 469, quoted in Matthew Jefferies, *Politics and Culture in Wilhelmine Germany: The Case of Industrial Architecture* (Oxford, 1995), 50–51.

56. Hermann Muthesius, "Wo stehen wir? Vortrag auf der Werkbundtagung 1911," quoted from Neue Sammlung, *Zwischen Kunst und Industrie*, 61.

57. In England, the confrontation between New Liberals and the traditional elites, represented politically in the House of Lords, reached crisis point in 1909. Social reforms were blocked by the Lords, and the Liberals retaliated with the famous "People's Budget," calling for taxes upon unearned increment on the sale of land and on land values, higher death duties, and a supertax on incomes above £3,000. Lloyd George singled out "the rich and the aristocracy" as the enemies of the new liberal Britain.

58. Hermann Muthesius, "Das Musikzimmer," in *Velhagen und Klasings Al-*

manach 1 (Berlin, 1908), 222–27. On Chodowiecki's cartoons, see C. G. Boerner, *Daniel Nikolaus Chodowiecki (1726–1801) und seine Zeit* (Düsseldorf, 2001); Renate Krüger, *Das Zeitalter der Empfindsamkeit. Kunst und Kultur des späten 18. Jahrhunderts in Deutschland* (Vienna, 1972); and Lothar Pikulik, *Leistungsethik contra Gefühlsethik, Über das Verhätnis von Bürgerlichkeit und Empfindsamkeit in Deutschland* (Göttingen, 1984), especially pp. 7–15 and 306–24.

59. The most famous example are two (three were originally planned) houses on the Rehwiese in Berlin, which were part of a landscaped ensemble that used a formal garden as a transitional space between the adjacent houses and the landscaped valley on which they bordered. These two houses—one of which was Muthesius's own home—served as advertisements for his work and can thus be regarded as the purest embodiment of Muthesius's views of the intersection of the land and the city.

60. The withdrawal from the public embodied in English Arts and Crafts houses is only surpassed by the mind-set that produced American gated communities, in which many U.S. Arts and Crafts houses are now located. The work of Bruce Price at Tuxedo Park, for example, is totally cut off from public view and cannot even be seen by appointment.

61. Review of Hermann Muthesius, *Die englische Baukunst der Gegenwart: Beispiele neuer Englischer Profanbauten* (Berlin, 1900), *Architect and Contract Reporter*, 65, 1673 (January 11, 1901): 27–28, and 1674 (January 18, 1901): 42–43; quotation, pt. 1, p. 27.

62. The most useful survey of the garden city movement's spread from England to Europe and America is Stephen V. Ward, *The Garden City: Past, Present and Future* (London, 1992).

63. Robert Beevers, *The Garden City Utopia: A Critical Biography of Ebenezer Howard* (London, 1988); Mervyn Miller, *Letchworth: The First Garden City* (Chichester, U.K., 1989).

64. Recent years have seen a flurry of new publications on Hellerau, including Klaus-Peter Arnold, *Vom Sofakissen zum Städtebau: Die Geschichte der Deutschen Werkstätten und der Gartenstadt Hellerau* (Dresden, 1993); Michael Fasshauer, *Das Phänomen Hellerau: Die Geschichte der Gartenstadt* (Dresden, 1997); *Entwurf zur Moderne: Hellerau, Stand Ort Bestimmung*, ed. Werner Durth (Stuttgart, 1996); Hans-Jürgen Sarfert, *Hellerau: Die Gartenstadt und Künstlerkolonie* (2d ed., Dresden, 1993).

65. Jefferies, *Politics and Culture in Wilhelmine Germany*, 81.

66. Walter Gropius, letter to Karl Ernst Osthaus, March 23, 1912, quoted from Hans Wichmann, *Aufbruch zum neuen Wohnen* (Basel, 1978), 102.

67. On Muthesius's reception of Mebes, see Julius Posener, *Berlin auf dem Wege zu einer neun Architektur: Das Zeitalter Wilhelms II* (Munich, 1995), esp. chap. on "Muthesius als Architekt," 127–59.

68. Lothar Pikulik, *Leistungsethik contra Gefühlsethik: Über das Verhätnis von Bürgerlichkeit und Empfindsamkeit in Deutschland* (Göttingen, 1984), and R. Krüger, *Das Zeitalter der Empfindsamkeit: Kunst und Kultur des späten 18. Jahrhunderts in Deutschland* (Vienna, 1972).

69. In reality, Goethe's garden house was not built "around 1800," as enthusiasts

like Schmitthenner et al. assumed, but dated from the seventeenth century. When Goethe took it over in 1776, he did have the house altered in several ways, yet it retained basic baroque features, notably the cubic pavilion shape and the steep *Walmdach*. It is true, however, that Goethe had some features added that became emblematic for the Biedermeier ideal, such as the two wooden garden gates. See Wolfgang Huschke, *Die Geschichte des Parks von Weimar* (Weimar, 1951).

70. Wolfgang Voigt, "Vom Ur-Haus zum Typ. Paul Schmitthenners 'deutsches Wohnhaus' und seine Vorbilder," in *Moderne Architektur in Deutschland 1900 bis 1950: Reform und Tradition*, ed. Vittorio Magnago Lampugnani and Romana Schneider (Stuttgart, 1992), 245–65; quotation, 245.

71. Hermann Bahr, *Secession* (Vienna, 1900), 40.

72. Nikolaus Pevsner, *Pioneers of Modern Design: From William Morris to Walter Gropius* (1949; rev ed., Harmondsworth, U.K., 1975). More recently, Maciuka, "Hermann Muthesius and the Reform of German Architecture," reiterated a reading of Muthesius as a precursor of high modernism.

73. Mark Jarzombek, "The Discourses of a Bourgeois Utopia, 1904–1908, and the Founding of the Werkbund," in *Imagining Modern German Culture, 1889–1910*, ed. Françoise Forster-Hahn (Washington, D.C., 1996), argues that the Werkbund was effectively a propaganda tool of a reactionary, nationalist "old boys' network" constituted from the Wilhelmine upper middle class. Similarly, an East German study by Kurt Junghanns, *Der Deutsche Werkbund: Sein erstes Jahrzehnt* (Berlin, 1982), regrets that much of the historiography perpetuates a positive view of Muthesius, whom Junghanns sees as an advocate of an exploitative industrial class that purposefully drove Germany into World War I. Schwartz, *Werkbund*, is similarly critical of the Werkbund, though he objects not so much to its allegedly reactionary politics as to its procapitalist orientation.

74. The category of "Heroic Modernism" was developed by Charles Jencks, *Modern Movements in Architecture* (Harmondsworth, U.K., 1985). The label refers to classical modernism in its most radical, uncompromising, and triumphalist mode. Yet it is confusing, in that the term "heroic" suggests that modernism's chief characteristic, the triumph of abstraction, can be likened to an achievement that is by definition idiosyncratic: the "heroism" of an individual.

75. On the 1919 Bauhaus manifesto, see *Bauhaus Weimar: Designs for the Future*, ed. Michael Siebenbrodt (Ostfildern, 2000), and Gillian Naylor, *The Bauhaus Reassessed: Sources and Design Theory* (London, 1985).

76. The controversy that led to this change is documented in *Die Zwanziger Jahre des Deutschen Werkbunds*, ed. Deutscher Werkbund and Werkbund-Archiv (Gießen/Lahn, 1982).

77. Karin Kirsch, *The Weissenhofsiedlung: Experimental Housing Built for the Deutscher Werkbund, Stuttgart, 1927* (New York, 1989); Richard Pommer and Christian F. Otto, *Weissenhof 1927 and the Modern Movement in Architecture* (Chicago, 1991), and Helge Classen, *Die Weißenhofsiedlung: Beginn eines neuen Bauens* (Dortmund, 1990). On the more mature Bauhaus style, see Judith Carmel Arthur, *Bauhaus* (London, 2000). On Mies's view of architecture, see Fritz Neumeyer, *The Artless Word: Mies van der Rohe on the Building Art*, trans. Mark Jarzombek (Cambridge, Mass., 1991).

78. Muthesius's dismissal of "style" in architecture dates back to his pamphlet *Stilarchitektur und Baukunst: Wandlungen der Architektur im 19. Jahrhundert und ihr heutiger Standpunkt* (Mühlheim-Ruhr, 1902). In 1927, shortly before his death, Muthesius published a review of the Weißenhofsiedlung in the *Berliner Tageblatt*. Though he acknowledged the validity of the project's aims, he criticized that the aesthetic perfectionism of the execution mitigated against practical use and spoke of the "tyrannical new form." Quoted from *Zwanziger Jahre des Deutschen Werkbunds*, ed. Deutscher Werkbund and Werkbund-Archiv, 117.

79. Vittorio Magnago Lampugnani, "Vom Block zur Kochenhofsiedlung," in id., *Moderne Architektur*, 267–81. About the ideological divisions in the Werkbund during this crucial period, see also "Mit der Zukunft im Bunde? Zur Geschichte des Deutschen Werkbundes, 1907–1934," in *Zwanziger Jahre des Deutschen Werkbundes*, ed. Deutscher Werkbund and Werkbund-Archiv, Reihe Werkbund-Archiv, vol. 10.

80. "Ein richtungsweisendes Beispiel der neuen Baugesinnung: Die Austellung Deutsches Holz für Hausbau und Wohnung," *Bauzeitung*, quoted from Lampugnani, *Moderne Architektur*, trans. the author.

81. The German title was Reichsforschungsgesellschaft für Wirtschaftlichkeit im Bau- und Wohnungswesen.

82. Reinhard Merker, *Die bildenden Künste im Nationalsozialismus. Kulturideologie—Kulturpolitik—Kulturproduktion* (Cologne, 1983).

83. Paul Schultze-Naumburg, *Das flache und das geneigte Dach* (1927).

84. The building regulations for the colonies are quoted in Lampugnani, "Vom Block zur Kochenhofsiedlung," 280.

85. Helge Pitz, "Die Farbigkeit der vier Siedlungen—Ein Werkstattbericht," in *Siedlungen der zwanziger Jahre—heute. Vier Berliner Großsiedlungen 1924–1984*, ed. Norbert Huse (Berlin, 1984), 59–809.

86. Gerhard Weiss, "Der Wohnungsbau Heinrich Tessenows: Eine baugeschichtliche und soziologische Untersuchung zum Wohnungsbau des 20. Jahrhunderts," in Gerda Wangerin and Gerhard Weiss, *Heinrich Tessenow: Ein Baumeister, 1876–1950* (Essen, 1976), 79–147.

87. The original, still in place today, reads "Unner en hooget Tak heuert en uprechten Minsken." According to an oral history interview with the present occupiers conducted by the author on February 10, 2003, the house was built in 1903–4 according to the architectural design of one Richard Schultze. The owner at the time, a Lutheran pastor, had the inscription painted onto the gable in the late 1920s, when the "Zehlendorfer Dächerkrieg" was at its peak.

88. Manfred Nerdinger, "Karl Schneider und die Moderne: Eine Ortsbestimmung," in *Architektur in Hamburg: Jahrbuch, 1992*, 152–59; *Karl Schneider: Landhaus Michaelsen*, ed. Elke Dröscher (Hamburg, 1992).

89. Josef Frank, *Architektur als Symbol* (Vienna, 1930). Similar views still dominate writing on the House Michaelsen today. It is termed "nicht stilrein" by Gerd Kähler, *Wohnung und Stadt* (Braunschweig, 1985), 132, and a "Zwitterwesen"—a hybrid—by Janis Marie Mink, "Karl Schneider: Leben und Werk" (Ph.D. diss. Universität Hamburg, 1990), 41.

90. *Bauhaus-Moderne im Nationalsozialismus: Zwischen Anbiederung und Verfolgung*, ed. Winfried Nerdinger (Munich, 1993). See also *Reichsautobahn, Pyramiden*

des Dritten Reichs: Analysen zur Ästhetik eines unbewältigten Mythos, ed. Rainer Stommer, with Claudia Gabriele Philipp (Marburg, 1982). An excellent new study of the state architecture of National Socialism, which combined modernist and neoclassical motifs, is Paul B. Jaskot, *The Architecture of Oppression: The SS, Forced Labor and the Nazi Monumental Building Economy* (New York, 2000). On Speer, see also Angela Schönberger, *Die neue Reichskanzlei von Albert Speer: Zum Zusammenhang von nationalsozialistischer Ideologie und Architektur* (Berlin, 1981).

91. Muthesius, "Bedeutung des Kunstgewerbes," 94.

5. *Passanti: The Vernacular, Modernism, and Le Corbusier*

This essay began as a lecture in the workshop "Modern Culture and the Ethnic Artefact" at the Internationales Forschungszentrum Kulturwissenschaften in Vienna, August 28–31, 1996, organized by Akos Moravánszky of the Eidgenossische Technische Hochschule in Zurich. A different version of the chapter appeared in the *Journal of the Society of Architectural Historians (JSAH)* 4, 56 (December 1997): 438–51, and in German as "Volkskunst, die Moderne und Le Corbusier," in *Das entfernte Dorf: Moderne Kunst und ethnischer Artefakt*, ed. Akos Moravánszky (Vienna, 2002), 249–78. I thank Professor Moravánszky and the workshop participants for stimulating discussions. I also thank Mardges Bacon, Sarah Williams Goldhagen, Harvey Mendelsohn, Christian Otto, and Eve Blau, who read drafts of the chapter and made useful suggestions.

1. Richard Pommer and Christian F. Otto, *Weissenhof 1927 and the Modern Movement in Architecture* (Chicago, 1991).

2. Eric Mumford, *The CIAM Discourse on Urbanism, 1928–1960* (Cambridge, Mass., 2000); Henry-Russell Hitchcock and Philip Johnson, *The International Style* (New York, 1932).

3. Le Corbusier, *Vers une architecture* (Paris, 1923), trans. as *Towards a New Architecture* (New York, 1927).

4. The principal publication of Le Corbusier's work is his own *Oeuvre complète*, 8 vols. (Zurich, 1929–70). For an overview of his whole career, the standard remains Stanislaus von Moos, *Le Corbusier: Elemente einer Synthese* (Frauenfeld, 1968), rev. English ed., *Le Corbusier: Elements of a Synthesis* (Cambridge, Mass., 1979). For an overview of Le Corbusier's early years, see H. Allen Brooks, *Le Corbusier's Formative Years* (Chicago, 1997) and the recent exhibition catalogue *Le Corbusier Before Le Corbusier*, ed. Stanislaus von Moos and Arthur Rüegg (New Haven, 2002). The literature by and on Le Corbusier, too vast to list here, can be found in two bibliographies: Darlene Brady, *Le Corbusier: An Annotated Bibliography* (New York, 1985), and Christopher Pearson, "A Selected Bibliography of Works on Le CorbusierPublished in the 1980s," *Bulletin of Bibliography* 51 (March 1994): 31–52.

5. Le Corbusier, *Le Voyage d'Orient* (Paris, 1966), ed. and trans. Ivan Zaknic as *Journey to the East* (Cambridge, Mass., 1987), hereafter cited as *Voyage*. His sketchbooks from the trip are published as Le Corbusier, *Voyage d'Orient: Carnets* (Paris, 1987), hereafter cited as *Carnets*. Other important documentation can be found in Giuliano Gresleri, *Le Corbusier: Viaggio in Oriente* (Venice, 1984).

6. Le Corbusier, *Voyage*, 19. The captain suggested the town of Baja, some 100 kilometers south of Budapest along the Danube.

7. Ibid., 16, 17.

8. Ibid., 42, 43.

9. Ibid., 21, 55, 116–17.

10. Particularly since the publication of Edward Said's *Orientalism* (New York, 1978), we are now more aware of the power games and epistemological difficulties lurking in any search for origins, or in any distancing from an *other*. For a recent anthropological perspective, see James Clifford, *The Predicament of Culture: Twentieth-Century Ethnography, Literature, and Art* (Cambridge, Mass., 1988). Zeynep Çelik, focusing mostly on Le Corbusier's projects for Algiers in the 1930s, finds colonial overtones in his interest in the non-Western world; but Sybel Bozdogan, focusing mostly on the "voyage d'Orient" of 1911, comes to the opposite conclusion: Zeynep Çelik, "Le Corbusier, Orientalism, Colonialism," *Assemblage* 17 (April 1992): 59–77; Sybel Bozdogan, "Journey to the East: Ways of Looking at the Orient and the Question of Representation," *Journal of Architectural Education* 41 (Summer 1988): 38–45, 61. For our purposes here, the issue of colonialism is marginal, since most of the vernacular and modernist architecture in question is European. It would be more interesting to explore, along similar lines, the implications of any notion of the vernacular, Western and otherwise, older and contemporary; but that would go beyond the limited scope of this chapter.

11. Adolf Max Vogt, *Le Corbusier: Der edle Wilde* (Braunschweig, 1996), trans. as *Le Corbusier, the Noble Savage* (Cambridge, Mass., 1998).

12. Le Corbusier, *Voyage*, 118–19.

13. Le Corbusier, *Carnets*, carnet 4, 69; the emphasis is Le Corbusier's. About the Balkans and Turkey: "Pourquoi notre progrès est-il laid? Pourquoi ceux qui ont encore un sang vierge aiment-ils prendre de nous le plus mauvais?" (Le Corbusier, *Voyage*, 170). And about the West: "le public . . . n'y comprend plus rien . . . Il a en lui aussi, l'épouvantable germe qui s'en va ruinant dans les pays chastes, les coeurs jusqu'ici simples et croyants, les arts jusqu'ici normaux, sains et naturels" (ibid., 121–22).

14. The passage "le public . . . naturels," quoted in the previous note, continues thus: "Ce que j'ai vu en route m'enlève à jamais tout espoir en la candeur des races neuves et je porte toutes mes espérances sur ceux qui, ayant commencé à l'alpha, sont déja bien loin, et connaissent beaucoup. C'est pourquoi je pense qu'il n'y a pas à réagir. Car l'épuration est une nécessité vitale, et, comme on fuit la Mort, par simple désir de vivre on reviendra,—oui, à la santé de cette époque, santé adéquate à nos contingences, et, delà, à la beauté" (Le Corbusier, *Voyage*, 122). In this passage, the term "races neuves" refers to premodern cultures, which are still virgin, chaste, and simple, to use Le Corbusier's terminology. And the phrase "ceux qui, ayant commencé à l'alpha, sont déja bien loin" refers to urban culture and modern art.

15. Other examples are Le Corbusier's Maison Citrohan (1921), an individual house type based on Parisian artists' lofts and cafés, and his Immeuble Villas (1922), an ideal apartment complex in which the unit type is based on the cells of Carthusian monasteries.

16. Thus, Le Corbusier claimed that the arrangement of one of his houses at the Weißenhof exhibition of 1927 had been derived from railway sleeping cars: Le Corbusier, "La Signification de la cité-jardin du Weissenhof," *Architecture vivante* (Spring 1928): 9–15. And while traveling to India in 1959, he carefully recorded some internal arrangements in his airplane, for later use in bathrooms and kitchens: Sketchbook P59 in Le Corbusier, *Le Corbusier Sketchbooks*, 4 vols. (New York, 1981–82), 4: 457.

17. Vogt, *Le Corbusier: Der edle Wilde*. The book as a whole argues for the importance of Rousseau in Le Corbusier's very education at home, in kindergarten and in elementary school. Pages 229–35 in particular deal with Le Corbusier's father, an early and enthusiastic mountain climber who was responsible for building two alpine huts, i.e., basic shelter in extreme conditions. By analyzing diary entries of Le Corbusier's father, Vogt shows that he viewed those conditions as a Rousseauian return to "natural" life. Vogt's point is important because it can easily be extended to Le Corbusier's interest in functional minimalism.

18. The ceremonial aspect of the Savoye ramp is noted in Moos, *Le Corbusier: Elements of a Synthesis*, 88 (see n. 4), and connected to Renaissance and baroque examples. A medieval precedent is suggested in Jürgen Joedicke, "Die Rampe als architektonische Promenade im Werk Le Corbusiers," *Daidalos* 12 (June 1984): 104–8. The importance of the ramp at the Villa Savoye is not diminished by the spiral service staircase to its left. The ramp is directly in front of the entrance, while the staircase is to the side and "shows its back" to the entrance; and the presence of this subordinate and duplicate itinerary only emphasizes the ceremonial quality of the ramp. It should also be noted that the exposed spiral staircase was not part of the initial concept and appeared only when the project was scaled down for budgetary reasons: in the first and grander project for the Villa Savoye, the service staircase was entirely hidden, as shown in Le Corbusier's *Oeuvre Complète*, 1: 186. Catholic churches have basins of holy water near the entry doors, and mosques have ablution fountains: for example, Hagia Sophia, visited by Le Corbusier, had one in the ceremonial court outside. It should also be noted that Le Corbusier intended the wash basin to have a more prominent location than the one it eventually received, partially hidden by a column. In the first and grander project for the Villa Savoye, the basin was framed by a sculptural curved screen. In the final reduced project, the basin is placed in front of the column, as the published plans show.

19. Le Corbusier to William Ritter, June 21, 1922. Bern, Schweizerische Landesbibliothek, Ritter Nachlass; copies at the Bibliothèque de la Ville in La Chaux-de-Fonds and at the Fondation Le Corbusier in Paris.

20. Three points about terminology are important here. First, the literal translation of the word *Sachlichkeit* is "factualness," but in German the word has a range of colloquial meanings that must be rendered by a number of English terms: "factualness," "matter-of-factness," "sobriety," "objectivity," "realism," "functionality," "practicality," "pragmatism." In the context of modernist architecture, the terms most used have been "sobriety" and "objectivity." I find the term "factualness" most precise because it explicitly incorporates the root "fact," *Sache*, a word that is often used alone in the writings of German theorists of the concept such as Karl Scheffler. The various meanings of the term are listed in Stanford Anderson, "Style-Architec-

ture and Building-Art: Realist Architecture as the Vehicle for a Renewal of Culture," in Hermann Muthesius, *Style-Architecture and Building-Art: Transformations of Architecture in the Nineteenth Century and Its Present Condition*, trans. Anderson (Santa Monica, Calif., 1994), 38n10. Second, for the sake of simplicity, I use the term *Sachlichkeit* as an umbrella to designate a broad cultural discourse extending from the 1890s to World War I. While the concept of *Sachlichkeit* was arguably the most common and early denominator in that discourse, other concepts, such as "type," "style," and "culture," provided focus as well. Which one of these terms best designates the whole discourse remains an open question. Third, before World War I, *Sachlichkeit* was invoked by both traditionalists and modernists. Naturally, it was the latter use of the concept that provided the direct springboard for the modernist generation after the war and that captured the attention of historians of modernist architecture (including myself). But it was precisely the traditionalist-modernist tension it accommodated that made this concept so fertile, as suggested later in this chapter. On *Sachlichkeit*, see Harry Francis Mallgrave, "From Realism to *Sachlichkeit*: The Polemics of Architectural Modernity in the 1890s," in *Otto Wagner: Reflections on the Raiment of Modernity*, ed. Harry Francis Mallgrave (Santa Monica, Calif., 1993), 281–323; Stanford Anderson, "*Sachlichkeit* and Modernity, or Realist Architecture," ibid., 323–62; Anderson, "Style-Architecture," in Muthesius, *Style-Architecture and Building-Art*; and Mitchell Schwarzer, *German Architectural Theory and the Search for Modern Identity* (Cambridge, 1995), passim. On the relevance of the concept for modernist architecture, the seminal essay remains William Jordy, "The Symbolic Essence of Modern European Architecture of the Twenties and Its Continuing Influence," *JSAH* 23 (October 1963): 177–87, which identifies "symbolic objectivity," i.e., symbolic *Sachlichkeit* as a central conceptual structure of modernist architecture. See also Fritz Schmalenbach, "The term *Neue Sachlichkeit*," *Art Bulletin* 22 (September 1940): 161–65, and Rosemarie Haag Bletter, introduction to Adolf Behne, *The Modern Functional Building*, intr. Rosemarie Haag Bletter, trans. Michael Robinson (Santa Monica, Calif., 1996), 1–83.

21. Loos developed this argument in various articles of 1897–1900, later gathered in his book *Ins Leere gesprochen, 1897–1900* (Paris and Zurich, 1921; reprint, Vienna, 1981). He further articulated the same argument in "Architektur," *Der Sturm* 42 (December 15, 1910), later translated as "L'Architecture et le style moderne," *Cahiers d'aujourd'hui* 2 (December 1912): 82–92, and in "Ornament und Verbrechen," first published in French as "Ornement et crime," *Cahiers d'aujourd'hui* 5 (June 1913): 247–56; both essays were later republished in German in his book *Trotzdem, 1900–1930* (Innsbruck, 1931; reprint, Vienna, 1982).

22. Loos, "Architektur." Loos does not use the expression "modern vernacular," but the sense of his essay clearly supports it. By the expression "modern vernacular," I mean something quite different from the "vernacular modernism" that Maiken Umbach discusses in Chapter 4. Umbach refers to such things as Hermann Muthesius's houses, which use vernacular (often rural) models and adapt them to modern suburban life: the forms are traditional, but their use is modern. I refer instead to the attempt to define a new vernacular that is characteristic of modern industrial civilization.

23. Nothing in Le Corbusier's correspondence suggests that he knew about

Loos at the time of the Balkan trip, although Loos's "Architektur" was published in *Der Sturm* in Berlin while Le Corbusier was there. In fact, just before boarding the ship on the Danube at the beginning of the trip, in a poignant missed encounter, Le Corbusier sketched a shop window on the Viennese Graben that caught his attention: it was the Knize store by Loos, not yet finished (Le Corbusier, *Carnets*, carnet 1, 56–57). But Le Corbusier casually annotated the sketch "a very nice store on the Graben"; he did not seem to know who Loos was, and this should not surprise us, because Loos's architecture and writings had been little published and mostly in Viennese publications not easily accessible to Le Corbusier. In late 1913, he read two of Loos's articles in French translation, as we know from his correspondence: these were "Architektur" and "Ornament und Verbrechen" (see n. 21 above). There is no record of further contact until 1920, when Le Corbusier met Loos in Paris and began seriously to come to terms with his thinking. On Le Corbusier's debt to Loos, see Stanislaus von Moos, "Le Corbusier and Loos," in *L'Esprit nouveau: Le Corbusier und die Industrie 1920–1925*, ed. Stanislaus von Moos (Berlin, 1987), 122–33.

24. On Muthesius as theorist, see Hans-Joachim Hubrich, *Hermann Muthesius: Die Schriften zu Architektur, Kunstgewerbe, Industrie in der "Neuen Bewegung"* (Berlin, 1981); Julius Posener, *Berlin auf dem Wege zu einer neuen Architektur* (Munich, 1979), 525–47; Anderson, "Style-Architecture," in Muthesius, *Style-Architecture and Building-Art*, with recent bibliography. On the German Werkbund, see Joan Campbell, *The German Werkbund: The Politics of Reform in the Applied Arts* (Princeton, 1978). On Muthesius's position about type and the 1914 debate at Cologne, see Stanford Anderson, "Deutsche Werkbund—the 1914 Debate: Hermann Muthesius versus Henry van de Velde," in *Companion to Contemporary Architectural Thought*, ed. Ben Farmer and Hentje Louw (London, 1993), 462–67, and Frederic J. Schwartz, *The Werkbund: Design Theory and Mass Culture Before the First World War* (New Haven, 1996), 121–50; 241n8 for bibliography. On the effect on Le Corbusier of the 1914 debate, see Winfried Nerdinger, "Standard und Typ: Le Corbusier und Deutschland, 1920–1927," in *Le Corbusier und die Industrie* (see n. 23 above), 44–53.

25. The full text of Muthesius's speech is found in Deutsche Werkbund, *Hermann Muthesius: Die Werkbund-Arbeit der Zukunft und Aussprache darüber . . . Friedrich Naumann: Werkbund und Weltwirtschaft . . . 7. Jahresversammlung des Deutschen Werkbundes . . . in Köln* (Jena, 1914), which also includes the "theses" and "countertheses" that preceded the speech, and the discussion that followed. Extensive extracts are found in Julius Posener, *Anfänge des Funktionalismus* (Frankfurt a/M, 1964), 199–227, and in Die Neue Sammlung, Staatliches Museum für angewandte Kunst, *Zwischen Kunst und Industrie, Der Deutsche Werkbund*), exhibition catalogue, ed. W. Fischer (1975), 85–115 (rev. ed., Stuttgart, 1987).

26. This whole discourse is admirably articulated in Schwartz, *Werkbund*: pp. 75–81 deal with the history of the disciplines of political economy and sociology, and pp. 121–46 deal specifically with the issue of type and with the evolving meanings of the German words *Typ*, *Typus*, and *Typisierung*, but the whole book is important for grasping the larger cultural implications of the debate. Particularly important as a precedent to Muthesius's speech was Friedrich Naumann's "Kunst und Industrie," *Der Kunstwart* 19, 2 (1906): 66–73, 128–31. Writing about the marketing of industrial products, Naumann spoke of "types or brands" ("Typen oder Marken") thus con-

necting the word *Typus* or *Typ* to industrial mass production. The most apt English term for *Marken* is "brands" (used in Schwartz, *Werkbund*, 128), but the full range of meanings is best conveyed by "brands," "trademarked products," and "trademarked models" taken together.

27. See n. 29.

28. The pardigmatic text of this attitude is Paul Schultze-Naumburg, *Kulturarbeiten*, 9 vols. (Munich, 1901–17). On Schultze-Naumburg see Norbert Borrmann, *Paul Schultze-Naumburg, Maler, Publizist, Architekt, 1869–1949* (Essen, 1989). Since 1897, Schultze-Naumburg had collaborated with *Der Kunstwart*, a periodical founded by Ferdinand Avenarius ten years earlier and an important forum from its inception for the discourse about *Volkskunst*. Schultze-Naumburg's reliance on the adaptation of traditional types would, in turn, underlie the iconic house designs of Heinrich Tessenow. It should be noted that Schultze-Naumburg was opposed not to industrialization per se but to its cultural ravages, as pointed out by Christian Otto, "Modern Environment and Historical Continuity: The Heimatschutz Discourse in Germany," *Art Journal* 43 (Summer 1983): 148–57. Naumann, Scheffler, and Muthesius shared that concern but differed in their analysis of cause and cure and, ultimately, in their political agendas.

29. For example, in 1897 Alfred Lichtwark praised the "*Typus*" of traditional Hamburg houses, developed during the Middle Ages around the needs and ways of life of shipmasters and fishermen, and then formalized by classicism during the eighteenth century: Alfred Lichtwark, "Das alte Hamburger Haus" and "Schiffer- und Fischerhäuser," later incorporated into his book *Palastfenster und Flügelthür* (Berlin, 1899). And in 1904, Schultze-Naumburg wrote that people in earlier times had been "wary of improvising quickly on their own what can only be the cumulative work of generations: creating the type, which the artist must fully master in order then to deviate from it according to the specific task" (hüteten sich davor, kurzer Hand aus Eigenem heraus das leisten zu wollen, was nur die Arbeitssumme von Geschlechtern sein kann: das Gestalten des Typus, den der Künstler auswending beherrschen muss, um ihn dann des Einzelaufgabe entsprechend abzuwandeln): Schultze-Naumburg, *Kulturarbeiten*, vol. 3, *Dörfer und Kolonien* (1904; new ed., Munich, 1908), 32. The notion that types emerge anonymously went back to Gottfried Semper, a source Muthesius mentioned explicitly in his speech "Wo stehen wir?" (1911), as noted by Schwartz, *Werkbund*, 123. Semper stressed that types arising from use and function (e.g., the type of a cup) are independent of time and place: Semper, *Kleine Schriften*, ed. Hans and Manfred Semper (Berlin, 1884), 269. Schultze-Naumburg used the same argument for more nationalistic purposes, focusing on more complex types characteristic of specific German situations.

30. Walter Riezler, statement during the discussion at Cologne. Full text in Deutsche Werkbund, *Werkbund-Arbeit der Zukunft*. Excerpt in Neue Sammlung, *Zwischen Kunst und Industrie*, 105–7.

31. As already suggested, by conflating the two discourses, Muthesius was building upon the thinking of his mentors Scheffler and Naumann, who had already co-opted a traditionalist and ruralist concept to support an industrial urban argument, for example, in 1901 and 1904, when they had pointedly used two words dear to the traditionalists, *Volkskunst* and *Volkstil*, to advocate an urban and industrial ma-

terial culture. Karl Scheffler, "Volkskunst," *Dekorative Kunst* 4 (January 1901) in *Die Kunst* 4 (1901): 140–44; Friedrich Naumann, "Die Kunst im Zeitalter der Machine," *Der Kunstwart* 17 (July 1904). Scheffler came back to this theme repeatedly in the first years of the century. And Naumann embedded it in the notion of type with his "Kunst und Industrie" of 1906 (see n. 26).

32. Le Corbusier, *Vers une architecture* (Paris, 1923), 106–7, in the chapter titled "Des yeux qui ne voient pas . . . III: Les Autos." This chapter was first published as an article two years earlier in *L'Esprit nouveau* 10 (Summer 1921). Without raising the question of its prewar German sources, Thilo Hilpert has already noted Le Corbusier's conflation of industrial and traditional ideals into an "industrial folklore" in Thilo Hilpert, *Le Corbusier, 1887–1987: Atelier der Ideen/Laboratory of Ideas/Laboratoire des Idées: Genius* (Frankfurt a/M, 1987), 19, 194.

33. Le Corbusier had certainly been exposed to the ideas of Karl Scheffler and Peter Behrens while working for the latter in Berlin in 1910–11; as mentioned in note 23, he could conceivably also have heard of Loos. But nothing in Le Corbusier's letters and notebooks of that time suggests an interest in *sachlich* ideas, other than Behrens's classicism. At that time, Le Corbusier was concerned with other issues. His tone changed only in 1913 after a trip to Germany, the probable acquisition of the *Jahrbuch des Deutschen Werkbundes* for 1913, and reading the two articles by Loos in French translation. By early 1914, articles and letters by Le Corbusier show that he was quickly absorbing the new ideas.

34. Brooks, *Le Corbusier's Formative Years*, 23–91. On the importance of Ruskin in his formation see esp. Patricia May Sekler, *The Early Drawings of Charles-Edouard Jeanneret (Le Corbusier), 1902–1908* (New York, 1977). Jeanneret began using the pseudonym Le Corbusier in 1920.

35. Alain Clavien, *Les Helvétistes; Intellectuels et politique en Suisse romande au début du siècle* (Lausanne, 1993). I thank Françoise Frey, the former curator of the Le Corbusier collection at the Bibliothèque de la Ville, La Chaux-de-Fonds, for suggesting this important reference to me.

36. On L'Eplattenier, see Sekler, *Early Drawings*, 1–47 passim, and the exhibition catalogue *Charles L'Eplattenier, 1874–1946* (La Chaux-de-Fonds, 1974).

37. Clavien, *Helvétistes*, 13–56.

38. Brooks, *Le Corbusier's Formative Years*, 185–91; Schweizer Baudokumentation, *Bauernhäuser der Schweiz* (Blauen, Switzerland, 1982), 1–12, with bibliography. Le Corbusier admired the farms of his region, and twice lived in them, during the winter of 1909–10 and then again in 1911–12, following his Balkan/Mediterranean tour. His reason for living in these isolated buildings had more to do with lifestyle than architecture. Architecturally, his serious interest began only in the second sojourn, and it reflects the changes in attitude occasioned by the tour, discussed later in this chapter. Brooks makes the important point that, in his late work, Le Corbusier came back to his experience of these farms, transforming their funnel-shaped hearths into the assembly spaces of the Assembly building in Chandigarh (1951–62) and of the church in Firminy (1960–65).

39. On Le Corbusier's stay in Germany during 1910–11 and, in general, on the influence of prewar Germany on him, see (listed here in order of publication) Winfried Nerdinger, "Le Corbusier und Deutschland: Genesis und Wirkungsgeschichte

eines Konflicts, 1910–1933," *Arch+* 90–91 (August 1987): 80–86, 97; Werner Oechslin, "Allemagne: Influences, confluences et reniements," in Centre Pompidou, *Le Corbusier, une encyclopédie* (Paris, 1987), 33–39, or, in German, "Le Corbusier und Deutschland: 1910/1911," in *Le Corbusier im Brennpunkt. Vorträge an der Abteilung für Architektur ETHZ*, ed. Werner Oechslin (Zurich, 1988), 28–47; Rosario De Simone, *Ch. E. Jeanneret–Le Corbusier: Viaggio in Germania 1910–1911* (Rome, 1989); Stanislaus von Moos, "Der Fall Le Corbusier: Kreuzbestäubungen, Allergien, Infektionen," in *Moderne Architektur in Deutschland, 1900 bis 1950. Expressionismus und Neue Sachlichkeit*, ed. Vittorio M. Lampugnani (Stuttgart, 1994), 161–84; and Brooks, *Le Corbusier's Formative Years*, 209–53.

40. There is no good biography of Ritter. Some useful information can be found in Josef Tscherv, *William Ritter, enfance et jeunesse, 1867–1889* (Melida, Switzerland, 1958); Josef Tscherv, *William Ritter 1867–1955* (Bellinzona, Switzerland, 1971); and Jean-Marc Rydlo, "Helvetus Peregrinus: William Ritter et la Slovaquie," *Hispo* (Bern) (October 1989): 7–20. My point of departure has been the substantial collection of works by Ritter kept at the Bibliothèque de la Ville, La Chaux-de-Fonds.

41. Ritter's antisemitism is particularly obvious in his novel *Fillette slovaque: Le Cycle de la nationalité* (Paris, 1903), and in his article "Magyars, Roumains et Juifs," *Demain* (Lyon) 1, 19 (March 2, 1906): 10–13. His antagonism toward urbanized Germans and to Americans can be inferred from Le Corbusier's correspondence with him.

42. This position was articulated by the review *La Voile latine*, published in Geneva from 1904 to 1910, on which see Clavien, *Helvétistes*. Ritter had a somewhat testy relationship with the review but shared its basic attitude, and a few months before Le Corbusier's grand tour, he recommended to him a book by the most extreme of the review's collaborators, Alexandre Cingria-Vaneyre's *Les Entretiens de la villa du Rouet* (Geneva, 1908), which used the racial theories of J. A. de Gobineau to support a Mediterranean identity for French-speaking Switzerland. On this book, see Paul Venable Turner, *The Education of Le Corbusier* (New York, 1977), 83–91.

43. Earlier in his life, Ritter had spent time in Bucharest, and had written extensively about the Rumanian painter Nikoulae Grigoresco. He had also written numerous articles about the artistic and political situation in Bohemia, Hungary, and Rumania; and he had especially addressed the situation of the Slovak minority in articles and two novels, *Fillette slovaque* (see n. 41 above) and *L'Entêtement slovaque* (Paris, 1910), the latter read by Le Corbusier before his trip.

44. At the time that he met Ritter, Le Corbusier was reading extensively and preparing a manuscript on urban design, eventually published as *La Construction des villes: Genèse et devenir d'un ouvrage écrit de 1910 à 1915 et laissé inachevé par Charles Edouard Jeanneret-Gris dit Le Corbusier*, ed. Marc E. Albert Emery (Lausanne, 1992); see Brooks, *Le Corbusier's Formative Years*, 200–207, on this. His notes mention Paul Schultze-Naumburg, the German theorist and preservationist whom we have already encountered. Le Corbusier also mentions Georges de Montenach and probably read Guillaume Fatio and Léandre Vaillat, three preservationists who wrote about Swiss vernacular architecture. All of these authors held ideas in line with those of Ritter, though Le Corbusier (a novice in their field) seems to have been interested mostly in technical points. Le Corbusier would rehash the ideas of Ritter and

of most of these authors in an article written without much conviction for a popular audience in the summer of 1913: Charles-Édouard Jeanneret, "La Maison suisse," *Les Etrennes helvétiques*, 1914: 33–39.

45. Behrens's classicism was itself part of the same *sachlich* interest in modern vernacular, because it was specifically inspired by German architecture around 1800, when the German bourgeoisie first attained a high level of self-consciousness. German critics contemporary with Behrens, like Alfred Lichtwark, Paul Schultze-Naumburg, Karl Scheffler, and Paul Mebes, saw classicism around 1800 (*um 1800*) as a sort of bourgeois vernacular. But little in Le Corbusier's letters suggests that he understood this implication of Behrens's style while he was working for him: his attention was focused on learning the formal discipline of classicism, an architectural language very different from that of the Arts and Crafts aesthetic in which he had been educated. On the return to classicism in early twentieth-century Germany, see Stanford Anderson, "The Legacy of German Neo-Classicism and Biedermeier: Behrens, Tessenow, Loos and Mies," *Assemblage* 15 (October 1991): 62–87.

46. "Voilà l'énorme lampe de sacrifice qui s'allume. Et combien il est dur de vivre chaque heure en sacrifiant!" Le Corbusier to Francis Jourdain, December 21, 1913, in Le Corbusier's copybook, Bibliothèque de la Ville, La Chaux-de-Fonds, LCms89.

47. Le Corbusier, *Vers une architecture*, 16, 48–63, 161–82: the famous definition reads, in full: "L'architecture est le jeu savant, correct et magnifique des volumes assemblés sous la lumière." Le Corbusier came back to the theme of proportions later in his life, with his book *Le Modulor: Essai sur une mesure harmonique à l'échelle humaine applicable universellement à l'architecture* (Paris, 1942).

48. On Le Corbusier's skyscrapers, see Francesco Passanti, "The Skyscrapers of the Ville Contemporaine," *Assemblage* 4 (October 1987): 53–65. On the proportions of the Villa Stein, see Roger Hertz-Fischler, "Le Corbusier's 'Regulating Lines' for the Villa at Garches (1927) and Other Early Works," *JSAH* 43 (March 1984): 53–59.

49. For a recent discussion of Le Corbusier's sources, see my essay "Architecture: Proportion, Classicism and Other Issues," in *Le Corbusier Before Le Corbusier*, ed. Stanislaus von Moos and Arthur Rüegg (New Haven, 2002), 68–97, esp. 77–81 and 83–86.

50. Pierre Reverdy, "L'Emotion," *Nord-Sud* 8 (October 1917), and "L'Image," *Nord-Sud* 13 (March 1918). Both essays are reprinted in his *Oeuvres complètes: Nord-Sud, Self defence et autres écrits sur l'art et la poésie (1917–1926)* (Paris, 1975), 52–60 and 73–75. In the first essay, Reverdy argues that a work of art is constructed through elements taken from life. In the second, he argues that the poetic image is born "from the bringing together of two more or less remote realities" ("du rapprochement de deux réalités plus ou moins éloignées"). Christopher Green has already pointed out the importance of Reverdy for the painting of Juan Gris in the late 1910s, and for that of Le Corbusier in the late 1930s: Christopher Green, *Cubism and Its Enemies* (New Haven, 1987), passim; Christopher Green, "The Architect as Artist," in Arts Council of Great Britain, exhibition catalogue, ed. Michael Raeburn and Victoria Wilson, *Le Corbusier, Architect of the Century* (London, 1987), 117.

51. "La poésie n'est que dans le verbe. Plus forte est la poésie des faits. Des ob-

jets qui signifient quelque chose et qui sont disposés avec tact et talent créent un fait poétique." Le Corbusier, *Vers une architecture*, 113, in the chapter titled "Des yeux qui ne voient pas . . . III: Les Autos" (see n. 32 above).

52. Mary Caroline McLeod, "Urbanism and Utopia: Le Corbusier from Regional Syndicalism to Vichy" (Ph.D. diss., Princeton University, 1985).

53. Stanford Anderson has addressed the question of continuity and change in architecture using a conceptual model derived from Karl Popper's theory of scientific knowledge. See, e.g., Stanford Anderson, "Architecture and Tradition," *Architectural Association Journal* 80 (May 1965); "Types and Conventions in Time: Towards a History for the Duration and Change of Artifacts," *Perspecta* 18 (1982): 108–17, 206–7, and Chapter 6 in this volume.

6. Anderson: The Vernacular, Memory, and Architecture

1. This strategy can be observed in the Museum of Modern Art's exhibition and publication of Bernard Rudofsky's *Architecture Without Architects* (New York, 1964).

2. Nancy Stieber, "The Professionalization of Housing Design: A Study of Collectivism and Cultural Pluralism in Amsterdam" (Ph.D. diss., Massachusetts Institute of Technology, 1986), and id., *Housing Design and Society in Amsterdam: Reconfiguring Urban Order and Identity, 1900–1920* (Chicago, 1998).

3. Cf. also Stanford Anderson, "Memory Without Monuments: Vernacular Architecture," *Traditional Dwellings and Settlements Review* 11, 1 (Fall 1999): 12–22.

4. Stanford Anderson, "Memory in Architecture / Erinnerung in der Architektur," *Daidalos* (Berlin) 58 (December 1995): 22–37.

5. Jack Goody and Ian Watt, "The Consequences of Literacy," in *Literacy in Traditional Societies*, ed. Goody (Cambridge, 1968), 30, 67.

6. Jacques Le Goff, *History and Memory* [*Storia e memoria* (Turin, 1977)], trans. Steven Rendall and Elizabeth Claman (New York, 1992), 57. See also André Leroi-Gourhan, "Les Voies de l'histoire avant l'écriture," in *Faire de l'histoire*, ed. Le Goff and Pierre Nora (Paris, 1974), 1: 93–105.

7. Goody and Watt, "Consequences of Literacy," 67–68.

8. In accounting for the "conquest and eradication of memory by history," Pierre Nora seems to me to glorify the conditions of "so-called primitive or archaic societies," and to show too little appreciation for the critical dimension of history in modern societies. See his "Between Memory and History," *Representations* 26 (Spring 1989): 7–26.

9. Aysen Savas, "Between Document and Monument: Architectural Artefacts in the Age of Specialized Institutions" (Ph.D. diss., Cambridge, Mass., MIT, 1994).

10. This section draws on Hermann Muthesius, *Stilarchitektur und Baukunst: Wandlungen der Architektur im XIX. Jahrhundert und ihr heutiger Standpunkt* (Mülheim-Ruhr, 1902), trans., with an introduction, by Stanford Anderson as *Style-Architecture and Building-Art: Transformations of Architecture in the Nineteenth Century and Its Present Condition* (Santa Monica, Calif., 1994). On Muthesius, see Chapter 4 in this volume and, with particular relation to his concern with domestic architecture, Laurent Stalder, "Wie man ein Haus baut: Hermann Muthesius (1861–1927) —

Das Landhaus als kulturgeschichtlicher Entwurf" (Ph.D. diss., ETH, Zurich, 2002).

11. Hermann Muthesius, *Das englische Haus: Entwicklung, Bedingungen, Anlage, Aufbau, Einrichtung und Innenraum*, 3 vols. (Berlin, 1904–5).

12. Muthesius, *Style-Architecture and Building-Art*, trans. Anderson, 96–97.

13. Ibid., 97; trans. slightly modified.

14. In the Introduction to this volume, the editors note the etymological tie of the word "vernacular" to the domestic realm.

15. Muthesius, *Style-Architecture and Building-Art*, trans. Anderson, 85.

16. William Morris, "An Address Delivered at the Distribution of Prizes to Students of the Birmingham Municipal School of Art" (n.d..) The word "architectooralooral" is quoted from ch. 27 of Dickens's *Great Expectations:* "'Why, yes, Sir,' said Joe, 'me and Wopsle went off straight to look at the Blacking Ware's. But we didn't find that it come up to its likeness in the red bills at the shop doors; which I meantersay,' added Joe, in an explanatory manner, 'as it is there drawd too architectooralooral.'"

17. Muthesius, *Style-Architecture and Building-Art*, trans. Anderson, 53.

18. See, e.g., *The Invention of Tradition*, ed. Eric Hobsbawm and Terence Ranger (Cambridge, 1983).

19. Jacques Le Goff, "Mentalities: A History of Ambiguities," in *Constructing the Past: Essays in Historical Methodology*, ed. id. and Pierre Nora (Cambridge, 1985), 166–80; *Faire de l'histoire*, ed. Le Goff and Nora, 3: 76–94.

20. Le Corbusier, *Le Voyage d'Orient* (Paris, 1966), ed. and trans. Ivan Zaknic as *Journey to the East* (Cambridge, Mass., 1987).

21. Rudofsky, *Architecture Without Architects*.

22. Stanford Anderson, "*Sachlichkeit* and Modernity, or Realist Architecture," in *Otto Wagner: Reflections on the Raiment of Modernity*, ed. Harry Mallgrave (Santa Monica, Calif., 1993), 322–60.

23. Sarah Menin, "Fragments from the Forest: Aalto's Requistioning of Forest Place and Matter," *Journal of Architecture* 6 (Autumn 2001): 279–305.

24. Colin St. John Wilson, *The Other Tradition of Modern Architecture: The Uncompleted Project* (London, 1995).

7. Czaplicka: The Vernacular in Place and Time

1. My point of reference here is, of course, John Brinckerhoff Jackson, "A Sense of Place, a Sense of Time," in id., *A Sense of Place, a Sense of Time* (New Haven, 1994), 154–63. The following essay is set against Jackson's understanding of the vernacular, which he developed with regard to the landscapes and cityscapes of the United States. The lucidity of his descriptions and the sensitivity to history exhibited by Jackson always seems informed by a will to discover the peculiarly American. The willingness limits the necessary critique of what is ordinary and common in the "American" landscape. In reflecting on the East, one might return to a critique of the "West" or, more particularly, of the ordinary and common in a capitalist economy's shaping of the built environment.

2. The comparison between East and West is largely implicit in this chapter.

3. The East-West similarities in the claim of a break with the past or the bent to-

ward a utopian and all-encompassing design, the degree of politicization, and the periodization of the modern (nineteenth century, interwar period, and communist era) are worth analyzing in a comparative manner. Differences in the pattern of industrialization (generally later in the East), the restrictions on the "artistic" creativity of the architect, and the role of internationalization are all research desiderata.

4. Indeed, this utopian aspect becomes a salient point of comparison and one that might suggest restrictions on the modernist paradigm in architecture in the respective political systems.

5. This is especially true in the former GDR, where demolition has begun in Hoyerswerda and in parts of the former East Berlin.

6. In cities such as L'viv and Riga, the modern has a different valence and character before World War I, in the interwar period, and after World War II. The late modernism of the Soviet Union was preceded by the monumental historicism of Stalinism, which succeeded the projections of a revolutionary modernism in the early Soviet period. In Poland after World War II, the reconstruction of historic city centers in what might be termed a postmodernist fashion (modern materials, modern configuration of interiors and space behind historicist façades) took place concomitant with the prevalence of a more typical socialist modernism.

7. In over sixty interviews with residents of the region in 1999, 2000, and 2001, many of whom lived in socialist housing, not once did my questioning about their "hometown" elicit any reference to the towers of reinforced concrete on the peripheries of Gdansk, L'viv, Riga, or Vilnius.

8. This is not to say that there were no local distinctions in Soviet architecture, but these were severely delimited by the mass production of prefabricated construction elements and the limited freedom allowed the architect. Focusing on Lithuania in his manuscript "East Bloc, West View, Architecture and Lithuanian National Identity," John Maciuika, assistant professor of architecture at the University of Virginia, makes a strong case for recognizing patterns of variation in structural rhythms and even Western influences in the Soviet system of building. Certainly, the truly distinctive modern buildings in cities such as Vilnius, Tallinn, or Riga that date from the late Soviet period are exceptions. How they respond to the international modernism in architecture as it developed in the West is beyond the scope of this chapter.

9. John Brinkerhoff Jackson, *Discovering the Vernacular Landscape* (New Haven, 1984), xii: "The beauty that we see in the vernacular landscape is the image of our common humanity: hard work, stubborn hope, and mutual forbearance striving to be love." Because Jackson's writings remain a touchstone in discussion of the meaning of the "vernacular" in the United States, one cannot but cite him in this context.

10. One could just as well look at the "vernacular landscape" of malls and gas stations Jackson loved to describe and call it an image of humanity molded by the market.

11. See Robert Riley, "Vernacular Landscapes," in Advances in *Environment, Behavior and Design*, ed. Ervin H. Zube and Gary T. Moore (New York, 130).

12. One might expand this to include the interiors of apartment buildings and residences built before the Soviet period that were transformed into communal apartments and "redesigned" by their occupants.

13. Again this is a generalization that needs to be both historically and locally contextualized. Blair Ruble's *Leningrad: Shaping a Soviet City* (Berkeley, 1990) provides an excellent overview of the Leningrad experience, and his *Money Sings: The Changing Politics of Urban Space in Post-Soviet Yaroslavl* (Cambridge, 1995) also offers a good perspective on the rise of historical preservation in a local environment during the late Soviet period. For various perspectives on the ideal of a socialist city and its various realizations, see *The Socialist City: Spatial Structure and Urban Policy*, ed. R. A. French and F. E. Ian Hamilton (New York, 1979), and R. A. French, *Plans, Pragmatism, and People: The Legacy of Soviet Planning for Today's Cities* (Pittsburgh, 1995). My general characterization of the socialist building programs does not reflect the nuanced historical understanding of changes in these studies nor the small variations on the concept of the socialist city that also affected the design in architecture. However, I would like to emphasize that planning was not done so much in detail or on a local level throughout the Soviet period, so that these variations are limited.

14. Especially significant in this pattern of denial, decay, and destruction was the loss of a traditional urban middle class that had cultivated local patriotism and culture.

15. See, e.g., Hartmut Häussermann, "From the Socialist to the Capitalist City: Experiences from Germany," in *Cities after Socialism: Urban and Regional Change and Conflict in Post-Socialist Societies*, ed. Gregory Andrusz, Michael Harloe, and Ivan Szelenyi (Oxford, 1996), 214–31. *Staging the Past: The Politics of Commemoration in Habsburg Central Europe. 1848 to the Present*, ed. Maria Bucur and Nancy M. Wingfield (West Lafayette, Ind., 2001), offers a good starting point. More detailed studies of bourgeois culture in eastern Europe prior to Soviet rule are needed, because local history and collective memory since the fall of communism relate closely to, and often derive from, local, ethnic, or national self-identification.

16. See e.g. Ruble, *Money Sings,* chap. 3, and on the city of L'viv and the role preservation had in the revolutions of 1989, see Padraic Kenney, *A Carnival of Revolution: Central Europe 1989* (Princeton, 2002).

17. The Vilnius Old Town Revitalization Strategy Project initiated after the old city center was inscribed in the UNESCO World Heritage List in 1994 is perhaps the most successful of the agencies that were founded in cities such as L'viv, Riga, and Tallinn to restore and revitalize historic districts. See *Vilnius Old Town Revitalization Strategy* (Vilnius, 1997). And see Janis Krastins, *Rîgas Râtslaukums* (Riga's Town Hall Square) (Riga, 2000) for one aspect of the reconstruction taking place in Riga.

18. Much of what I write here could, of course, be applied to poor-quality modern architecture outside the Soviet Union as well.

19. One could, for instance, understand the peculiar Baltic wooden architecture in Riga and the highly representative Jugendstil apartment houses as part of the vernacular of that city.

20. Dolores Hayden's *The Power of Place: Urban Landscapes as Public History* (Cambridge, Mass., 1995), with its careful articulation of ethnic neighborhoods in Los Angeles and their alternative histories of the city, is very suggestive in this regard.

21. One of the very focused individual studies relating this conception is King-

ston Wm. Heath, *The Patina of Place: The Cultural Weathering of a New England Landscape* (Knoxville, 2001).

22. See Kenney, *Carnival*, and Padraic Kenney, "Lviv's Central European Renaissance, 1987–1990," in *Lviv: A City in the Crosscurrents of Culture*, special issue of *Harvard Ukrainian Studies* 24 (2000): 303–11.

23. Vilnius became a World Heritage City in 1994, Riga in 1997, and L'viv in 1998.

24. See *Composing Urban History and the Constitution of Civic Identities*, ed. John J. Czaplicka, Blair Ruble, and Lauren Crabtree (Washington, D.C., 2003).

25. See Janis Krastins, *Riga: Art Nouveau Metropolis* (Riga, 1996).

26. The concepts of *Kunstgeographie* or *Kulturlandschaft* may be applicable terms here, but their explanation in this context would involve a careful articulation of the concept of region set against that of place or locality. See *Borders in Art: Revisiting Kunstgeographie*, ed. Katarzyna Murawska-Muthesius (Warsaw, 2000).

27. They are the remains of the wooden suburbs of the city built after the destruction of their predecessors in 1812, when all the wooden buildings of the Riga suburbs were burned down in anticipation of an attack by the advancing forces of Napoleon.

28. This distinctive wooden architectural heritage will probably not survive or only survive with vinyl siding replacing the wood and mass-produced fittings replacing historical details. The inability to preserve this architectural heritage derives in part from the current lack of distinction between architecturally significant wooden architectural monuments and what might be termed wooden shacks. The inventory of wooden architecture in Riga recently completed by the State Inspection for Heritage Protection may rectify this situation. Jurgis Dambis and Andis Cinis in Riga and Jurate Markeviciene in Vilnius were kind enough to introduce me to the wooden architecture of these cities. The treatment it deserves cannot be gone into here.

29. See Akos Moravánszky, "Materiallandschaften," *Kritische Berichte* 28, 2 (2000): 20–28.

Subject Index

In this index an "f" after a number indicates a separate reference on the next page, and an "ff" indicates separate references on the next two pages. A continuous discussion over two or more pages is indicated by a span of page numbers, e.g., "57–59." *Passim* is used for a cluster of references in close but not consecutive sequence. Page numbers in italics refer to the endnotes. The editors thank Thomas Volker Stachel for his work on this index.

Index of Names

In this index an "f" after a number indicates a separate reference on the next page, and an "ff" indicates separate references on the next two pages. A continuous discussion over two or more pages is indicated by a span of page numbers, e.g., "57–59." *Passim* is used for a cluster of references in close but not consecutive sequence. Page numbers in italics refer to the endnotes.